I0137355

Family and Court

Middle East Studies Beyond Dominant Paradigms

Peter Gran, *Series Editor*

At the entrance to a house in the old city of Jaffa. From a postcard produced by the studio of Bonfils in Beirut, late nineteenth century.

Family & COURT

*Legal Culture and Modernity
in Late Ottoman Palestine*

Iris Agmon

SYRACUSE UNIVERSITY PRESS

Library of Congress Cataloging-in-Publication Data

Agmon, Iris.
    Family and court : legal culture and modernity in late Ottoman Palestine / Iris Agmon.— 1st ed.
        p. cm.— (Middle East studies beyond dominant paradigms)
    Includes bibliographical references and index.
    ISBN 0-8156-3062-X (hardcover (cloth) : alk. paper)
    1. Domestic relations (Islamic law)—Palestine.   2 Family—Palestine—History.
3. Social change—Palestine—History—19th century.   I. Title.   II. Series.
KMQ1054.A946 2005
346.569401'5—dc22   2005021504

In memory of Yael Saar-Agmon

For who in this world can give anyone a character? Who in this world knows anything of any other heart—or of his own?

—Ford Madox Ford,
The Good Soldier: A Tale of Passion (1915)

Fiction here is likely to contain more truth than fact. . . . Lies will flow from my lips, but there may perhaps be some truth mixed up with them; it is for you to seek out this truth and to decide whether any part of it is worth keeping. If not, you will of course throw the whole of it into the wastepaper basket and forget all about it.

—Virginia Woolf,
A Room of One's Own (1929)

Iris Agmon is a professor in the Department of Middle East Studies at Ben-Gurion University of the Negev in Israel. Educated at the University of Haifa and the Hebrew University of Jerusalem, where she earned her doctorate, Agmon has published several articles on the social, cultural, legal, and economic history of the modern and early-modern Middle East, in particular the history of women and gender. Her essay "Muslim Women in Court According to the *Sijill* of Late Ottoman Jaffa and Haifa: Some Methodological Notes" appeared in *Women, the Family, and Divorce Laws in Islamic History,* edited by Amira El-Azhary Sonbol and published by Syracuse University Press in 1996.

◆　◆　◆

Contents

Part Four: **Reshaping Solutions**

Illustrations

♦　　♦　　♦

Foreword

PETER GRAN

PROFESSOR IRIS AGMON'S WORK fits into this series, Middle East Studies Beyond Dominant Paradigms, on several grounds. Not only does Agmon
present cogent arguments backed by a wealth of evidence challenging the established paradigm of a dominant Oriental despotism, with its numerous in-
sinuations of a static and irrational Eastern society crying out for foreign
intervention, but she does so from the vantage point of family history, as revealed by specific court cases.

Palestinian history is often taken in Middle East studies as a foil for modernity. According to this view, the Ottomans brought a minor semblance of
order to tribal anarchy in late-nineteenth-century Palestine, and then were followed by the British, who more decisively created Mandate Palestine, giving
birth to modern Palestine. The Zionist leader Theodor Herzl summed up this
view by writing, "It was a land without a people for a people without a land."
Further, according to this paradigm, when the British arrived, they had to
wrestle with the "backward" Islamic legal and cultural system inherited from
the Ottomans in order to bring about modernization. It has been also assumed that things do not change quickly in the Holy Land and that, as a result,
modernization for Palestinians was difficult because there was no recent experience with change. In making use of such premises, the dominant paradigm
turns to Weber and looks at the court system in terms of "kadi-justice," something regarded as in serious need of replacement by British positive law. The
dominant paradigm also assumes that where Muslims live, one has an Islamic
city, and that this perception likewise reflects the rigidities and lack of trust

one associates with premodernity. In recent years, however, the conclusions of numerous studies have gone against those of the dominant paradigm, but rarely if ever do their authors make much of this fact. In this highly revisionist work, Iris Agmon challenges much of the traditional picture, either directly or by implication.

The legal system that Agmon presents for the reader was one undergoing continuous change in the nineteenth century. It was a system profoundly affected by the rise of legal advocacy as well as by the breakdown of judiciary's direct knowledge of the plaintiffs and defendants; urban migration had created cities full of strangers. These discoveries about this period go a long way toward undermining the idea of kadi-justice. They seem to leave us with a picture of a system evolving according to local conditions. Agmon does not glorify or demonize this system. Here was something that existed and that worked.

This work is an achievement not only on the level of paradigm challenge, but also in terms of the use of sources. Court proceedings in the hands of many previous scholars seemed like a few random cases pulled out of a large juridical archive. Court proceedings here are integrated into a grounded microhistory. Agmon uses her sources to show many different kinds of interactions among involved parties, interactions that in different ways also suggest things about the larger society. At the same time, she is very careful about the dangers of overstatement. There are, as she writes, limitations to looking at a few cases about the family in the manner of microhistory.

It is obviously the case that in the contemporary study of social history, the study of family history is one of the main points of convergence of interest among many scholars. This is especially the case for the field of Middle East history, for which family history is also relatively new. Agmon explains that although several routes have brought scholars together to work in this area, one route in particular has been important: the move in women studies to gender history. As that move has taken place, the study of the family has become increasingly logical.

What Agmon is able to offer as her contribution to the field of family history is a sense of the strategies used by men and women in struggling against each other in court as well as of strategies used by judges interested in protecting children, orphans, and those left in a vulnerable situation. Here one sees historical patterns within a fairly specific context, for, as Agmon also points out—and this gives her work a considerable specificity—the old and highest upper classes did not use the court system, nor did the very poor, meaning that what we have gained access to is the changing nature of the middle strata and its mores. Examples of these mores include ideas of intimacy and privacy, which she shows to have arisen from a shared usage of property among those dwelling close to one another. Through their neighborliness and close proximity, these groups became "semirelatives"—people perhaps living in the same house and even sharing in each other's lives but unrelated by blood or marriage.

For a number of reasons, therefore, this book is an important work for Syracuse to publish expeditiously. Family history is an important area now. Much of it is naïve and reproduces older paradigms, so Agmon's work is a good corrective. Palestinian history is a subject of obviously great importance because its construction(s) are so politically charged. It strongly needs a touch of science, which Agmon provides. Moreover, the insights she brings us about orphans, divorce matters, and marital rows are rich and complex; they make one think. She sweeps aside the old idea that such work is impossible in Middle East studies because there are no sources or that such subjects lie outside of history. This book is a pioneering work.

◆　◆　◆

A Note on Transliteration

THE SOCIETIES EXPLORED in this study were characterized by a linguistic mixture of Arabic and Turkish. To reflect that typical mixture, I have used names and terms in their original languages in transliteration according to the following principles:

1. Terms that relate to the Ottoman administration and hierarchies, titles of state employees, and proper names of people of Turkish origin or from Turkish-speaking regions are transliterated following modern Turkish, with certain modifications.

2. Legal terms used in the court records and the proper names of people from the Arab provinces are transliterated from the Arabic. All diacritical marks have been omitted.

3. Sometimes the same term appears in two different forms. The term referring to a *shari'a* judge, for instance, is *kadı* in Turkish and *qadi* in Arabic, and in certain sections both versions may appear.

Arabic: All diacritical marks are omitted.

ʿ   ayn
ʾ   hamza

Turkish pronunciation:

C, c   "j" as in *justice*
Ç, ç   "ch" as in *church*
Ğ, ğ   soft "g"; pronunciation depends on the adjacent letters
I, ı   undotted I, pronounced like "ea" in *earnest*

Ö, ö	as "ö" in German
Ş, ş	"sh" as in *sheet*
Ü, ü	as "ü" in German
^	denotes Ottoman long vowels (a, i, u) in certain words
ʿ	ayn; it is transliterated only in certain words
ʾ	not pronounced; denotes the Arabic *al* (the) in certain names

◆   ◆   ◆

Acknowledgments

THIS BOOK BRINGS a long personal journey to its conclusion. The task of writing it alone took me somewhat more than a year. However, a much longer process of research and self-education preceded it, a process that brought me to venues that I had not anticipated and shook some of my basic assumptions. Granted, no previous project had ever thrilled me the way writing this book did. But it was also an extremely distressing time. Fortunately, however, I found on this bumpy road some true friends, sometimes in the most unexpected places and circumstances, and learned more than in any time in the past the meaning of friendship. Inevitably, the list of people who encouraged and helped me in one way or another and to whom I am deeply grateful is quite long.

First of all, I wish to thank a few friends and colleagues whose continuous advice and support along the way and at certain crucial points in my project were invaluable. My deep gratitude goes to Tal Shuval, from whom I learned the meaning of dignity and whose friendship and advice I cherish. I am also grateful to Siham Daoud, whose common sense, courage, and individualism I admire, and to Ursula Woköck, whose intellect and open-mindedness I appreciate so much; they always generously gave their advice and insights. I am not able to thank Şevket Pamuk enough for good advice and support that always came at the right moment. I am also profoundly grateful to Amira Sonbol for her continuing encouragement and trust.

Three people were directly involved in the production of the book and in turning this process into an encouraging and highly constructive experience: Ann Ussishkin, who edited my manuscript from the very first draft and from whose high professional standards and linguistic sensibility I greatly benefited; Peter Gran, the editor of this series, whose original thinking and intellectual curiosity turned the publication process into an instructive dialogue; and Mary Selden Evans, the acquisitions editor of Syracuse University Press, whose competence, dependability, and sweeping good spirit were a constant source of encouragement for me. I feel so privileged to have passed through my first publishing experience with the three of them. I am also indebted to the rest of the staff at Syracuse University Press, who have been so helpful and support-ive, and to Annie Barva, who meticulously copyedited this book. I thank my friend Zipi Birak-Bizanski, who generously helped me to prepare the illustra-tions for the book; and Avi Rubin, who prepared the index.

When I began this project, I consulted with Tania Forte, Leslie Peirce, Donald Quataert, Ehud Toledano, and Ursula Woköck about the structure and synopsis of my book. I am grateful to them for their thoughtful com-ments and good advice. After I finished writing, several friends and colleagues read the manuscript and reflected on it: Beth Baron, Haim Gerber, Aharon Layish, Avi Rubin, Ido Shahar, Amy Singer, and Ehud Toledano. I benefited immensely from their comments and suggestions, as well as from the careful reading and helpful remarks of an anonymous reader for Syracuse University Press. In addition, a few friends and colleagues read and commented on spe-cific sections of my study or shared with me historical documents that came into their possession. For these contributions, I am indebted to Jun Akiba, Be-shara Doumani, Mark LeVine, Tal Shuval, Ursula Woköck, and Mahmoud Yazbak. For countless hours of conversations on philosophy, modernity, and postmodernity that time and again made me reconsider my subject matter, I thank my friend Ilana Arbel. I am grateful to my colleagues at Ben-Gurion University—Ilana Krausman Ben-Amos, Iris Parush, and Niza Yanay—for their solidarity. I am also indebted to my former teachers and advisors Gad Gilbar and Amnon Cohen and to Israel Gershoni for their encouragement.

The Haim Herzog Center and the Faculty of Humanities and Social Sciences at Ben-Gurion University awarded my project financial support. The staff of the Departments of Microfilms and Rare Books at the library of the University of Haifa generously gave excellent service, and the staff of the Müftülük in Istanbul tendered warm hospitality and help in tracing documents.

During the course of my research, I was fortunate to meet with members of the Karaman family. I am grateful to Suad and Darwish Taher Karaman for hosting me in their home at Ibtin and sharing with me their memories and family stories. I remember with fond appreciation Taher Darwish Taher Karaman and the late Bushra Karaman, whom, to my deep regret, I came to know only a couple of years before her untimely death. She was remarkable for her intriguing insights and enthusiasm and for her willingness to help me in collecting more evidence.

The academic year of 2001, which I spent in Istanbul affiliated with Sabancı University, constituted a formative period in constructing my view of this book. I am grateful to my colleagues at the Faculty of Art and Social Sciences there, in particular Tülay Artan and Halil Berktay for inviting me in the first place, for awarding me a generous fellowship, and for being so kind to me. I thank Tony Greenwood and Gülden Guneri for making so pleasant my stay at the American Research Institute in Turkey (ARIT), my home away from home. A substantial number of scholars spent relatively long periods of time at ARIT during that year, and we turned into a small community sharing personal events, dinners, holidays, research experiences, and, inevitably, also arguments. I thank them for their companionship. In particular, Sjnezana Buzov, Shirine Hamadeh, Karen Kern, and John Walbridge gave not only their friendship, but also insights and advice in our numerous conversations. I am indebted to my friends and neighbors Virginia and Çağlar Keyder for their generosity and to Hakan Erdem for all his help. I am also deeply grateful to Jun Akiba, Dilek Akyalçın, and Nurullah Şenol for their invaluable advice and assistance in my struggle with the Ottoman documents.

Finally, I thank my close friends and family for tolerating my prolonged seclusion and for being so patient and sympathetic. I am especially grateful, much more than I can hope to put into words, to my parents for their unconditional love and support. Their humanity, integrity, and modesty have lighted my way.

* ◆ ◆

Abbreviations

Archival Sources

HCR	Haifa Court Record*	SA dos.	*Sicill-i ahval dosyaları*
JCR	Jaffa Court Record*	SA def.	*Sicill-i ahval defterleri*

* Titles and numbers of volumes of court records from both cities are noted according to what appears on the label or opening page. When these marks are missing, only the dates covered by the respective volume are mentioned.

Official Ottoman Publications

Düstur 1	*Düstur*, birinci tertib (1st ed.)
Düstur 2	*Düstur*, ikinci tertib (2d ed.)
Al-Dustur	*Düstur* 1 translated into Arabic
Mecelle	*Mecelle-i Ahkam-ı Adliye*
Salname VB	*Beyrut Vilayeti Salnamesi*
Salname VS	*Suriye Vilayeti Salnamesi*

Dates

In citations to archival materials, dates are designated as "16 S 1276/14 IX 1859," signifying the day, month, and year of the Hijri and Gregorian calendars, with months given either as capital letters for dates within the Hijri calendar or as capital roman numerals for dates within the Gregorian calendar. When sources give only Mali dates, they are designated as "9 Nisan 1291." The Mali calendar, a combination of the lunar and solar calendars, was introduced in the nineteenth century by the Ottoman administration.

Part One

◆　　◆　　◆

Entering a Sociolegal Arena

1

Historical Settings

Grandmother was said to have been born in the year of the Ottoman law on growing tobacco. My father did not know her birth date. In his notebook, bound in faded leather, he calculated the date by referring to other important events in the life of Grandfather Jubran. But, as I have said, the oral tradition puts Grandmother's birth in the year the Ottoman tobacco law was published. Had I not chanced upon the 1874 volume of the Lebanese journal *al-Jinan,* I would not have known that my father had actually been correct in his calculations. (Shammas 2001, 7)

ANTON SHAMMAS OPENS HIS NOVEL *Arabesques,* a breathtaking intricate saga of a Palestinian family in a Galilean village, with the narrator's memories of his grandmother ʿAlia's death. In this study, in a rather similar manner, I try to weave bits and pieces of historical evidence of various types and origins into a meaningful story about a family. This is not a specific family, but rather an abstract, historically contingent grid of human bonds and relations. Unlike Shammas's family, this one is urban, and I examine it in the *shariʿa* court setting.

The popular image of Muslim societies is one in which both family and *shariʿa* court, institutionally and conceptually, oppose modernity. The Muslim family has a reputation of being a monolithic, patriarchal, unchanging social framework. The connotation of the *shariʿa* court is of a traditional, religious, narrow-minded legal institution, which strengthens this image. Modernity, according to this line of thinking, is in total polarity to both court and family and pertains to new, rapidly changing, rational, efficient, and flexible social institutions.

The present study draws an entirely different picture from this popular view. In Jaffa and Haifa, two growing port cities in late Ottoman Palestine, family is a variegated social structure, and the *shari'a* court is a dynamic institution, able to adjust to rapid and rather profound changes to its long-standing pattern—indeed, to play an active role in generating these changes. Court and family interact and transform themselves, each other, and the society of which they form parts. This study develops a hermeneutic reading of court records and questions prevailing assumptions about family, the courts, and the nature of modernity in Muslim societies in concrete historical terms.

My interpretive strategy is inspired by hermeneutic philosophy, a field dealing with the interpretation of texts that has a significant influence on theoretical thinking in the social sciences. This field was originally linked to religious texts, then considered part of theology. In the nineteenth century, it became a distinct philosophical discipline relating to texts in general. Its further development in the twentieth century has been influenced mainly by the ideas of H. G. Gadamer. As opposed to poststructuralist philosophers, Gadamer assumes that texts have a true meaning that, in principle, is intelligible. However, he does not consider hermeneutics a scientific method aiming at providing conclusive explanations for texts. Rather, the aspiration is to understand them better, the very meaning of interpretation.[1]

I explore family as both a social and a cultural construct. It constitutes a useful conceptual framework as a melting pot of emotions and interests of the individuals in society, a crossroad of micro- and macrounits of analysis. Because of these very features, it also provides a highly valuable prism for observing the urban communities of Ottoman port cities in Palestine, in particular their growing middle classes,[2] at a historical juncture: the age of reform and shifting political order, an unconscious twilight of empire.[3]

In the course of the "long nineteenth century," the Ottoman Empire un-

1. See, for example, Levy 1986; Dostal 2002; Grondin 2003.

2. I use *middle class* as a descriptive term rather than as a sociological category. See the explanations at the end of chapter 2.

3. At the height of the First World War, Muhammad Bahjat and Rafiq al-Tamimi, two young Ottoman-Arab officials, wrote a profound report on the state of the province of Beirut (Bahjat and al-Tamimi 1917–18). Their report does not indicate at all that the possibility that the empire was about to lose the war and disappear even crossed their minds. See Rubin 2000, 28–45. See also Bahjat and al-Tamimi's comments at the end of this chapter.

derwent a profound series of reforms that continued in spite of many obstacles and interruptions. During the same period, incorporation of the empire into the capitalist world economy accelerated considerably. Both processes had significant repercussions on the urban and human settings of Jaffa and Haifa, the two main port cities on the southeastern shores of the Mediterranean. They were small harbor towns at the beginning of the nineteenth century; by the turn of the twentieth century, however, they had developed into flourishing port cities, attracting immigrants in large numbers and continually growing. During this period, their population experienced rapid growth, social mobility, state intrusion, and bureaucratization that touched every aspect of daily life.

It is obvious that this era was one of major transformation, of an accelerated passage to modernity, of many state-designed and even more unintended changes. It is the concrete historical content of these changes—the mechanisms that generated them, their specific local nature, and the meaning of widely used categories such as modernity and premodernity—that requires investigation. By *modernity,* I mean both certain practices that substantially differed from premodern ones and a discourse organizing such practices. I presume that the existence of the discourse of modernity (which includes, by definition, *premodernity*) in the period under discussion does not require to be proved, but rather needs to be explored. This is where family as a conceptual framework and historical object provides an analytical perspective.

It is difficult to overestimate the significance of the family as a social unit for both individuals and society at large. Family is the basic framework of belonging for every individual, so it is pertinent to the most essential concerns of human beings as individuals and social creatures. At the same time, it constitutes the cornerstone of society and of the social and political order. Consequently, it is a sensitive seismograph. As a fortress of individual emotions and interests in society, the construction of the family will not easily lend itself to change despite or possibly because of the fact that it is constantly exposed to conflicts and pressures. Yet no significant change should be expected to pass it by. Thus, both continuity and change are noteworthy in the construction of the family. The information may contribute to a better understanding of the family itself, of the society in which it functioned, and of the way individuals experienced their family and society and took part in the major transformations of their time.

The conceptual advantages of the family notwithstanding, it is methodologically a category that is difficult to pin down in the history of the Middle East. Direct historical evidence is rare, whereas prejudice about the "traditional Muslim family" is abundant and deep rooted. This is where the *shariʿa* court comes in: its record contains serial accounts covering thousands of proceedings, most of which legally fall under the category of family law. In fact, the court provides more than a record: it is an intriguing social and cultural arena. The texts of its record, however, are highly structured by legal discourse. Therefore, their use for investigating the family requires a deconstruction as well as a reconstruction of court practice. Hence, the court itself provides both the setting for this story about the family and an object for historical investigation. In other words, this study is about family *and* court.

In the course of nineteenth-century reforms, the *shariʿa* courts, the principal state court system for centuries, lost a wide range of jurisdiction to newly established courts of the *nizamiye* system operating on the basis of new legal codes.[4] Hence, *shariʿa* courts turned into "family courts" by default. Although *shariʿa* law remained as the basis of their decisions, these old institutions underwent vigorous reorganization and procedural reform. At the same time, they redefined their position in society in relation to both the newly established courts and their own clientele. In the process, their legal culture underwent significant changes. The interaction between the changing courts and their clients—the dynamic urban communities of Jaffa and Haifa, whose members sought legal remedy for their family problems—is the focus of this study.

The court records, despite their highly formal and uniform structure, are far from being unbiased. Precisely because of their features and the fact that

---

4. In the literature on legal reform the *nizamiye* courts are often inaccurately called "civil courts." In fact, however, the *nizamiye* system was responsible for all legal fields except for those covered by the *shariʿa* family law (namely *waqf* and inheritance, marriage, divorce, and children) which were left under the jurisdiction of the *shariʿa* courts. Furthermore, the *nizamiye* courts also adjudicated cases of public law. Ottoman legal reform did not distinguish between civil and public law, a distinction typical of the French legal tradition, whose influence was otherwise dominant. Thus, in this study I use the term *nizamiye* when referring either to the entire new court system or to certain courts, whereas I use the term *civil court* only with regard to a specific court (in Jaffa or Haifa) dealing with civil cases. I owe this observation to Avi Rubin and Ursula Woköck.

they provide historians with a centuries-long documentation of the everyday business of ordinary people, they tend to mislead the reader into believing that they contain an account of what really happened, the way it actually happened. The court records are the product of a long tradition of official documentation carried out by a socioprofessional group. The education, concepts, relations, and interests of the members of this group are inscribed in the texts they produced. Moreover, this socioprofessional group operated under ever-changing historical circumstances. Reading court records thus requires contextualizing them historically rather than seeing them simply as a bank of historical data.

This study, then, aims at exploring the court records of late Ottoman Jaffa and Haifa—their textual conventions, their orthography, the legal procedures of their production, and the background of their producers—for the sake both of learning about the legal culture of these courts and of improving the methodology used for drawing on court records as a historical source. Comparing the records of two neighboring and highly similar cities, Jaffa and Haifa, enables one to explore the local and contingent aspects of the records in order to understand them better as historical products (Ze'evi 1998; Agmon 2004c).

The period under discussion spans mainly the late nineteenth century and the early twentieth century—namely, the phase during which most of the reforms pertaining to *shari'a* courts were implemented in Jaffa and Haifa and for which we have court records from both cities. This is the period during which, as I show in the rest of this chapter, many other changes and processes of growth considerably accelerated there, as in other port cities. However, in order to explore and historicize the changes that occurred in this period, the discussion of various issues goes back to the late eighteenth and early nineteenth centuries. Furthermore, the sections in chapter 2 that deal with the historiography of the family and the methodology of reading court records relate to a broader time span that starts around the time of the Ottoman conquest of the Arab provinces in the sixteenth century in order to provide the present study with a broader historical and historiographical background.

Jaffa and Haifa in the Age of Ottoman Reform

In the past few decades, a wide range of studies on Ottoman history has considerably changed our knowledge about this vast, multifaceted, long-lived empire (Faroqhi 1999, 174–203; Toledano 2002; Hathaway 2004; Peirce 2004).[5] A major leitmotiv that appears in almost any study on the Ottoman state in any period is its adaptability to changing circumstances and cycles of reform. As the research on the early-modern history of the Ottoman Empire becomes more detailed and refined, the similarities between human dilemmas and solutions typical of different eras seem more prominent than the differences. Hence, it is sometimes tempting to generalize and conclude that the division between premodernity and modernity results only from modern discourse, but that, as far as human experience is concerned, it is impossible to draw a meaningful line between them. Besides the fact that a discursive line is nonetheless a line, judging changes by looking at human experiences in everyday life might conceal major changes that can be detected when looking at larger time spans. In this regard, the Ottoman reforms of the nineteenth century are different from previous reforms and transformations, despite some similarities and much continuity.

A few decades ago the nineteenth-century reforms were attributed largely to an Ottoman effort to avoid military defeats and the loss of territories by superficially adopting European military techniques, combined with an attempt to appease the European powers that constantly increased their pressure on the Ottoman Empire in the course of the nineteenth century. The uniqueness of this period as the beginning of the modern era in the empire was described mainly in these terms. However, the growing number of studies challenging the paradigm of the alleged Ottoman decline have also altered the focus of research on the nineteenth-century reforms. First of all, the periodization has changed. In the hitherto established historiography, the Tanzimat (1839–76 C.E.), or the reforms initiated and led by high-ranking bureaucrats who served under the sultans Abdülmecit and Abdülaziz, was considered as a single reform period divided into two waves. The reforms of

5. The survey presented in the rest of the chapter is based on Lewis 1968; Cohen 1973; Shaw and Shaw 1977; Findley 1980, 1986; Owen 1981; Schölch 1982; Fawwaz 1983; Agmon 1985, 1995; Gerber 1985; Mannaʿ 1986; Abu-Manneh 1990; Kark 1990; McCarthy 1990; Pick 1990; Keyder, Özveren, and Quataert 1993; Divine 1994; Quataert 1994; Hanıoğlu 1995; Kayalı 1997; Bonine 1998; Deringil 1998; Schilcher 1998; Toledano 1998; Yazbak 1998; Eldem, Goffman, and Masters 1999; Faroqhi 1999; Keyder 1999; LeVine 1999; Rogan 1999; Quataert 2000; Philipp 2001; Clancy-Smith 2002; Gilbar 2003; and Ginio 2003.

Selim III in the late eighteenth century and those of Mahmut II in the early nineteenth century, preceding the Tanzimat, were seen as failed attempts to save the empire through instant modernization; the reign of Abdülhamit II, following the Tanzimat, was presented as a counterrevolutionary phase; and the Young Turks were seen as the beginning of the inevitable nationalist era (Lewis 1968).

In more recent historiography on the nineteenth century, the Tanzimat is still considered a crucial phase of reform. However, it is seen as part of a continuing process, "the long nineteenth century," which, when judged according to standards of modernization, starts somewhere around the turn of the nineteenth century and terminates with the end of the Ottoman Empire in the First World War (Toledano 1998, 252–53; Quataert 2000, 54–73). The present study also sustains this periodization of the age of reform, particularly regarding the late nineteenth century and the beginning of the twentieth century, and looks at it, from the point of view of the small provincial unit, the subdistrict *(kaza)*, as an uninterrupted phase of reform.

The concept that the reforms constituted a shallow imitation passed for the purpose of gaining more time for the empire has already been refuted quite successfully, so there is no point in beating this dead horse any further. It is necessary, however, to stress that the nature of the nineteenth-century reforms was such that they not only showed continuity with previous reforms, but also represented significant change. The Ottoman dynasty and power elite were typically reforming the state mechanisms of control over their vast territory and heterogeneous society in order to maintain its frontiers, to collect enough revenue, and to reconcile the various pressure groups. The specific modifications made and the ruling methods adopted over the centuries varied considerably, and in the process the nature of the Ottoman state underwent far-reaching change. Yet it was only in the course of the reforms of the nineteenth century that some of the basic foundations underlying the relations between the Ottoman center and its provinces and between the Ottoman ruler and his subjects were gradually transformed.

In the age of reform, the entire state apparatus was reorganized. The army, the government, the financial and legal systems, land tenure, the provincial administration, education, and the infrastructure underwent continuous changes. The reforms in these spheres were meant to enable the Ottoman state to deal better with external and internal forces that challenged its sovereignty. They aimed at unifying the administration of the empire, rationalizing its methods by creating hierarchies of authority down to the lowest provincial level and by centralizing state control over its domains, while eliminating power groups and clusters that competed at different levels with the central government. Although the models and inspiration for many reforms initiated in the Ottoman capital were European, their specific shape and methods of implementation, the new class of state bureaucracy to which they gave rise, and the numerous mechanisms of change they set in motion were indigenous, in line with the long Ottoman tradition of reform (Shaw and Shaw 1977; Findley 1980; Quataert 1994; Göçek 1996).

The characterization of the nineteenth-century reform as a shallow imitation of European practices has been refuted, but most of the scholarship revisiting Ottoman reform has focused so far on the imperial center, thus replacing the imitation paradigm with a description of top-down reform, based on a culture identified solely with the high-ranking Ottoman bureaucracy. Only recently have historians tackled the challenge of reconstructing Ottoman reform as experienced in certain provinces by studying various contributions by provincial figures and social groups and the ways in which local realities and aspirations shaped the transformations. Furthermore, recent studies focusing on the nineteenth-century Ottoman center have shown that the center, too, was not monolithic. Among its various aims, the present study seeks to contribute to the pluralization of the history of Ottoman reform insofar as provincial perspectives and exchanges between the capital and provincial regions are concerned.

Reform and the Port Cities

For the purposes of this study, two spheres of reform require special attention: the reorganization of the provincial administration and legal reform. The Ottoman government issued various rules regarding provincial administration in the first half of the nineteenth century, particularly after the retreat of the Egyptian army and administration from the Syrian provinces and the restoration of Ottoman rule in 1840. However, the most systematic step in this direction was the promulgation of the Law of the Provinces late in 1864, a law that was modified in 1867 and 1871 for implementation in all provinces. This law redefined a unified hierarchy for the administration of the provinces (sing. *vilayet*), organized their chain of control and accountability, and in the process created some new institutions and positions. An aspect of this law that had a direct impact on the development of Jaffa and Haifa was the creation of a new administrative unit, the subdistrict *(kaza)*. The term *kaza* previously referred to a judicial unit, but was then adopted for the new level in the provincial administrative structure, thus unifying the administrative and judicial hierarchies. It was defined as the unit below the district (sing. *liva*, or *sancak*) and above the smallest unit, the county *(nahiye)*—a group of villages with one village serving as county center. The *kaza* was included as the lowest unit in the chain of control and accountability to the central government. Below the subdistrict, in the counties, control remained local (Cohen 1973, 173–74; Findley 1986).

Before the Tanzimat, Jaffa had been the center of a small administrative district that, together with the district of Gaza and Ramla, were considered as unattached units within the province of Damascus. Judicially, according to the pre-Tanzimat terminology, Jaffa was part of the *kaza* of Jerusalem, which administratively was a center of another district belonging to the province of Damascus. Haifa was annexed both administratively and judicially to the district of Lajjun, which belonged to the province of Damascus, but from time to time Haifa and its surrounding area was annexed to the province of Saida (Cohen 1973, 121–22, 139–52; Yazbak 1998, 7–25). The implementation of the provincial law meant that Jaffa and Haifa, both administratively and judicially, became centers of subdistricts (the new *kaza*). They were attached to the district centers of Jerusalem and Acre respectively, and, owing to the implications of the new law, they also became part of the larger setup. Their institutions and officials became part of the state hierarchy; the approval of appointments, payment of salaries, and the submission of financial reports were channeled via the center. In addition, some of the new institutions established during this period were required to open a subdistrict branch. One result of these changes was an administrative upgrading of the two cities to the level of other subdistrict centers. Jaffa experienced upgrading in spite of the fact that hitherto it had been a district that became a subdistrict center. State offices were built, and more positions in government offices for junior staff, servants, guards, and other workers became available for the local population. In other words, this administrative change joined many others that stimulated economic and urban growth and the immigration of new social and ethnic elements to the two towns.

Another result of this law was the establishment of an administrative council *(meclis-i idare)* in each city, including representatives of the local reli-

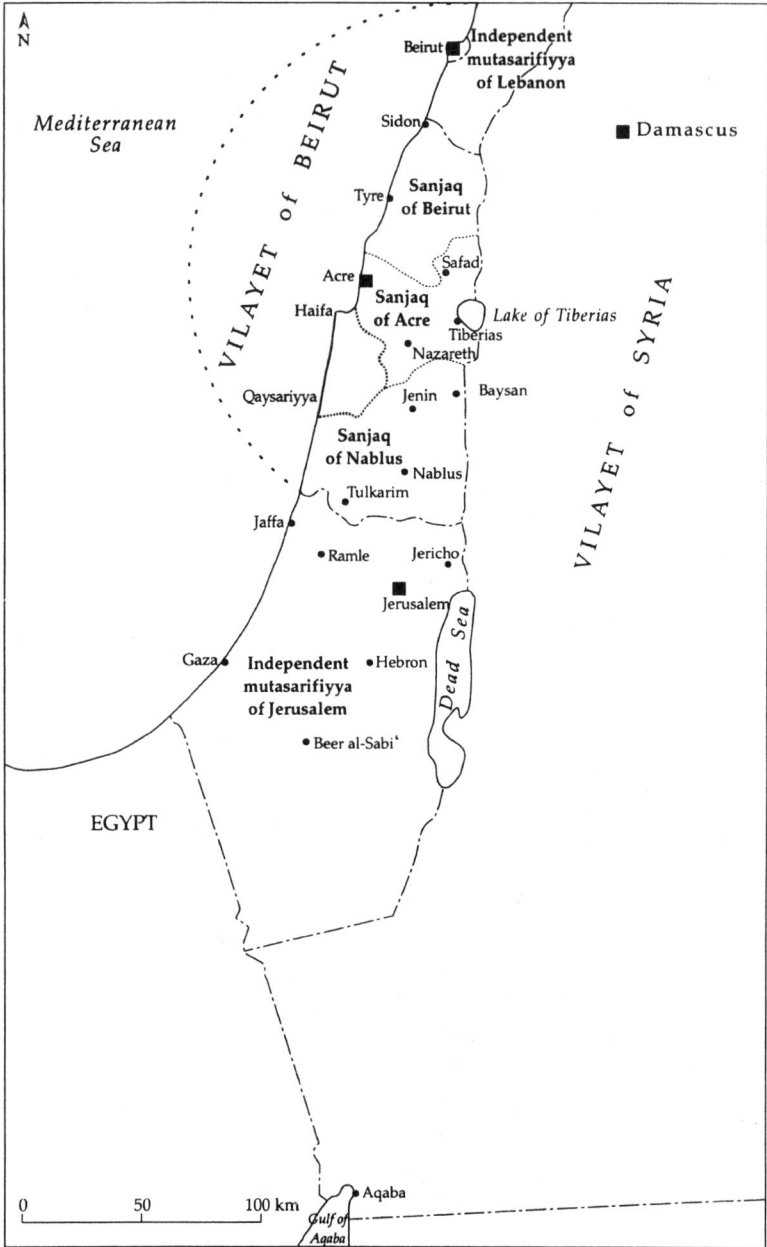

Map 1. Late Ottoman Palestine. From Yazbak 1998, 30. Courtesy of Brill Academic Publishers.

gious communities and certain officials who were ex officio members. This innovation had initially been introduced during the decade of Egyptian rule in the region (1831–40). The law of 1864 further developed the idea of the participation of representatives of the local communities in government. Two new elements were introduced owing to the foundation of the councils, albeit in a restricted form: the participation of the subjects of the empire in government and the representation of the various religious groups in this initial step toward self-rule. The councils created another site of social activity and local power relations, mainly for the notable families of Jaffa and Haifa because the council members were elected from among them. Although not defined by provincial law, the municipality was another institution whose impact should be considered together with that of the local council. In addition to bringing new positions and responsibilities to the local scene, these institutions reinforced the prominence of the Christian and Jewish communities at the local level. The diverse composition of the population in religion, ethnicity, language, citizenship, and various combinations thereof was a salient feature of both Jaffa and Haifa. The participation of members of the major non-Muslim communities in the institutions of local government fostered the position of these communities, particularly of their notable families, in the two cities (Gerber 1985, 94–142; Kark 1990, 204–38; Yazbak 1998, 28–88; LeVine 1999, 47–85).

When seen from the perspective of the *shariʿa* court, the legal reform caused a significant reduction in the court's jurisdiction and the loss of its long-held status as the principal state court and public-record office. From the point of view of the entire judicial system, however, legal reform was not meant to reduce the system, but rather to expand it considerably and radically to reshuffle its juridical sources. The larger picture included the promulgation of a series of new law codes, most of which were based on European examples (penal code, commercial law, and civil code or the *Mecelle-i Ahkam-ı Adliye*, which was based eclectically [*takhayyur*] on the Hanafi civil law); the establishment of new courts *(nizamiye)* and the introduction of new laws of procedure for the criminal, civil, and commercial courts; and eventually the drawing up of the Constitution. The smaller picture consisted of countless regulations and modifications issued in Istanbul, dealing with the details of these reforms and their implementation, a process that continued throughout the long nineteenth century.

As stated, legal reforms, including their implications for the *shariʿa* courts, contributed to the upgrading of the two cities as subdistricts and sites of administrative activities. Jaffa had a longer history as an administrative center than Haifa. Furthermore, judicially, Jaffa had interrelations with Jerusalem long before it administratively became part of the district of Jerusalem, whereas Haifa was not attached to Acre for most of the pre-Tanzimat period. I discuss the way this difference affected legal culture at the *shariʿa* courts of the two cities in chapter 3. However, in both cases, the volume of legal operations grew. Before the reforms, for instance, the *shariʿa* court in Jaffa functioned as an extension of the court of Jerusalem. The judge was literally a deputy *(naib)*[6] of the judge of Jerusalem, and both were often members of ulama families in Jerusalem, sometimes even of the same family. This dependency restricted the administrative impact of the court on the development of Jaffa. Hence, although the reforms limited the jurisdiction of the court, they also elevated its position in the court system by decreasing its dependency on Jerusalem. Moreover, the *shariʿa* court became part of a broader local judicial system: in late-nineteenth-century Jaffa and Haifa, *nizamiye* courts of first instance *(bidayet)* also operated, and, at the turn of the twentieth century, orphan funds were attached to the *shariʿa* courts (see chapter 5). Other institutions were established during the reforms, and the amount of bureaucratic activity grew substantially and contributed to the economic and social impact of reform.

The Port Cities and the Capitalist World Economy

The contribution of the reforms to the growth of the port cities constituted only one factor in a process that had begun before the reforms and had been building up momentum in the course of the nineteenth century. One of the most powerful factors that shaped this process was the incorporation of the Ottoman Empire, like other peripheral economies, into the capitalist world economy.[7] This process, which had begun earlier, accelerated considerably in

6. The term was also used for "subdistrict judge" after the legal reforms, yet its meaning changed. See chapter 3.

7. Within the analytical framework of the world economic system, Ottoman reforms are seen as yet another aspect of the process of integration and peripheralization of preindustrialized economies into the capitalist world system (Owen 1981; Schölch 1982; Keyder, Özveren, and Quataert 1993; Göçek 1996, 14–18; Eldem, Goffman, and Masters 1999, 125–28, 196–206).

the nineteenth century. During this period, the Ottoman economy underwent many structural changes, triggered in almost every economic sphere by incorporation into the world economy. Foreign trade played a major role, so the port cities of the empire became a focus of rapid growth. However, because this development caught each port city in a different situation, economic growth and its numerous repercussions were not identical in all cities, despite many similarities. First of all, neither Jaffa nor Haifa ever reached the scale of growth of Beirut, Alexandria, and other larger port cities on the Mediterranean shores. Both were small harbor towns at the turn of the nineteenth century, Haifa being even smaller than Jaffa, and both grew into medium-sized port cities in the course of the century, developing along somewhat different lines.

At the turn of the nineteenth century, Jaffa was a small harbor town with a population of several thousand (Cohen 1973, 157); it was an entry port for pilgrims on their way to Jerusalem and for regional and some international sea trade. During the eighteenth century, Jaffa had gradually grown and symbolically taken on a more urban appearance when the Ottomans enclosed it with walls and watchtowers for protection. Churches of several Christian denominations were also built during that period. By the turn of the century, however, it had suffered a ruthless siege by the French army. Plagues caused further harm in the first years of the nineteenth century, and the population decreased as a result of death or emigration (Kark 1990, 146). However, the governor of Jaffa from 1807 to 1818, Muhammad Abu Nabut, restored the city walls and renewed the development of the town. During his rule, Jaffa returned to its previous position as a gradually growing harbor town connected to a large agricultural hinterland. The immigration of Jews began in the 1820s. In the following decade of Egyptian rule (1831–40), the town developed further, and local councils and other administrative innovations were introduced. Considerable Egyptian immigration to Jaffa began in this period, when former Egyptian soldiers settled in what later became the neighborhood of Manshiyya, to the north of the old city. Several European consuls also resided in Jaffa. Thus, when the Ottomans restored their administration in Jaffa in 1840, the major development patterns typical for Jaffa during the following eighty years—urban and administrative expansion, immigration, and ever-growing foreign trade and agricultural production—had already taken shape.

During this same period, Haifa developed under somewhat different circumstances. It had originally belonged to the district of Lajjun, and its history as a growing harbor town had begun only in the second half of the eighteenth century, when Dahir al-ʿUmar (1762–75) recognized its potential. He destroyed Haifa in its original location, rebuilt it a couple of kilometers to the southeast, in the Bay of Acre, and surrounded it for the first time by walls. Located only a few kilometers from Acre, the major Ottoman administrative center and harbor on the southern coast of Syria, Haifa had until the change attracted smugglers and pirates and had constituted a constant source of concern for the Ottomans. Before Dahir al-ʿUmar, the Ottomans had attempted to change the situation in Haifa and encourage the immigration of "positive" elements by exempting newcomers from taxation. They also attached Haifa administratively to Saida. Their policy was inconsistent, however, so ultimately it failed. Dahir al-ʿUmar's more successful project that followed was continued at the turn of the nineteenth century by a powerful governor *(vali),* Ahmet Paşa, better known in history as al-Jazzar (the Butcher), whom the Ottomans appointed in order to regain their authority in the region. Under his rule, Haifa escaped the fate of Jaffa during the French invasion at the turn of the nineteenth century. Haifa was conquered easily, without too much damage, and then became a base for the French army's long, cruel, yet unsuccessful siege on Acre. Thus, Haifa was saved owing to its proximity to Acre, the very proximity that for a relatively long period had kept it in the position of a mere small coastal town (Cohen 1973, 137–44; Yazbak 1998, 7–18).

In the late eighteenth century, Acre had reached its peak as the largest urban and administrative center on the southern Syrian coast, with considerable agricultural hinterland and sea trade. In addition to the French siege, various circumstances slowed down its growth and then in the course of the nineteenth century encouraged its gradual decrease in size (Cohen 1973, 128–37; Philipp 2001). Haifa, a promising harbor town at the beginning of the nineteenth century, was rather small, with about only a thousand residents (Schölch 1982, 57). In 1831, the Egyptian army repeated Bonaparte's strategy, this time successfully; it conquered Haifa rapidly and used it as a base for a harsher siege of Acre, which dealt another blow to the city's slow recovery from the previous siege. Like in Jaffa, the decade of Egyptian administration in Haifa introduced some of the features that later became typical of its nineteenth-century development: the council of local notables; constant immigration, including Christian families from Acre; and the residence in Haifa of several European consuls.

With the restoration of Ottoman administration (1840), the development of both Jaffa and Haifa intensified. In the following forty years, until the late 1870s, the two port cities witnessed steady growth and expansion that accelerated in the last phase, from the 1880s until the First World War. The incorporation of the Ottoman Empire into the world economy became particularly forceful and apparent in shaping the development of the two cities in this period, to an extent that highlighted the similarities rather than the differences between them. Foreign trade grew in volume and value at unprecedented rates until the 1880s and even more so afterward. Its composition in terms of types of commodities, the sources of import and destinations of export, and the rate between export and import changed considerably, encouraging structural and social changes as well (Schölch 1982; Agmon 1985; Kark 1990; Yazbak 1998, 189–201; LeVine 1999, 47–130).

The growing demand for certain agricultural products on the world market encouraged an export-oriented agriculture. The most salient example was the expansion of citrus orchards. In the course of this period, the orange industry developed from one growing fruit mainly for local and regional consumption to one producing large quantities of a commodity in high demand, mainly by Great Britain. The constant demand for these quantities triggered other economic developments. Much uncultivated land and land previously cultivated for growing products less in demand were turned into citrus orchards, particularly around Jaffa. The production and export of the oranges created many opportunities for workers in fruit picking and packing and in porterage. It also encouraged a search for and the introduction of new types of oranges that would be more durable for maritime transport. The first direct steamship line from Europe to Jaffa was established by a British company, especially for the export of oranges to Liverpool. A small industry producing boxes for packing the oranges also developed, after packing methods improved and enabled the use of boxes instead of baskets in order to reduce damage during transport (Schölch 1982, 17–18; Agmon 1985, 60–64).

The development of this and other labor-intensive agricultural industries entailed a growing demand for seasonal workers, mainly residents of the neighboring villages and members of tribes, but also even bedouins and villagers from more distant locations. The immigration, attracted to both cities by these and many other job opportunities, encouraged the expansion of the built-up area inside and outside the walls of the two cities. New urban quarters were gradually built outside the walls. In the vicinity of Jaffa, neighboring villages such as Abu Kabir practically became suburban neighborhoods. The city walls around both Haifa and Jaffa were eventually demolished. The immigration of manual workers changed the range and structure of the urban lower classes and hence of the entire urban stratification either because of their moving into the towns or as a result of the expansion of the town to include nearby villages and suburbs.

Expanding agricultural production in general, specifically that of the citrus orchards, illustrates the multifaceted impact of the growth in foreign trade. Owners of citrus orchards and orange merchants made a fortune. Some of the upper-class families who owned orchards in the vicinity of the town built large houses in or next to their orchards and moved there, thus changing their lifestyle and adopting an upper-class taste that developed during that period, detached from the growing urban lower classes and the highly populated urban quarters. Some middle-class families also managed to join this flourishing industry by purchasing small orchards to improve their socioeconomic position—thus contributing to changes in the nature of the middle class or in some cases joining the upper class. Oranges and other profitable export and import commodities also attracted merchants from other port cities in the region and from other countries to the two port cities, further increasing the heterogeneous character of the urban communities (Kark 1990, 53–134; Agmon 1995, 150–65; Yazbak 1998, 189–201; LeVine 1999, 50–85).

The export of grain also illustrates the role that incorporation into the world economy played in shaping the development of the port cities. Grain was always in high demand by a variety of markets all over the world, in addition to the constant demand by the local and regional markets. As a crop that fits the natural conditions of almost all regions of the country, its cultivation was widespread. In the present context, its export illustrates the development of the infrastructure that foreign trade encouraged and the impact of foreign trade on the growth of Haifa at the expense of Acre. The crops of Mount Hawran—"the granary of Syria"—had for a long time been transported by animals to the port of Acre and exported from there. Whereas access to the port of Acre was problematic owing to rocks and other factors, the Haifa bay was more accessible. Trade through the Haifa harbor had grown ever since the town was rebuilt in the late eighteenth century and its harbor improved. In the course of the second half of the nineteenth century, the natural advantage of the Haifa harbor over the Acre harbor was reinforced as steamship transport became more important, particularly in foreign trade. Nonetheless, the export of grain via the port of Acre continued.

Meanwhile, already in the early 1880s, the construction of a railway from the Hawran to the port of Acre was planned, and British and French companies struggled to get a concession or to prevent their rivals from obtaining one. The railroad between Damascus and Beirut was under French control. A French company also constructed the railway from Jaffa to Jerusalem in the early 1890s, but a parallel line connecting the Hawran to the Mediterranean was not built, apparently owing to French efforts to maintain their control over railways in Syria—yet another illustration of the effect of the incorporation of the region into the world economy. At the turn of the twentieth century, the Ottomans eventually embarked on the construction of an extension to the Hijaz railway, starting from Darʿa in the Hawran mountains and ending at the coast. At first, the plan was to connect both Acre and Haifa to this railroad. The Acre connection was postponed until 1913, whereas the construction of the railroad to Haifa was accomplished in 1905, thus channeling the lion's share of grain export to the Haifa port and further stimulating both the port's and the city's development. The port, the railway station, the customhouse, and the growth in the volume of foreign trade created job opportunities, which in turn attracted more immigrants of various origins and social strata (Agmon 1985, 53–56, 112–16, 162–66; Pick 1990; Bonine 1998; Schilcher 1998).

Thus, the cities of Jaffa and Haifa were marked by immigration and a rapid population growth, the heterogeneous character of their urban communities, and social mobility. In addition to the larger groups of Ottoman subjects—Muslims, Orthodox and Catholic Christians, and Sephardi and Ashkenazi Jews—the urban communities in both cities were composed of smaller groups of non-Sunni Muslims; various other Christian denominations; non-Arab Ottomans, such as Armenians and Turks; Persians (the Bahaʾi center in Haifa); and other non-Ottomans. These smaller groups were mainly merchants and clergymen from Mediterranean countries (Greece, Malta, Italy, Spain) and from western Europe (France, England, Austria, and Germany)—especially the Templars from Germany, who established two of their colonies in Jaffa and Haifa; American settlers (in Jaffa); and finally Zionist immigrants mainly from eastern Europe.

Moreover, the "hard core" of upper-class Muslim and Christian Ottoman-Arab families included several newcomers from the region. Even several of those families who had deeper roots in Jaffa and Haifa had settled there in the mid–seventeenth century at the earliest, unlike some of their counterparts in the large inland cities of Palestine and greater Syria who had a longer history in their towns. The Ottoman-Arab middle and lower classes also comprised many immigrants from both nearby and more distant towns, villages, and tribes. Furthermore, it ought to be emphasized that these features of hetero-geneity and mobility were typical of populations that, on the eve of the First World War, numbered only approximately forty thousand in Jaffa and twenty thousand in Haifa (Kark 1990, 151; Yazbak 1998, 89–111). These figures show a rapid growth when compared with the estimates for the early nine-teenth century, yet in absolute terms they represent medium-sized, albeit highly vibrant and socially mobile, urban communities.

In the summer of 1915, two Ottoman-Arab officials, Muhammad Bahjat and Rafiq al-Tamimi, arrived in Haifa. They had been sent by the governor of the province of Beirut to explore the situation in the province and to report their assessment of its socioeconomic conditions. In a chapter of their pro-found account "The Social Conditions in Haifa," the two enthusiastic young authors wrote: "One cannot find [another] town like Haifa where contrasts and strange differences in social life are [so] evident. To notice this all one needs to do is to stand in a corner of any one of the city markets and watch the appearance of the passers-by. Then one could not find a generalization that fits all the residents of Haifa as this is a town comprising all nations" (Bahjat and al-Tamimi 1917–18, 1: 246). The two Ottoman-Arab travelers, who earlier had had a chance to visit and live in larger cities such as Beirut, Istanbul, and even Paris, did not visit Jaffa during their tour because it was not included in the province of Beirut. Had they visited there too, their impressions of it would most probably have been similar to their view of Haifa.

Seventeen years earlier, in 1898, the German kaiser had visited Palestine, an occasion that inspired the Lumiere brothers to produce one of the very first documentary films. Several years ago the material cut from their film was used to produce the fifteen-minute feature *A Spectacle of Cinematography*. This fascinating film shows a visit to Palestine that started in the port of Jaffa, continued through its streets and markets, and from there proceeding by train to Jerusalem, where the filmmakers toured the streets of the old city, and then returned to Jaffa. The part showing the visit in the streets of Jaffa offers a visual depiction of what Bahjat and al-Tamimi reported about Haifa in 1915.[8]

8. Educational Television of Israel, *The Treasury of Old Films: "A Spectacle of Cinematography,"* directed by Yosi Ha-Lahmi. For a discourse analysis of Bahjat and al-Tamimi's report and a reconstruction of their Orientalist concepts, see Rubin 2000.

2

Family and Court

Family History in Middle Eastern Historiography

FAMILY HISTORY is a relatively new and little-used tool in the social history of the Middle East. Not a few scholarly works on the Middle East can be categorized *post factum* as "history of the family." However, historical investigation conducted within the conceptual framework of family history proper, examining the family as a unit of analysis with a deep awareness of the interdisciplinary approach, has not yet been attempted in many scholarly works on the Middle East. A great number of studies in practice deal with family issues, but, until quite recently, family history as a viable field has been neglected.

In light of the significant role that the family has played in various Middle Eastern societies, the tardiness with which it has become a distinctive field of research on the Middle East seems rather surprising. This is especially so if one considers the fact that in the historiography of both Europe and North America, which has inspired the development of many fields of historical investigation in the Middle East, family history has been a flourishing, well-established field for almost half a century (Stone 1981, 51–52; Tilly 1987; Hareven 1991). Family history has intrigued historians studying several non-Western societies (Hareven 1991, 97), but only recently has its use begun to develop in the Middle East.

The explanations for this relative neglect lie in the type of historical sources available and in the scholarly agenda of Middle East studies. The former is straightforward: there is a lack of sufficient historical sources pertaining to the "realities" of family history, particularly with regard to social strata other than the power elite. Moreover, most of the available sources do not lend themselves easily to a reconstruction of such significant dimensions as family ties and relations and their meanings for members of different groups, as well as of other dimensions based on ordinary people's perspectives. The reason for this scarcity is the nature of the historical sources: they were written exclusively by a relatively small number of people who had access to power in their society. The voices of people who belonged to other societal groups that, because of the prevailing power relations, had no access to power—such as women, children, urban lower classes, villagers, nomads, and slaves—are silenced in these sources.

The other reason for the delayed interest in the study of the family in the Middle East may be seen against the background of broader scholarly historical agendas for the history of the early-modern Middle East. In several cases, social historians of the Middle East began their research from perspectives other than the family, but are ultimately ending up seeking answers to their questions in family history. A rather similar pattern characterized the development of family history in Europe and North America several decades earlier, in the 1960s and 1970s (Stone 1981, 52–56). Yet in the study of the history of the Middle East, scholars have arrived at this field via a longer route (roughly between the 1970s and the late 1990s), motivated by a different impetus.

How did this trend develop? Since the 1970s, and even earlier, many scholarly paradigms in the history of the Middle East have been queried as part of a broader shift in post-colonial[1] historiography on this region and other Third World regions. Behind this shift stood a painful process of decolonization that occurred in many Third World countries, combined with the maturing of some new approaches in social sciences that challenged the foundations of prevailing scholarly notions of Western academia. The revisionist wave of the 1980s was composed of neo-Marxian paradigms, on the one hand, and the philosophy of Foucault and poststructuralist theories, on the other. The most salient contribution of the latter, though not necessarily the first in Middle East studies, is Edward Said's *Orientalism* (1978; see also Kramer 1989; P. Burke

---

1. I use the presentation *post-colonial* (with the hyphen) when referring to the period of de-colonization and formation of independent nation-states and to scholarship written in this period and when dealing with colonial and post-colonial situations in general. I use *postcolonial* (without the hyphen), however, to refer exclusively to scholarship written within a certain, mostly poststructuralist, analytical framework.

1995; Iggers 1997; Agmon 2004c). In Ottoman history, a major issue on the scholarly agenda of this phase, which continued well into the 1990s and beyond, has been the refutation of the paradigm of Ottoman decline. This paradigm has been criticized for lacking historicity, being Eurocentric, and being based on nationalist anachronistic presumptions.

The project of refuting the paradigm of decline has taken the form of concrete historical studies of political institutions and elite culture, as well as local histories of Ottoman provinces. Within these topics, the politics of households in the Ottoman capital and the provincial centers has been recognized as central to the revision of early-modern Ottoman history.[2] Historians who discuss these issues raise questions about the households of the power elite, seen as exhibiting a patron-client system, and about the political and social significance of these structures. Two monographs in particular illustrate this type of revision of the paradigm of Ottoman decline: one deals with the Ottoman capital and the other with provincial centers. By dealing with the politics of households, these studies have inadvertently pursued a scholarly interest in family history.

In *The Imperial Harem* (1993), Leslie Peirce discusses one of the main tropes of the Ottoman decline paradigm, the period known as "the sultanate of women" in the capital in the sixteenth and seventeenth centuries. She analyzes the politics of the imperial household and shows how women of the royal family played an accepted role. By investigating the networks that women of the royal family formed and used for pursuing political goals inside as well as outside the imperial harem, she focuses on the Ottoman culture of sovereignty and patronage. Contrary to the image of decline, this focus shows a culture that involved the royal women in Ottoman politics. The research suggests an entirely different understanding of the period of "the sultanate of women" than the one previously prevailing and at the same time turns the spotlight on the Ottoman household and its significant role in Ottoman elite culture.

The second revisionist work is Jane Hathaway's *The Politics of Households in Ottoman Egypt* (1997). Ottoman decline has been presented in terms of an emergence of local dynasties in the provinces (for example, the Mamluks in

2. See, for example, Abou-El-Haj 1974; Kunt 1983; Peirce 1993; Hathaway 1997; Khoury 1997; Toledano 1997; Shuval 2000.

the case of Egypt). Hathaway, however, deconstructs the Mamluk-Ottoman dichotomy in Egyptian history, together with the paradigm of the Ottoman decline that this dichotomy allegedly indicated in the seventeenth and eighteenth centuries. She achieves this goal by studying the emergence of the Qazdağlı household in Egypt, showing that it was a typical provincial Ottoman household in its main features and in its patronage of both local relationships and those with the imperial center.

The significance of studying the structure and formation of households for a reconsideration of early-modern Ottoman political history has not been restricted to the Ottoman dynasty or to a few prominent figures from among the Ottoman ruling elite. Historians have also recognized its potential contribution to the analysis of the local Ottoman provincial upper class.[3] Studies on households of the power elite draw on sources that contain direct evidence on the topic and are relatively abundant in Ottoman archives and libraries. However, the study of households of the local elites and even more so of other strata requires a different kind of sources, most of which do not easily lend themselves to historical examination: *sharīʿa* court records, collections of *fatawa* (legal opinions issued by muftis), travel literature, chronicles, and Ottoman demographic data.

These types of sources lead us to demographic history. In nineteenth-century Ottoman censuses and other data that serve as the main source material for demographic historians, the Ottoman authorities used the household (in its technical sense—namely, covering a group of people who shared the same house and constituted an economic unit) as their main formation. Initially, scholarly interest in this field was connected with economic history and questions of modernization in the late Ottoman period. Because the late Ottoman censuses are quite systematic, historians have been able to employ quantitative methods and statistical calculations for studying rates of demographic growth, various cross-sections of the population, and demographic movements.[4] Inspired by the Cambridge Group for the History of Population and Social Structure,[5] social historians of the Ottoman Empire—mainly (but

---

3. See, for example, Schilcher 1985; Fay 1993; Zeʾevi 1996; Yazbak 1998; Meriwether 1999; Cuno 2001; Reilly 2002.

4. See, for example, Raymond 1984; Karpat 1985; McCarthy 1990.

5. See, for example, Wall, Robin, and Laslett 1983; Reay 1996.

not exclusively) urban historians looking for evidence about household formation and structures among all urban social strata—have been using demographic sources for their purposes. Their studies have made an extremely
important contribution to uncovering the variety of household structures that
existed in premodern Ottoman societies, challenging the common knowledge
about the "traditional" family household, which allegedly was extended and
multigenerational; most of these studies have shown that no single typical
household structure existed and certainly not the large joint (more than one
married couple, with or without children) household.[6]

Haim Gerber's (1989) discussion on the nature of households in sixteenth-
century Istanbul and seventeenth-century Bursa is a case in point. Drawing on
shariʿa court records and a state survey of endowments, Gerber concludes that
the simple household (one couple and their children) rather than the joint
household was typical in these regions, mainly owing to socioeconomic and
political conditions, a finding that contradicts the accepted wisdom about "the
traditional family."[7]

These studies paved the way for other social historians who, like their
counterparts in European and North American family history and in family
histories of other Third World regions, gradually recognized the potential of
combining demographic and family history. Some historians were initially interested in the formation and structure of households for studying issues such
as the emergence of local Ottoman elite groups, the politics of notables, the
political economy of certain Ottoman provinces, and the incorporation of
the empire into the world economy. While looking for tools and concepts suit-
able for fitting the household into their various conceptual frameworks, some
shifted their focus to family history proper.

A study that illustrates this shift to family history is Kenneth Cuno's "Joint
Family Households" (1995). Drawing mainly on *fatawa* literature, Cuno shows

---

6. See Rafeq 1970; Barbir 1980; Raymond 1985; Duben 1985, 1990; Gerber 1989; Duben
and Behar 1991; Establet and Pascual 1994; Cuno 1995, 1999; Fargues 2003; Okawara 2003. A
similar interest in household studies has developed in the history of East Asia. See, for instance,
Wolf and Hanley's (1985) collected volume on China and Japan. I explain the terminology I use
for types of households and family structures in the next section.

7. Following Laslett, Gerber's use of the term *family* (1989, 410) refers to what is defined
here as *household* or *family household*.

that the joint household was the dominant form among rural notable families in nineteenth-century Egypt. Through this type of household, families preserved and reinforced their social and political status, which depended on their landed property and their ability to avoid its fragmentation during a period of profound change in the system of landholding.

In "Endowing Family: Waqf, Property Devolution, and Gender in Greater Syria, 1800 to 1860," Beshara Doumani (1998) compares the notion of family—particularly in terms of kinship, gender, and property—in Nablus and Tripoli (Syria) in the first half of the nineteenth century, drawing on family *waqf* endowments.[8] He finds that family patterns in Nablus tended to stress the patrilineal structure and property-devolution strategies tended to exclude the female line of descent, whereas in Tripoli family patterns were more conjugal, and property devolution was more egalitarian genderwise. He suggests that this unexpected difference between two rather adjacent societies should be understood mainly in terms of the different political economies of the two cities.

By discussing the role of gender relations in the construction of the family, Doumani's article brings attention to another rapidly growing field of research on the Middle East—the history of women and gender. The scholarly works on these topics are closely connected to the post-colonial agenda and have ultimately led some historians to family history. A major goal of revisionist approaches to the history of the Middle East has been to challenge the concept of the stagnant and passive Orient, whose history was allegedly determined exclusively by external forces. The paradigm of Ottoman decline was only one aspect of that concept. For historians of women and gender, the agenda has been to revisit concepts of stagnation and passiveness twice: first, with regard to the Orient as a whole, and, second, in relation to the construction of societal groups in the Middle East, mainly women, as both passive and unchanging (Agmon 2004c).

8. *Waqf* is a legal framework that allows property owners to endow a revenue-producing property for charity and religious goals and to allocate its revenues to designated people and goals (see chapter 7, note 18). Property owners used the *waqf* to exclude certain assets from the *shari'a* inheritance law by endowing them and designating specific family members as beneficiaries and by defining the principle of passing on beneficiary rights to all future generations. On the colonial roots of scholarly biases in the study on *waqf*, see Powers 1989.

Bringing women back into history ("back" not because they had been there before, but rather because history was incomplete without them) initially required that women would first become a category of historical investigation. However, this process frequently defeated its purpose because it resulted in a separate instead of an integrated history of women. Joan Scott's essay "Gender: A Useful Category of Analysis" in her 1988 book *Gender and the Politics of History* was a call for breaking the dichotomous history of men and of women without giving up the awareness of the cultural sex differentiation and the power relations it reproduced (see also Scott 1995, 52–58). It should be noted that the two categories, women and gender, are not synonyms, although they are quite often used as if they were (Scott 1988, 31–32). The analytical category "women" refers to a distinctive social group defined by sex. Hence, women's history deals separately with the past of women, feminine subgroups, and individual women. Gender, in contrast, has two dimensions. It is a category, a societal group defined by social roles and cultural meanings attributed to its sexual distinction in society, but at the same time it is an analytical perspective focusing on the differences between sex groups in society and the ways they are constructed in all spheres of life. Hence, from the perspective of gender, women cannot be looked at separately, but rather must be viewed in relation to men, and vice versa, and the history of women ceases to be a supplement of history, men's history (Scott 1995, 56–57).

The movement from the category of women to that of gender in the history of the Middle East—occurring roughly since the mid-1990s—has offered a particularly important contribution to understanding the role of women in nationalist movements and modernity (or, rather, an illustration of their potential contribution because only a few scholars have so far chosen to make such a move).[9] It has also enriched the analysis of historical sources and literature required for the interpretation of evidence from the classical period and the Middle Ages, for which source material for social history is extremely limited and problematic.[10] In addition, it has helped to introduce discourse analysis into social history at large. For some historians who shifted their frame of inquiry from women to gender, the next logical move was to family. In this regard, the passage from the category of historical analysis of women to the

9. See, for example, Baron 1993, 2005; Kandiyoti 1998; Najmabadi 1998, 2005; Booth 2001.

10. See, for example, Malti-Douglas 1991; Sanders 1991.

analysis of gender and then of family may be viewed as a move toward the pluralization of women's history.

A recent work by one of the most prolific scholars in the field, Judith Tucker, serves as an illustration here. Tucker, who to my knowledge wrote the first monograph on the social history of women in the Middle East (Tucker 1985), for a long time defined her conceptual framework as the history of women, employing quantitative methods for analyzing *shariʿa* court records. Nevertheless, her analysis of the position of lower-class Egyptian women even in her earlier book cannot be described as an autonomous women's history. In her recent book *In the House of the Law: Gender and Islamic Law in Ottoman Syria and Palestine* (1998), she has explicitly shifted to gender while adding sources and focusing on qualitative rather than quantitative methods in her analysis. She discusses the legal realities of gender roles and relations in seventeenth- and eighteenth-century Ottoman Jerusalem, Nablus, and Damascus, drawing on both *shariʿa* court records and *fatawa* literature. She examines court cases and *fatawa* on marriage, divorce, child rearing, and sexuality. By analyzing the legal discourses of gender, she shows that the Islamic legal system in early-modern Syria, although based on a patriarchal bias, was both in theory and in practice rather flexible, sometimes even compensating for that bias.[11]

The shift from the history of women to the history of gender has not been easy. In fact, the shift to gender analysis, which chronologically became an option in Middle East studies before family history, has in many cases never been accomplished beyond the level of the use of the title "women and gender" for studies on women. In European and North American historiography, the interest in family history preceded the focus on women and gender. By contrast, historians of the Middle East who specialized in the history of women apparently did not even consider the family as a category of analysis. In the post-colonial context of Middle Eastern historiography, the family had a subconsciously negative connotation as a category that identifies women with the domestic sphere, a linkage that historians tried to sever.[12] Therefore, the recent conceptual turn to the family has been neither clear-cut nor inevitable.

11. See a discussion on both of Tucker's monographs in Agmon 2004c.

12. See, for example, the review of Tucker's book on Egyptian women (1985) by Andrea Rugh (1988). Rugh blames Tucker for using Western criteria when attributing higher social status to women who were involved in economic and social activities in the public sphere. In her

As mentioned, the shift has also been a function of the nature of the source material used—namely, legal sources, in particular *shari'a* court records. The Ottoman *shari'a* court records have emerged as one of the most important sources for social history, including that of women and gender, in the early-modern and modern Middle East (Ze'evi 1998; Moors 1999; Agmon 2004c). These records clearly emphasize the significance of the family as a major social, cultural, and political unit. Even when the inherent legal bias toward certain aspects of domestic life is taken into account, the logic of employing the family as a unit of analysis can hardly be ignored. The structure of scholarly works by legal historians who explore social issues and use *shari'a* court records intensively (as reflected in the table of contents of their monographs) well illustrates the emphasis on the family.[13] Another important legal source frequently employed by historians of women and gender, *fatawa* literature, also underscores the importance of the family. Thus, it was only a matter of time before Middle East historians of women and gender would turn to family history to seek better (or, at least, more) answers to their questions. When some of them made this move, their paths crossed those of historians, such as Doumani and Cuno, who came to family history from the perspective of provincial and local history. Both historiographic currents have shared the experience of drawing on *shari'a* court records and *fatawa* literature as major source material.[14]

Three methodological approaches in the current historiography on the family, two of which are closely interrelated, have also contributed to this shift. First, discourse analysis, borrowed mainly from the field of literary criticism, focuses on the role of language, vocabulary, and text structure in the description of historical reality (Kramer 1989, 99–107). It is particularly useful for reading sources that at first glance do not look like the "natural" choice for the historian of the family. In other words, by employing this method, some historians have been able to utilize sources that were previously considered

---

view, the domestic sphere, the family, is the source of women's social status in Egyptian society (119–20). Although Rugh's critique sustains my point about the family and shows sensitivity to problems of positioning in historical investigation, her view may at the same time sustain a reproduction of the very Orientalist vision she clearly means to criticize. See also Toledano 1989.

13. See, for example, Layish 1975, 1991; Shaham 1997.

14. See also Meriwether and Tucker 1999, 6–8.

mute and therefore useless for the writing of family history. For example, Leslie Peirce discusses in one of her articles (1997) the discourse of gender in legal and administrative texts of sixteenth- and seventeenth-century Ottoman Anatolia. These sources were written by Ottoman statesmen and thus represent a masculine, state-oriented perspective. Nevertheless, by employing discourse analysis, Peirce convincingly extricates from them various cultural concepts about domestic cycles of men, women, and families that prevailed in the observed society. Yet the potential of poststructuralist methods, as demonstrated in this article and in a few other studies, is still far from being fully recognized and properly articulated in the field of family history or in the social history of the Middle East.

The second approach is the result of the influence of anthropology on historical methodology (Adams 1981; Cohn 1981; Davis 1981, 1990; P. Burke 1995; Sharpe 1995). The impact of anthropology has been particularly tangible because several anthropologists have used the *shariʿa* court records, and a few have studied contemporary *shariʿa* courts as participating observers and have written ethnographies about them. Some social historians have been inspired by these studies and by their conceptual frameworks, including family and kinship, which are pivotal issues in cultural anthropology.

The third approach, also linked to the impact of anthropology, deals with the size and nature of the unit of observation. Historians writing on Ottoman provincial history have been immensely inspired by the Annales school; by studies in local history, such as Le Roy Ladurie's *Montaillou;* and by the concepts *histoire totale* and the *longue durée* defined in Braudel's *La Mediterranée et le monde méditerranéen à l'époque de Phillipe II* (1966).[15] In the 1980s, when most of the wide-scale studies on the history of the Ottoman provinces were conducted, quantitative methods and large-scale units of observation and periodization dominated social history of the Middle East (Agmon 2004c). Consequently, provincial *longue durée* histories became more abundant. When these historians continued their research in more recent years, however, after accomplishing their *longue durée* dissertations, some of them looked for smaller units of observation in order to pinpoint more subtle social processes and

---

15. See, for example, Raymond 1973–74; Gerber 1988; Marcus 1989; Doumani 1995; Zeʾevi 1996; Khoury 1997. Most of these monographs are based on dissertations for which research was conducted in the 1980s. On the Annales school, see P. Burke 1990.

mechanisms of change that had attracted their attention during their initial research. Opting for a focus on the family meant a reduction in the scale of the unit of analysis, which is yet another characteristic of anthropological methodologies. For instance, Doumani's *Rediscovering Palestine* (1995) is a provincial history of the Nablus region in the eighteenth and nineteenth centuries based on his dissertation. In his later work (1998, 2003), however, he concentrates on certain aspects of his previous work and develops them within the conceptual framework of the family. For historians who shifted from women and gender studies to family history, the change in the unit of analysis was not so much in its size, but rather in its nature: from a unit defined by a group (sex group, in this case) and by a hierarchy of power relations (gender) to a structure that is socially and culturally constructed in history—the family.

After this long incubation period, the current shape of family historiography in the Middle East is, perhaps not surprisingly, rather similar to the basic characteristics of its European and North American counterparts in the early 1980s, as described by Lawrence Stone (1981, 55–56). The similarity is evident at least insofar as interdisciplinary approaches are concerned. As in European and North American family history in the early 1980s, five salient approaches may be discerned in the current writing on the Middle East: the demographic, legal, economic, social, and cultural approaches illustrated earlier. In his review article on Euro-American family history up to the 1980s, Stone suggests another classification—"history from below" and "history from above." These categories, however, seem almost irrelevant to the state of family history in the Middle East at the turn of the twenty-first century.

This state of the field may be attributable to the time lag between the commencement of research on Euro-American family history and the commencement of research on Middle Eastern family history. The approach known as "history from below" first emerged within social history before the methodological changes encouraged by the "cultural turn," mainly discourse analysis, reshaped the field. Later came the development of these methods for inducing source material to "speak" with the voices of various social strata, groups, and individuals that were not initially apparent. These new perspectives rendered the term *history from below* very inaccurate. E. P. Thompson's definition of *history from below* as a reconstruction of the past experience of ordinary people and the understanding of that experience in their own terms does not do justice to the wide range of methodologies and types of inquiry that the newly developed approaches encouraged (Sharpe 1995, 26, 35–38). At a time when Euro-American "history from below" inspired research on the social history of the Middle East, many of these innovative methods and lines of inquiry were already firmly established.

Moreover, the nature of most of the source material for social history (family history included) in the Middle East is such that it does not lend itself to writing "history from below" as defined by Thompson. Diaries, memoirs, and other such sources are not known to exist for strata of Middle Eastern societies other than the upper ones, and even for them they are not very abundant. Legal sources, used intensively for European medieval history to extrapolate past experiences of ordinary people, provide too "thin" a description for this kind of historical analysis in the case of the Middle East.[16]

Thus, scholarly works dealing with notables and members of the upper class and those focusing on ordinary people require similar methodological sophistication, and both portray a historical picture for which their classification as either "history from above" or "history from below" lacks explanatory capacity. Peirce's *Morality Tales: Law and Gender in the Ottoman Court of Aintab* (2003) may well illustrate my point. In order to contextualize the construction of gender and local justice in a concrete historical setting, Peirce reconstructs the interrelations between the *shari'a* judge and other Ottoman officials in sixteenth-century Aintab, on the one hand, and Aintaban men and women who sought legal solutions for their problems in court, on the other. Her main argument is that the local court was an arena in which law was continually negotiated and interpreted by both the judge and the local community. Her sources were produced by Ottoman officials of various ranks in the judicial, military, and fiscal administration—members of the ruling elite and local established families. By virtue of her focus on interactions that took place in court, she deals with both local people of different social positions and state officials belonging to the power elite. The reconstruction of the latter could be defined as "history from above" owing to their status and the fact that the sources represent their perspectives, whereas the reconstruction of local ordinary people, women in particular, would certainly be defined as "history from

---

16. See the exemplary works in European history by Le Roy Ladurie 1978; Ginzburg 1980; Davis 1983; and Sabean 1990, 1998.

below": by employing discourse analysis, Peirce skillfully reads ordinary people's points of view into sources they themselves did not write. However, the interactions between these groups and the urban and regional setting would be difficult to define one way or another. Moreover, whether these aspects in Peirce's work are easy or difficult to define, such a definition is not worthwhile, for it would defeat the very purpose of her work.[17]

The historiography on the family in the Middle East also seems to be divided thematically. The structure of the first collection on family history in the Middle East, *Family History in the Middle East: Households, Property, and Gender* (2003), edited by Beshara Doumani, illustrates this division. The volume consists of four parts: two are thematically defined, *(a)* family and household, and *(b)* family, gender, and property; the other two deal with sources and methodology—the *shariʿa* court records as a source for family history and the family as discourse, respectively. The first two parts reflect the current thematic disintegration of the field. This situation is also reflected in the fact that all the contributions by anthropologists in the volume are assembled in the second section on family, gender, and property, whereas the section on households includes articles authored by historians. The editor of the anthology highlights the disintegration of the field in his introduction, although he interprets it as "a healthy sign" (Doumani 2003, 2–3). This disintegration is also apparent in some of the articles themselves and in other studies in family history proper.

The thematic division is twofold: the family serves as a loosely tied framework within which various studies are in fact dealing with either household formation and structures or property and gender. Except for falling under the broad headline of family history, the two areas have little in common. The other aspect of this division is the lack of integration between the discussion on family structures—namely, households—and the discussion on family sentiments and relations. This separation may also be described in terms of form and substance; the meaning of the household is restricted to form, whereas human relations that developed within this form are discussed in isolation as the quintessence of the family. An important exception to this pattern is represented by Duben and Behar's (1991) study on Istanbul households. In addition to writing one of the earliest monographs on family history proper, the authors combine a discussion of household structures and formation with

17. For further discussion on Peirce 2003, see Agmon 2003a, 2004c.

questions of family ties and sentiments. However, in their analysis, they adopt a binary concept of the passage from "traditional" (or "indigenous") to "modern" ("westernized") family values, which perhaps inadvertently reproduces earlier scholarly notions that they initially meant to revisit in their study. Generally speaking, however, the studies in the field of family history deal either with whoever was included in the family household in technical terms (relatives by kin, marriage, patronage, service, and slavery) or with gender roles and relations, emotional bonds, and economic interests. Only the issue of property and economic interests is dealt with in both contexts.[18]

The thematic division appears to reflect two features of the state of the field. One feature is the fact that family history is still in its initial phase as a field in the social history of the Middle East; its territory has not yet been clearly defined in terms of historical questions, methods, and sources. The different circumstances and the various fields from which historians have moved to family history are in some cases more salient in their studies in family history than the new framework they have adopted (Doumani 2003, 2). This is likely to change as time goes by. The second feature is more inherent in the definition of the field: the multidimensional nature of the family as a unit of analysis and the fact that it has a bearing on so many aspects of historical investigation. This feature, provided that it becomes a bit more balanced, constitutes to my mind a major benefit of this field because it leaves much desirable space for historical imagination.

Family and Sociocultural Analysis

As noted, family history became a distinctive field of study in Western academia in the 1960s, as part of the development of social history. From the outset, social historians determined their objective as twofold: to reconstruct past experiences of marginalized individuals and societal groups—those who had no access to political power, economic wealth, and high social status, and hence were not considered historical subjects—and to analyze the role these individuals and groups played in macrohistorical transformations, which entails rewriting the history of these changes accordingly.[19] The family was recognized as a useful unit of analysis for this enterprise (Tilly 1987; Hareven

---

18. See also Agmon 1998, 493–95, where I made only an initial comment on the matter. A similar criticism about Chinese family studies is included in Zhao 2001, 39.

19. For a recent critical survey of the state of social history, see Magnússon 2003.

1991). Like other fields of social history, family history borrowed approaches, methods, and models from other disciplines, notably social sciences. Economy, sociology, and demography provided quantitative tools for the analysis of serial sources in search of family structures, household formations, kinship, and property devolution. Anthropology, psychology, and literary criticism inspired terminology, conceptual frameworks, and theoretical thinking. In the course of the 1970s and 1980s, as historians tackled postmodernist challenges, the latter influence grew stronger while generating questions on family and gender, discussions on family discourses, and microanalyses of the meanings of family bonds and sentiments.[20]

At first, historians sought answers to a wide range of questions on the passage of Western societies to modernity and social transformations at large in the realm of family life. And the research on household structures and family relations in premodern western Europe indeed changed some hitherto accepted conventions. For instance, the belief that premodern families in western Europe tended to live in large joint households and that industrialization reinforced the notion of the simple family was profoundly undermined. The development of the field encouraged family historians to expand their "territory" and to explore family life in ancient societies, such as the Roman Empire and ancient Greece. At the same time, family history gradually became a distinctive field of study in the history of other societies as well—North America, eastern and southern Europe, Asia, Africa, and Latin America (Hareven 1991, 97). In the writing of Middle East history, however, this development occurred, as described, much later.

A number of themes of family history are pertinent to my study. In studying family households, historians have often combined quantitative demographic methodologies with anthropological terminology and research strategies.[21] In the historiography on the Middle East, the common wisdom

20. See my review article (Agmon 2004c). Magnússon (2003) offers a different periodization for and evaluation of the influences of postmodern philosophy on social history. He argues that postmodern challenges affected this historiography only since the late 1980s and that then the changes were insignificant. His analysis, however, is based on a separation between the development of microhistory and cultural history in the 1970s and 1980s, on the one hand, and the "linguistic turn," on the other. In my view, this separation is flawed as far as understanding the shifts in historical writing is concerned.

21. See, for example, Sabean 1990 and 1998.

enhanced by modernization theories was that the "traditional" (that is, the ahistorically Muslim/Arab premodern) family lived in an extended household serving as a socioeconomic unit headed by its patriarch. Social, economic, and demographic historians who have questioned this myth have analyzed demographic and fiscal data, land registrations, inheritance inventories, and *waqf* endowments. As noted earlier, in their studies on family household structures and on the formation of these structures in certain societies at specific periods, these historians have shown that a variety of household structures prevailed in premodern Middle Eastern societies. Moreover, they have linked their findings about household formation and family structures to various aspects of family life and to the family's interaction with broader processes in society, such as changes in land tenure, commercialization of agricultural production, urbanization, and processes of state formation—thereby revisiting the narratives on these macroprocesses.[22]

I do not undertake quantitative research on the reconstitution of families and forms of households here, but I do study several questions relating to these issues and employ certain terminology that requires elaboration. I define *family households* as either "simple" or "joint." A *simple household* contains one married couple and their children. In the literature on family history, sociology, and anthropology, this structure often appears as either *nuclear* or *conjugal*. I use the term *nuclear* when referring to a structure or notion of "family" (composed of a married couple and their children), as opposed to *household*— namely, the same group of relatives dwelling together and constituting an economic unit. I use the term *conjugal* to stress a simple-family notion or family structure to which a person belongs through matrimony (as opposed to a person's family by birth, or the *natal* family).

As noted earlier, a *joint household* contains more than one married couple, with or without children. This term covers various combinations of family structures. The *extended household*—a multigenerational structure headed by the elder father and including unmarried daughters and all married sons and their conjugal families—is only one such combination. For instance, a joint household may include a number of brothers with their conjugal families, unmarried sisters, a divorced mother, or any combination thereof. It may also include

22. To name but a few: Raymond 1973–74; Duben and Behar 1991; Peirce 1993; Cuno 1995; Doumani 1998; Shuval 1998; Meriwether 1999.

polygamous families. In the literature on family history, there are specific terms for some of these combinations. For instance, a joint household comprised of two or more brothers and their conjugal families is called *frèrèche,* and a polygamous household is called a *compound.* For brevity and simplicity, I use the term *joint household* for all variations and describe the composition of each case I discuss. In addition, I use the term *extended family* when referring to a group of nuclear families related to each other both horizontally through kin and marriage among the same generation, and vertically among kin of three generations, but not necessarily living under one roof.

The families under investigation in this study belonged to urban communities undergoing rapid demographic growth, which raises questions about living conditions and the cultural ideals that pertained to the boundaries between men and women who were not relatives, particularly among the middle and lower classes. Two intertwined sets of issues of family history are relevant here: one links family with questions on migration, family networks, neighborly relations, and family space; the other pertains to family and gender. Several scholars have already established that a large joint-family household was not a common structure among urban populations in Ottoman towns even before the nineteenth century (Raymond 1985; Gerber 1989; Marcus 1989; Duben and Behar 1991; Establet and Pascual 1994; Shuval 1998). The present study employs microanalytic methods in sustaining similar findings about the existence of various household structures among the urban middle class in Jaffa and Haifa. It further deals with physical proximity among neighbors and notions of family space developed in a situation involving the constant immigration of a variety of people to the port cities, people who often moved there alone or only with their nuclear families. This situation, in addition to scarcity of housing and high rents, entailed smaller family structures and more proximity among nonkin. At the same time, there was *chain migration,* in which newcomers' kin, friends, and neighbors from their hometown or village followed them and settled nearby.

The implications of immigration and urban growth also bring to the fore the issues of family and gender. As noted, these two categories are complementary. A number of questions linked to gender and certain methods for analyzing them in the literature on the family are pertinent to the present study. Gender is essential for the discussion of the family as both a discourse and a socially constructed unit. Here, legal notions of family and the changes these notions underwent with regard to gender roles and relations constitute major themes. The patrilineal family is a core element of legal notions of family, which entail a clear male dominance in family and society. However, other aspects of legal discourse and changes that transpired in the legal arena and in other spheres of life in the course of the nineteenth century in Jaffa and Haifa also played a role in constructing both family and gender. When investigated within this framework, the category of gender highlights concepts of social justice in the legal discourse on the family. I discuss gender in relation to two other categories essential for studying the family: children and matrimony. The category of children, combined with gender, raises questions about parenthood and the distribution of labor between parents as well as between them and other relatives. I link this issue in the present study to contested family notions: for example, the patrilineal family versus the conjugal family (the family unit that a man and a woman establish through marriage). The historical circumstances in the changing Ottoman Empire described in chapter 1 contributed to accelerate tensions between the two family notions. The analysis of children's material and emotional well-being in the rapidly growing urban communities of Jaffa and Haifa highlights these tensions and the underlying dynamics.

One of the approaches I employed for understanding family and gender is *life-course analysis* of individuals in their families. This approach is meant to introduce a dynamic dimension into the historical investigation of families by reconstructing the experiences of individuals at various stages in their domestic cycle and in their interactions with other family members along the way. It is also meant to sustain the development of *family time,* a measurement pertaining distinctly to family history (Hareven 1991, 106–8). Like many other approaches in family history, life-course analysis is used mainly as part of quantitative research.[23] The present study inclines toward microanalysis, so I employ this life-course approach on a small scale to improve understanding of the interplay between family and gender and to get some sense of what it was like to be, for instance, a minor girl, a wife, a mother, or a grandmother; to move from one stage to another in the domestic cycle; and to provide an idea of what choices men and women of a middle-level social background had in the nineteenth-century port cities.

23. See, for example, Magnússon 1995.

In addition to class or socioeconomic levels, another significant factor in reshaping family notions I consider here is the Ottoman state and the profound restructuring it underwent. The interrelations between family and state, frequently discussed by family historians with regard to processes of the formation of modern states, constitute an important issue in the present study by virtue of its setting: the legal arena and the historical circumstances of Ottoman reform. My discussions on interrelations between family and state in turn reaffirm the conceptual inseparability of the categories of family and gender and their historical bearing on the societies under investigation: any change that state reform policies introduced in the balance between state and family was reflected in the construction of the family, first and foremost in terms of its gender roles and relations.

Court Records and Historical Reconstruction

Since the 1970s, the Ottoman *shari'a* court records of various periods and places have been used as source material in a wide range of scholarly works on the history of the Middle East and the Balkans. These studies were written mainly within the perspectives of political, social, and legal histories. The methodologies applied for using the records as a historical source have also varied in kind and sophistication, ranging from quantitative to impressionistic and qualitative methods, or (mostly) combinations thereof (Ze'evi 1998; Moors 1999; Agmon 2004c).

For centuries, the *shari'a* court system constituted the judicial backbone of the Ottoman state. It sustained the reproduction of its identity, status, and raison d'être as a Muslim empire. The four schools of *shari'a* law (especially the Hanafi school adopted by the Ottoman Empire), the ad hoc laws and regulations of the state *(kanun),* the way of life of the empire's subjects, their norms and beliefs, as well as various customs and local practices—all were constantly processed by the on-going work of this court system. All that remain of the multifarious forms of daily human interaction at a large number of courts throughout the empire are the surviving records, a huge collection documenting a variety of daily legal procedures. Present-day historians have the rare opportunity of access to what appear to be the past experiences of a wide range of people who lived in different eras and regions.

This offer is irresistible for social historians, particularly so for the social historians of the Middle East. Since the emergence of social history as a distinctive field of study in the history of the Middle East in the early 1970s, the latter historians have watched longingly as their colleagues produce fascinating social histories of medieval Europe based on serial legal documents. With regard to their own situation, they knew that historical reconstruction based only on law books and manuals of etiquette leaves out most of the people who actually lived in the past and ignores many aspects of their lives. Such reconstruction requires substantiation, and to achieve it, sources of empirical nature are essential. Thus, seeing this sort of serial documentation, the *shariʿa* court records, as useful was initially a source of such excitement that some historians were carried away. They too often considered the records positivistically as a mine of information just waiting "out there" to be picked up and to tell us exactly what "really happened" in the past (Agmon 2004c). As Linda Lewin, who specializes in the family history of Brazil, argues, "by not sufficiently distinguishing legal requirements from social practices, historians may have been reading the former as the latter. By the same token, they may have erred by confusing common social practice with the law's routine provisions" (1992, 353).

However, with the passage of time, scholars have become more critical about the use of this source for historical reconstruction. In addition, since the 1980s several scholarly works on the anthropology of law dealing with contemporary Muslim societies have been published. These studies may be broadly defined according to three conceptual emphases and scholarly traditions. First, a number of studies have been influenced by the European, mostly British, academic tradition of social anthropology that focuses on social relations, such as Bernard Cohn's studies on India (1965, 1996), John Bowen's on Java (1988), June Starr's on Turkey (1992), Martha Mundy's and Anna Würth's on Yemen (both 1995), and Ziba Mir-Hosseini's on Iran and Morocco (1997, 1998). Second, works written within the American (mostly Geertzian) cultural anthropology focus on structures of meanings: Lawrence Rosen's on Morocco (1989), Barbara Yngvesson's on a Muslim court in New England (1993), and Brinkley Messick's on Yemen (1993). At the same time, Messick has produced one of the salient works in the third group, which may be defined as "postcolonial anthropology," focusing on power relations, hegemony, inequality, and resistance. Another characteristic of some of the studies in this third group, well represented by Messick's work, is the focus on history in ethnographic work. Messick's work represents a synthesis of the cultural and postcolonial anthropologies of law.

Other studies in the postcolonial group are Allan Christelow's on Algeria

(1985), Susan Hirsch's on Kenya (1994, 1998), Erin Moore's on India (1994), Annelies Moors's on Palestine (1995), and Ido Shahar's on the Israeli *shariʿa* court in Jerusalem (2000a, 2000b). Interestingly, only a few among these scholars actually conducted participatory observations in courts of law, and except for Messick and to a lesser extent Shahar (2000a), none pays particular attention to the production of court records and other legal documents. The interest in courts of law, however, may be growing: in two recent dissertations (Kogacıoğlu 2003; Shahar 2005), the court is the main site of observation, studied as a sociolegal arena.[24]

Anthropological studies have inspired historians investigating court records in terms of approaches, interpretation strategies, and the critique on the use of historical court records.[25] In recent years, some critical articles and scholarly debates on the nature of the court records and on the scholarship based on them have been published.[26] At the same time, historians have been paying more attention to the construction of the text of court records and to the process of their production. This alternate focus has had an impact on the interpretation of the records. Yet two major lacunae still exist in the research.

First, a map and typology of the various collections of *shariʿa* court records are needed. Historians have substantiated their research by "the *shariʿa* court record," inadvertently obscuring the fact that the records, although showing a high level of uniformity owing to their adherence to certain textual formulae and calligraphic conventions, also reflect a wide range of differences that require historization.[27]

Second, our knowledge about the work of the *shariʿa* court system and its personnel is quite sparse. Obviously, the court records constitute the only remaining section of a large number of court activities. In order to understand better how the texts of the records relate to past realities both inside and out-

24. There are probably more studies, yet this list gives a general idea of the field. Two additional studies are difficult to define as belonging in any one of the categories: Hill 1979 and Berk-Seligson 1992. I am grateful to Ido Shahar for sharing his observations with me.

25. Cases in point are Gerber 1989, 1994; Agmon 1995; Zeʾevi 1998; Peirce 2003; Ergene 2004.

26. See Ghazzal 1996, 1998; Raymond 1998; Zeʾevi 1998; Agmon 2004c. See also "Court Records Discussion" and "Qadi Court Records Workshop" at http://socrates.berkeley.edu/~mescha.

27. "Court Records Discussion" at http://socrates.berkeley.edu/~mescha.

side the courtroom, we need to investigate the court itself, the people who worked there, and the record they produced (Ze'evi 1998). Such a contribution is Jun Akiba's pioneering dissertation exploring the education and administration of the Ottoman *shari'a* court judges during the Tanzimat reforms.[28] This prosopographic study has contributed significant insights about the court records integrated in my study. Two recently published books also make an important contribution: one by Boğaç Ergene (2003) dealing with the courts of seventeenth- and eighteenth-century Çankırı and Kastamonu, two neighboring district centers in northern Anatolia (see also Ergene 2004, forthcoming); the other, by Leslie Peirce (2003), dealing, as noted earlier, with the sixteenth-century court of Aintab in southeastern Anatolia (see also Peirce 1997, 1998a, 1998b). However, much more needs to be explored in this sphere, particularly with regard to the work of *shari'a* courts and their personnel in the different provinces.

The legal aspect is also, perhaps surprisingly, somewhat problematic and requires further efforts. Social historians whose research is located in the legal sphere must acquire substantial knowledge of legal history in order to understand these texts and the entire arena of their interpretation. They correctly assume that the legal sphere is just yet another site, albeit important and unique, of social interaction and power relations operating within a specific historical context, so that, as in any other interdisciplinary research, their appeal to legal history for tools and perspectives to help historical reconstruction is reasonable. However, although Islamic law and historical investigation are common denominators of both legal and social histories, the rich Muslim legal history is still to a large extent inaccessible to social historians. At the same time, in most (but certainly not all) cases when legal historians use empirical legal sources, such as *shari'a* court records and *fatawa,* and discuss social issues in their investigation, the parameters they use depart only very cautiously from purely legal ones.

The reason for the poor communication between social and legal historians seems to be the difference between the scientific traditions of the two fields. The roots of this situation can be found in the sociology of knowledge on Muslim societies. As a discipline, Muslim legal history more resembles

---

28. Akiba's dissertation is written in Japanese. However, a number of his papers and articles are based on this work (Akiba 2000, 2003, 2005).

intellectual rather than social history. Its main frame of reference is the vast body of normative legal literature, and its discourse is legalistic in nature (Powers 1989; Hallaq 2002–2003). The development of social history, in contrast, originally resulted from a call for the historization of exactly this type of approach (Moors 1999). The ineffective communication undermines the interests of both spheres of knowledge, and the challenge of more productive dialogue stands at the doorsteps of both social and legal historians.

A major aim of my study is to contribute to overcoming the second lacuna by looking at the court records of late Ottoman Jaffa and Haifa as a historical object and by offering a methodology for contextualizing them. To achieve this aim, I have investigated the following aspects of the court records: calligraphic, stylistic, and orthographic phenomena; textual formulae; recording procedures; routines of court work; ranks and hierarchies of judges and other court personnel; and judges' and scribes' social backgrounds and career paths.[29] I do not deal with these issues separately, but rather as an integral part of the discussion of other themes. This part of my hermeneutic strategy aims at demonstrating that the context of the court records (or of any other source material for that matter) and the main historical themes of research are inseparable. In other words, my intention is to pursue the idea of the departure from the methodological division between historical sources serving as an external arena and the historical reconstruction "stemming" from these sources—a division that inadvertently renders historical sources an extraterritorial status, which in turn is bound to damage the quality of the historical reconstruction.

At the same time, although this study also employs discourse analysis and deems the structure and the language of the court texts records extremely important, it by no means gives up on a historical reconstruction of past processes, events, and experiences. On the contrary: I employ these various approaches as vehicles to improve the historical reconstruction of past realities. Moreover, although acknowledging the pitfalls of historical reconstruction based on court records and the uniqueness of the court arena, I nevertheless insist on a reconstruction of the events, relations, and processes that took place both inside and outside the courtroom. The underlying assumption is that knowing past realities—in fact, also present ones—as they

29. For a social biography of a judge in rural Morocco, see Eickleman 1985.

"really happened" is always an unfinished and uncertain business. Yet that does not necessarily mean that the surviving texts provide historians with access only to "the eye of the beholder," specifically the producers of the texts, nor does it mean that past realities and the poetics of the texts describing these realities are historically equal.[30]

Another assumption I make here is that although the court arena is indeed socially unique, it is nevertheless not isolated. Although a site of authority and sacred knowledge, the *shariʿa* court was not detached from people's daily lives and was actually open to them. I show that the reformed *shariʿa* court preserved the feature of accessibility to all by stressing the characteristics of mediation and arbitration typical of the judge's functioning. Furthermore, I argue that in the course of redefining their position in the wake of the reforms, the *shariʿa* courts of Jaffa and Haifa reinforced their open-door attitude, which in turn encouraged mainly (though not exclusively) people of modest background to use their services. Thus, the strategy I adopt stresses a continuum from the court arena to the social arena at large, allowing some leeway for speculation and consideration of the plausibility of interpretations offered.

I use two other major sources, both Ottoman administrative records, for the contextualization of the court records. One is the collection of rules, regulations, and instructions, *Düstur,* issued by the Ottoman government during the Tanzimat and post-Tanzimat reforms, available in two published multi-volume editions (*Düstur* 1, *Düstur* 2), which include many regulations relating to the work of the *shariʿa* courts, judges, and other relevant issues. The second source consists of two sets of personal records providing information on Ottoman *shariʿa* judges and other officials of the religious administration *(ilmiye),* dating from the late nineteenth century and kept at the Ministry of Şeyhülislâm in Istanbul (Fetvahane, or Bab-ı meşihat), the bureaucratic organ in charge of the *shariʿa* court system. One set *(Sicill-i ahval dosyaları)* is literally a collection of dossiers, each including different papers with information about the career of a certain judge, such as a history of his education, other biographical details, a curriculum vitae, official correspondence regarding his service, and other such papers. The dossiers differ from one another in size and composition. The other set *(Sicill-i ahval defeterleri)* consists of seven

---

30. On a methodology for recovering the lost voices of enslaved people and writing their social history, see Toledano forthcoming.

volumes of summaries of judges' careers registered by the officials of the Fetvahane. Some judges were registered in both sets, and others only in one. In addition, there were judges who were not registered in any one of these sets of documents. The logic behind the variations in the dossiers and summaries is not clear. What is clear, however, is that the dossiers were prepared earlier than the summaries. The former followed career paths as they evolved chronologically, whereas the summaries must have been registered during the last few years of the empire because the career paths summarized include information up to those years, except in the cases of judges who had died or retired earlier (Albayrak 1996; Zerdeci 1998; Agmon 2004b).

Jaffa and Haifa Court Records

In the second half of the nineteenth century, both Jaffa and Haifa served as subdistrict *(kaza)* centers in the reformed Ottoman administrative system. Jaffa belonged to the district *(liva)* of Jerusalem and Haifa to the district of Acre. A *shari'a* court rendered legal services to the population of each port city and to the villages in its subdistrict. In the Jaffa court, the record that survived starts in 1799 and includes more than one hundred volumes, covering the entire nineteenth century and the first two decades of the twentieth century, as well as additional volumes from the British Mandate period. The number of volumes from the first half of the nineteenth century is smaller than the number of those from the second half. In addition, not all the years are covered. However, no gap exceeds a few years, so that in terms of decades the entire nineteenth century is covered. In Haifa, only a few dozen volumes, beginning in 1870, remain. These records include references to volumes that existed both before and after 1870 but did not survive (Agmon 2003b, 203–5, 2004a). The development of the courts in Jaffa and in Haifa in somewhat different directions (discussed in chapter 3) during the course of the eighteenth and nineteenth centuries might have had an impact on the fact, among other things, that the record that survived in Jaffa was more intact than that from Haifa.

Be the reason for this difference as it may, the result is that only the Jaffa court record includes volumes from the period preceding the reforms of the Tanzimat in addition to volumes that cover the period of all the reforms of the legal system, which, as far as the *shari'a* court system was concerned, date from the 1850s. This means that I substantiate the discussion on changes in court culture—a major theme and methodological factor in this study—by a diachronic comparison of Jaffa court records, but a synchronic comparison of the Jaffa and Haifa court records.

Generally speaking, all volumes include records of a variety of legal proceedings chronologically structured. Several major changes over time can be detected by checking the volumes more closely. In the earlier volumes, the design and style of handwriting resemble those of Ottoman formal decrees and similar documents; the handwriting tends to be curly and somewhat square, and the lines are wavelike. As to the division of space on the pages, the unwritten space in the margins and between the lines is very small, and scribbles prevented the addition of unauthorized text on sections of the pages left empty. In later volumes, the handwriting tends to be smaller and more rounded; the lines are straighter; sometimes ready-made lines are drawn on the pages; the margins and space between lines are wider; and unwritten sections are not always scribbled over—and when they are, the scribbles tend to be less stylish. These changes are connected to various modifications introduced in the production of formal texts, in the concept of authorizing documents, and in the technology of documentation.[31]

Most of the records in the volumes consist of summaries of the cases and their respective court decisions. Since around the 1860s, however, some volumes contain detailed accounts of court proceedings, and as we approach the 1890s, this type of record develops into full protocols of court proceedings documented along different lines from the summaries (for discussion of protocols, see chapter 4). Another change in the content of the volumes relates to their organization according to legal categories. Whereas the earlier volumes and many of the later ones include records of cases dealing with all kinds of legal issues, some volumes from the late nineteenth century "specialize" in a certain kind of legal proceedings, such as giving power of attorney *(wikala),* registering inheritance *(tarika),* or adjudicating lawsuits *(da'wa,* pl. *da'awi).*

The range of legal issues dealt with at court also reflects changes. During the nineteenth-century reforms, the jurisdiction of the *shari'a* court was re-

---

31. See the supplement for Hagopian 1907, which includes examples of a variety of handwritten official documents and calligraphic styles, among them the Divanî style (supp., p. 28), typical of some of the earlier volumes of the court record of Jaffa, and the Rik'a style (Hagopian 1907, supp. 32), typical of late-nineteenth-century Ottoman administrative documents, encompassing most of the court records from both Jaffa and Haifa.

duced to family matters. The jurisdiction over the other legal fields was transferred to new courts (*nizamiye,* including criminal, commercial, and civil courts)[32] with their own codes, and this multiplicity in the court system also reduced the function of the *shariʿa* court as a public-record office. Officially, then, the composition of the court records should have changed dramatically along these lines. Practically, however, the change appears to have been less dramatic than expected: imperial decrees, state appointments, and to a certain extent criminal cases did not form a major component of the earlier court records, probably owing to the lower rank of the Jaffa and Haifa *shariʿa* courts in the pre-Tanzimat judicial administration. Hence, the exclusion of these matters from the court records in the late nineteenth century caused a moderate change, and civil cases continued to be adjudicated and recorded in the *shariʿa* courts in spite of the existence of a civil court of first instance *(bidayet)* in both Jaffa and Haifa from the early 1880s. Furthermore, the number of volumes of court records did not decrease with the exclusion of major legal fields from the authority of the *shariʿa* court. On the contrary, the court record of Jaffa contains more volumes from the second half of the century than from the first half.

Family, Court, and Social Change

The present study aims at addressing two intertwined sets of questions: concrete historical questions and methodological ones. At the empirical level, the broader question underlying this study is the historical sine qua non problem of social change, or simply put: Why, how, where, and when did social changes evolve? As our knowledge of past realities becomes more concrete and detailed, the question of change becomes less a matter of "catching" changes and nailing them down under labels—big change, small change, Westernized change, authentic change, no change—than of following the mechanisms of change—the countless wheels, big and small, premeditated and contingent— that create social dynamics: in other words, the historicizing of change processes. I deal with a historical phase—the Ottoman reform era of the long nineteenth century—that clearly witnessed significant changes, particularly in the settings under discussion. These changes have a major impact on our understanding not only of the past but also of the present, as well as on our

---

32. See note 4 in chapter 1.

worldview and political positions. Thus, despite the fact that a concrete and detailed knowledge of the changes that took place in that era is especially important, the relatively small number of existing studies that undertake this kind of investigation is particularly astonishing.

In the past few decades, the vast project of revisiting Ottoman history and rethinking Ottoman modernity has focused on undermining the grand narrative of a linear passage from a declining empire in the seventeenth and eighteenth centuries, through the stage of an empire in need of rescue—"the sick man of Europe"—in the nineteenth century, to the final, allegedly inevitable dismantling of that empire. In addition, historians with this agenda have focused on the hitherto neglected point of view of the provinces. They have undermined the decline paradigm and the lack of agency it attributed to Ottoman societies. Both of these currents have contributed important studies on the Ottoman provinces between the sixteenth and mid–nineteenth centuries. In the process, however, the social history of the Arab provinces in the second half of the nineteenth century (Egypt excepted) has, generally speaking, been neglected.[33]

The reforms and social transformations of the nineteenth century should be perceived as a nexus between a long history of Ottoman reforms and the twentieth-century processes of change in post-Ottoman societies. Exploring the nineteenth-century transformations as they evolved in various Ottoman provinces is essential for understanding the nature of this era of change and, at the same time, is bound to have implications for our understanding of the preceding and following phases. Moreover, as centralization and further integration of the Arab provinces in the Ottoman Empire constituted a major objective of nineteenth-century reform, exploring the reform in these provinces is likely to contribute not only to the history of the provinces, but also to our understanding of the mentality of Ottoman reform at large. The accumulated historical knowledge on Ottoman modernity shows that neither the Ottoman center nor the provinces (nor even a specific province) were monolithic. Hence, Ottoman history written from an integrative perspective might portray a much more pluralistic and dynamic picture than one written from the perspective of either the Ottoman center or its provinces.

33. This lacuna seems to have received more scholarly attention recently owing to several research projects in progress or recently accomplished.

While this study observes the nineteenth century with the general question of historical change in mind, it is also motivated by social historians' wider interest to reconstruct the way ordinary people lived through these major transformations, the way they experienced them, and the extent to which they shaped them. The achievement of this reconstruction is bound in its turn to contribute to a better understanding of the transformations (Toledano 1998, 276–83). In order to learn about the lives of ordinary people, however, we need to reduce the scale of the unit of observation. Microhistory has challenged social history's strong inclination toward using quantitative methods when approaching historical transformations and toward using large structures when writing about them. The main problem microhistorians identify in sociology- and economy-oriented social history is that the explanations they provide deal with large social structures, long time spans, and macrolevel processes, thus failing to show how ordinary people actually lived with, made sense of (or otherwise), and shaped these transformations, which, we may recall, was the social history's original endeavor. Microhistorians claim that when an individual, a family, a small community, or a single event is examined, these grand structures lack any explanatory capacity. They further argue that whereas social historians approach large-scale structures through quantifications, they by definition stress average behavior patterns and hence lose sight of what Giovanni Levi has defined as "the contradictions of normative systems . . . the fragmentations, contradictions and plurality of viewpoints which make all systems fluid and open" (1995, 107).[34]

Microhistory, therefore, focuses on small-scale units of analysis, a choice that not only means giving up on statistical typicality, but also highlights the significance of exploring extraordinary cases, such as the sixteenth-century Italian miller Menocchio (Ginzburg 1980), or unusual events, such as the return of an absent villager, Martin Guerre, to his village in sixteenth-century southern France only to discover that an impostor had managed to take his place in the village, his family, and his marital bed (Davis 1983). Studying such individuals and events requires a thorough reconstruction of everyday life in order to con-

---

34. Levi argues that the main theoretical point regarding the scale of the unit of analysis is not its reduction, but rather the social contextualization attained by the alteration of scales of analytical units (1995, 107–8). However, in practice, this idea results mainly in reducing the scale of analytical units owing to the predominance of macroanalysis in social history.

textualize them historically, to learn about the "normality" of their "exception" and about the form that large-scale processes took in their realities. Against this background, the contradictions and ambiguities of the past as well as forms of resistance and choices made by people otherwise often depicted as lacking agency are reinforced. By virtue of these features, studies in this field are often structured as narratives: "telling events," as Natalie Z. Davis defines affairs that are bound to make good microhistories (1990, 31), need to be told, and individuals whose choices in life qualify them to be protagonists of microhistories require that their biographies be written.

Another genre of microhistory, focusing on the everyday life of analytical units such as a single village or town (rather than one individual or event), does employ quantitative methods and longer time spans. Studies in this genre are often structured analytically rather than narratively. Thus, this genre, developed mainly by French and German historians, is connected to microhistory (in whose development Italian historians are the most salient) by virtue of its everyday-life feature and the relatively small community that forms its unit of analysis.[35]

In the social history of the Middle East thus far, microhistory is relatively rare. In 1993, Edmund Burke III edited a volume of biographies offering a remarkable picture of ordinary people's agency and illustrating the potential of this approach. In 1998, Nelly Hanna published an intriguing microhistory dealing with a seventeenth-century Egyptian merchant. In the same year, Leslie Peirce (1998a) presented the story of a sixteenth-century unmarried pregnant village girl in southeastern Anatolia, and recently (2003) she published an intricate microhistory dealing with a single year, 1540–41, in the *shariʿa* court of Aintab and the people of that town and province.

In this study, I observe several relatively small units and approach them via microanalysis. In the Ottoman administration, I explore the low level of the subdistrict; in the Syrian provinces, the relatively small harbor towns Jaffa and Haifa are the objects of my investigation; in the societies of these towns, I examine the smallest social unit—the family. I also investigate another entity, the Ottoman state, as embodied in the *shariʿa* court system, at the level of the

---

35. On microhistory, see Davis 1990; Muir and Ruggiero 1991; Ginzburg 1992, 1993, 30–35; Levi 1995; Reay 1996; Iggers 1997, 101–18; Gregory 1999; Magnússon 2003, 709–16; Agmon 2004c.

subdistrict local court. And, finally, I sustain the discussion by a microhistorical analysis of a handful of court cases. Each case record serves as a unique story, capturing bits and pieces of the social reality of which it formed a part, along with the people who produced the text and told it. The narrative and registration of each case in the records are also unique, yet they are not necessarily exceptional. At the same time, they do not form any average or representative sample according to statistical criteria, which are irrelevant in microanalysis. As noted, I use a hermeneutic approach in telling the stories of individuals and families inscribed in the case records. Moreover, I aim at engaging the readers in my interpretive considerations, which is yet another aspect of microhistory (Levi 1995, 105–6).

Family is in itself a relatively small unit sensitive to social change and cultural conventions. Moreover, it is composed of individuals whose particular personalities and interrelations also contribute to its social construction. As noted, I look at changes in the structures of family households, family relations, and urban space, and at life individuals' experiences and their notions of family and gender. I investigate these aspects of the family within the arena of the court. Family members come to court when necessary for a variety of reasons and intentions. However, they run their lives, maintain their numerous interrelations, and weave their social networks elsewhere, not at court. Many of them live their entire lives without attending court or engaging in legal proceedings even once. Moreover, when people do come to the court, they enter a distinct domain. They bring their baggage with them, yet at court this baggage is unpacked and presented in the court's specific terms. For historians, this is not necessarily a disadvantage, as I hope is apparent from this study. Admittedly, the arena of the court poses its own restrictions and creates its own conditions for observing the family. Yet, provided that these conditions are taken into consideration, this arena sheds a unique light on a variety of relations within different families as well as between families and other structures, mainly the court and the state it represents.

Thus, the arena of the court delineates this study, which is composed of two layers. The broader framework is divided into four parts, metaphorically reflecting a visit to a *shariʿa* court, where a typically structured lawsuit is deliberated through three stages: claims, negotiation, and solution. This skeleton highlights the significance of the legal arena and echoes a major theme in the discussion of court culture—namely, the function of the court, in particular of the judge as a mediator in domestic disputes, and the conduct of the court as being "user-friendly" at a time of growing bureaucracy. Although it is true that the court was not the family's natural setting, I intend to show how it made itself more available, mainly to families of modest means and background, than might be expected under the circumstances of population growth and expanding legal bureaucracy.

At the same time, the framework of starting with claims and ending with solutions achieved by negotiation and mediation reflects my own view of historical investigations that face methodological problems of the sort mentioned earlier: it is the framework of an adventure. Historians may have high hopes of recovering lost voices and turning the landscape of historical knowledge upside down, and they may be well equipped with thought-provoking theories when they embark upon a research endeavor. But along the way they face unexpected barriers and traps posed by their source texts, and before they know it, their dreamy voyage turns into endless negotiations with these sources as their only traveling companions. The methodological solutions they reach may lead them to places they had no intention to visit, not necessarily better or worse places, only different. But is this not what adventure is all about?

The narrative of investigation in the chapters of parts two, three, and four forms the second structural layer. It further develops the figurative visit to a court and observation of family members who bring their problems before the judge—a visit that ultimately leads the observer to follow these people when they leave the court and return to their daily routine. The voyage already began at the nineteenth-century port cities of Jaffa and Haifa in chapter 1 and locates them in the realm of present-day historical interest and debate in this chapter. We then enter the Jaffa and Haifa courts in chapter 3, observe the interactions between families and court cultures in chapters 4, 5, and 6, and then follow family members as they leave the court and go back home in chapter 7. This narrative also echoes the study's anthropological perspective.

The first chapter's discussion of legal reforms and some of their repercussions on the work of the Jaffa and Haifa courts and on the social texture of these cities continues in chapter 3 by examining the implementation of new regulations regarding the court personnel and analyzing their impact on court culture. I compare the legal traditions of the Jaffa and Haifa courts to one another and look at how each court adjusted to the changing routines during the legal reforms, a process that resulted in somewhat different versions of court culture. The main themes in chapter 3 are the local court culture as an encounter between successive judges, who were outsiders, and local scribes who served long terms, as well as the changing balance of power at court between the judge and the scribes, who belonged to the same socioprofessional group and were interested in redefining the position of the court in local society. I look at the interrelationship between litigants, scribes, and judges through a microanalysis of a case from Jaffa in which the plaintiff was a judge of local origin enjoying a "leave of absence" and at which an elderly judge from Damascus, who worked at an unusually slow pace, presided. While discussing the deliberations of this case at the court of Jaffa, I also unfold the story of the Damascene judge and his family.

A major aspect of the court's work was the production of the record. During the reforms, the routine of documenting and keeping records changed considerably, and innovative procedures for recording detailed protocols were introduced at the Jaffa and Haifa courts. In chapter 4, I assess the multilayered impact of these procedures, which at first seem purely technical. A case of domestic dispute from Haifa, covered in several records, illustrates both the empirical and the methodological questions discussed in this chapter. The implementation of the recording procedures at the Jaffa and Haifa courts increased the scribes' workload and reinforced procedural aspects in both the records and the deliberations inscribed in them. These procedural innovations involved the people attending court: they had to confirm the records that documented their legal family and other matters. This aspect of the innovative procedures raises the main question in chapter 4: To what extent might the involvement of lay people in the proceedings dealing with their family relations have strengthened their legal notion of the family? A related question is, Were all people at court equally involved in these procedures? A comparison of the implementation of the recording procedures in the Jaffa and Haifa court records shows that the personnel in the two courts understood somewhat differently the instructions they received from Istanbul. Therefore, the litigants in the two cities might have experienced involvement in the new procedures in different ways. In addition, litigants, mainly from the upper class, who did not attend court but rather authorized attorneys to represent them, were not exposed to the change. The court thus served as an arena mainly for the growing and rather fluid middle class.

Chapter 5 offers an analysis of the legal notions of gender and social justice. The analysis reveals a considerable overlap between the two legal concepts and links them to the legal notion of the family that underpins the patrilineal family, while stressing the vulnerability of certain weaker individuals within it. Two case records, one from Jaffa and the other from Haifa, illustrate the notions of gender and social justice. It is an accepted wisdom that family law was left untouched by the legal reforms, so the legal notion of the family was not exposed to change. But I challenge this understanding by a discussion of a new institution, the orphan funds, that was established as part of the reforms. The case on which I focus shows that the orphan funds represented an initial intrusion by the state into a particular family domain, the responsibility for minor children, in a way that to some extent strengthened the notion of the simple conjugal family and the position of women and children. At the same time, the position of minor children, in particular females, in the legal concept of the family remained vulnerable, and their security was considered secondary to the reinforcement of the patrilineal family.

Chapter 6 revisits the battered Weberian thesis of "kadi-justice" from an angle that has not yet been explored: the emergence of professional attorneys at the *shari'a* courts. A microanalysis of two case records of domestic disputes sustains a comparison between the way the judge used his discretion when he dealt with a lawsuit single-handedly and when he shared the stage with two rival attorneys. This analysis reinforces the mediation feature in the judge's discretion while highlighting the significance of legal procedure for the role played by judges. It also shows how a new concept of legal representation was adjusted to court culture, while pointing to additional aspects of the legal notions of family and social justice. The discussion of the emergence of professional attorneys at the court also highlights the social stratification of the court's clientele: attorneys were hired mainly by upper-class families, which tended to keep away from the court, leaving the arena to their middle- and lower-class counterparts. This situation corroborates the impressions that the reformed *shari'a* court stressed aspects of social justice in its legal notion of the family as one way of maintaining its accessibility to a wide range of people and that this approach shaped the redefinition of the court's position toward its clientele.

Chapter 7 represents the passage from the courtroom to the houses, alleys, and neighborhoods where families lived and maintained the relations that brought them to court in the first place. Some of the cases unfolded in earlier chapters are reconsidered in this discussion, which focuses on family space and relations in the diverse urban middle class. Household structures, housing conditions, immigration, interrelations with neighbors and housemates, as well as notions of intimacy and seclusion, family boundaries, gender and family loyalties are the main topics of discussion. The aim of this analysis is twofold. At the empirical level, it presents a preliminary outline of a simultaneous "re-constitution" of family and class among the fluid middle class in the port cities.[36] At the methodological level, it represents a provisional summary of the potential of court records for studying past realities in general and the family in particular. In order to portray a more accurate picture of middle-class family experiences and at the same time to get an idea of the sort of information on the family that the court records lack, I compare these experiences to those of upper-class families using the memoirs of a childhood in an established family in late Ottoman Jaffa.

In the conclusion, I evaluate both the methodology employed to combine court records with family history and the nature of the transformations reconstructed in this study. I point to the conceptual nexus between family and court that led me to focus on the growing urban middle class. This evaluation allows for more general observations about modernity and historical reconstruction.

◆   ◆   ◆

As mentioned, the population of both Jaffa and Haifa was highly diversified in terms of religious, ethnic, and other collective identities. The dividing lines between the various groups were significant, yet there were also intensive interrelations among them, and most communities were not isolated. Furthermore, even after the legal reforms that in principle should have eliminated non-Muslims' motivation to bring their legal business to the *shariʿa* court, the court records show that they continued to attend the court to some extent. Mainly Orthodox and Catholic Arab Christians, Jews (including Zionist immi-

---

36. The Cambridge Group for the History of Population and Social Structure uses the word *reconstitution* as a technical term describing the methods for processing serial data included in sources such as parish registers to reconstruct family structures. Therefore, I use a slightly different spelling, *re-constitution,* for the word's regular meaning, namely "reconstruction" or "reproduction."

grants), and sometimes citizens of Mediterranean and European countries were among the court's clientele. Arab Christians were the most prominent attendants. Like other non-Muslims, they brought to court mainly issues of real-estate transactions and disputes, but in addition also inheritance matters, and at times even cases of domestic dispute. However, generally speaking, the lion's share of the clientele of late-nineteenth-century courts in Jaffa and Haifa was Muslim. Thus, "the family" in this study is a Muslim family, and the legal case records that are used for microanalysis involve Muslim family members. Many family patterns and relations discussed here are also relevant for non-Muslim families, however, especially those who lived in mixed neighborhoods.[37]

As stated, I concentrate on the middle class in the urban communities of the port cities. Like other social strata, maybe even more so, the middle class was a fluid and not clearly distinct social level in circumstances of constant immigration, urban growth, and reforms. Thus, it may be defined by default as neither upper nor lower class. It was not a tightly knit social group, but rather a number of loosely interrelated segments in the observed urban communities, whose socioeconomic characteristics and cultural conventions are further described in upcoming chapters. Therefore, the term *middle class* as employed here is descriptive rather than technical, and it does not relate to one closely defined social group.[38]

37. See, for example, al-Qattan 2002.

38. Alternately, I use either *higher middle class* or *lower middle class* to describe more accurately the socioeconomic position of people whose legal proceedings I discuss. On conceptual problems faced by historians who deal with non-Western middle classes, see Göçek 1996, 9–19.

Part Two

◆   ◆   ◆

Presenting Claims

3

The Court Arena

OBSERVING THE WORK of the *shari'a* courts in late Ottoman Jaffa and Haifa more closely, this chapter concentrates on the personnel of the courts and particularly on the judges and scribes and their interrelations in court. First, I survey the development of the two courts during the eighteenth and nineteenth centuries. This description provides the historical background to a discussion on new work regulations in the courts. I compare the two courts and show the differences between their legal cultures. I examine court culture through the microanalysis of a situation in which a judge of local origin came to court at Jaffa as a plaintiff to claim a debt. The presiding judge at that time—the turn of the twentieth century—was a relatively elderly judge who belonged to the pre-Tanzimat generation. He was approaching retirement and was not functioning at full capacity in court. In what seems to have been a joint effort, both the judge and the scribes took care of their colleague, the plaintiff judge, in a way that did not exceed the legal restrictions, yet guaranteed his interests. The deconstruction of the record of this unique case and reconstruction of the plausible situation behind it sustain my analysis of the local nature of the court culture in a relatively small yet fast-growing city—Jaffa.

The Jaffa and Haifa Subdistrict Centers and Their Courts

As described in the first chapter, Jaffa and Haifa at the turn of the nineteenth century were two small harbor towns on the southeastern shores of the Mediterranean. Jaffa was somewhat bigger and higher ranking in the provincial administration than Haifa. During the nineteenth century, the position of both cities in the Ottoman provincial hierarchy underwent a profound change.

Jerusalem, to which the court of Jaffa belonged, was originally also a district center *(sancak)* in the province of Damascus (al-Sham). From the perspective of the Ottoman capital, Jerusalem was one of many rather remote district centers in the Arab provinces. During the nineteenth century, however, Jerusalem gradually became a focus of foreign religious and political interests, and consequently many foreign institutions and individuals, mainly from Europe, became actively involved in the city.[1] In the course of the Tanzimat reforms, the central government had decided to deal with the situation by first turning Jerusalem into the center of a larger district comprised of all the new subdistricts of southern Palestine and later to control this district's affairs directly. Thus, in 1872 the district of Jerusalem became autonomous, a district that was not part of or elevated to the status of a province *(vilayet),* but was directly subordinate to the central Ottoman administration *(liva-ı gayr-ı mülhaka)* (Abu-Manneh 1990, 8–9).[2]

These administrative moves did not result in changes in Jaffa's status in the legal hierarchy; rather, they reinforced its connections with Jerusalem by turning it into a subdistrict subordinate both judicially and administratively to the district of Jerusalem. Functioning as the port for Jerusalem, Jaffa grew immensely during the nineteenth century, a growth stimulated by that of Jerusalem and the attention it attracted worldwide. At first, Jaffa was rather exclusively dependent on the administration and sociopolitical networks of Jerusalem. However, in the last third of the nineteenth century, as Jerusalem became more important and the central government became more deeply involved in its affairs, Jaffa's situation also changed, its administration and politics becoming increasingly complex.

At the beginning of the nineteenth century, the legal proceedings at the *shariʿa* court of Jaffa were conducted by a deputy *(naib)*[3] of the Jerusalem

1. A broader discussion of this and other processes of change in international power relations are beyond the scope of this study. See, for example, Ma'oz 1968, 212–40.

2. See the Provincial Law of 1864 and its modifications of 1871, *Düstur* 1, 1: "Vilayet nizamnamesi," 7 C 1281/7 XI 1864, 608–24; and "İdare-i umumiye vilayeti nizamnamesi," 29 L 1287/22 I 1871, 625–51.

3. The use of the term *naib* in the literature is somewhat confusing. Before the Tanzimat, this term meant the delegation of legal authority by a senior judge *(qadi),* often by leasing out the position of conducting legal proceedings in a lower-ranking court under his jurisdiction to a junior judge *(naib,* literally "deputy") in exchange for the future revenues of the lower court. The entire system of recruiting and appointing provincial judges was reorganized as part of the legal

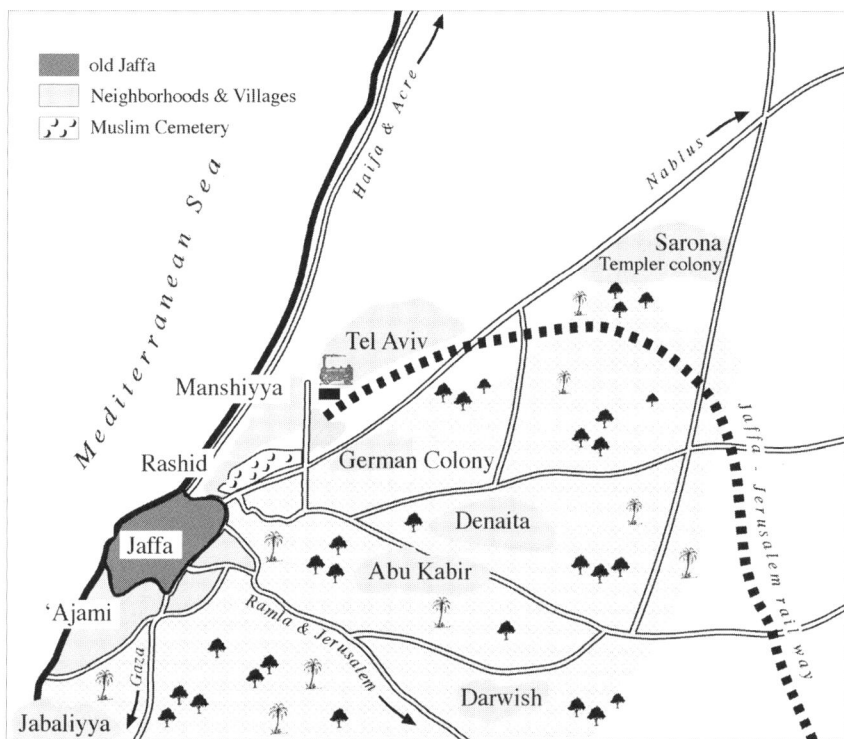

Map 2. Late Ottoman Jaffa. Courtesy of the author.

judge. The deputy was appointed by and reported to the Jerusalem judge *(qadi)* and the Jaffa court was virtually part of the Jerusalem court well into the century. Ulama from the families prominent in the legal system of Jerusalem, mainly the Khalidi family, were appointed at the beginning of their judicial careers to serve as deputies to the judges in Jaffa and other subdistricts and then promoted to legal institutions in Jerusalem.[4] At the same time, ulama

reforms of the nineteenth century. The method by which senior judges delegated judicial authority to juniors was gradually replaced. Under the new system, judges of all ranks were appointed by the central government, and the term *naib* was used for all ranks (except for a few high-ranking judges, who were still entitled *qadi*). In 1913, the use of the term *qadi* was resumed. See also Kupferschmidt 1986, 125.

4. For instance, ʿAli Efendi al-Khalidi was appointed deputy judge for Jaffa by his brother Musa, the judge of Jerusalem in the early nineteenth century. A few years later, when his brother was promoted and became one of the highest-ranking judges (*kazasker* of Anatolia), Sheikh ʿAli took up his position as judge in Jerusalem (Mannaʿ 1995, 135–36, and 53, 142, 183). See also Mannaʿ 1986, 174–80, 253–58; Abu-Manneh 1990, 14–15.

1. A view of the old city of Jaffa from the sea, c. 1910.

from local Jaffa families were appointed to other legal positions in town. The Dajani family emerged as particularly prominent in the Jaffa legal system during that period. The position of mufti of Jaffa, for example, was held without interruption by members of this family from the 1820s until the end of Ottoman rule (SA def. 1, 25; *Filastin,* 9 Nov. 1912, 3; Dabbagh 1988, 4: 290–92; Manna' 1995, 170–72; Albayrak 1996, 1: 309).

Thus, when the legal system was intensively reformed from the mid–nineteenth century on, and the central Ottoman judicial administration took over the appointment of judges down to the level of the subdistrict, the Dajanis were already well established in the legal institutions and the local elite of Jaffa. At the same time, however, reform also revived the old norm that the *shari'a* judge would not be recruited from among the local ulama. This norm was maintained rather strictly in both Jaffa and Haifa, particularly since the early 1870s, when many other judicial reforms were implemented in the Arab provinces (Agmon 2004a; Akiba 2005).[5] Thus, a judge of the Dajani family (or

5. About this policy in Haifa, see Yazbak 1998, 46–49. With regard to Nablus, Yazbak (1997) mentions the names of several local ulama who served as *shari'a* judges in their hometown. It seems, however, that most of them served in the first half of the nineteenth century. Doumani claims that most of the judges who served in Nablus after 1866 were of Turkish origin (1985, 164). See also Messick 1993, 176–82; İnalcık 1991, 4. Several historians mention the principle of not allowing judges to serve in their hometowns as an accepted norm for earlier periods. The specific content and implementation of this policy changed over time (İnalcık 1965,

of any other local family, for that matter) was rarely appointed in Jaffa during that period. The appointment of court scribes, however, did remain at the local level. In the Jaffa court record, therefore, we come across many scribes who bore the name al-Dajani (in addition to the position of mufti, which the family continued to hold for the entire century). Thus, in the course of the reforms, the prevailing control of elite families from Jerusalem over legal and other institutions in Jaffa was redistributed between three elements: the former ulama families from Jerusalem, the central government, and local elite families from Jaffa. In the *shariʿa* court, this redistribution meant the successive presence of Dajanis as scribes and chief scribes, although the judges were changed more or less every other year in line with another regulation of the reform.[6] This situation shaped the legal and administrative culture of the *shariʿa* court of Jaffa somewhat differently from that of Haifa.

Although Haifa also became a subdistrict center during the nineteenth century, its relations with Acre, the district center, developed along different lines. As described in the first chapter, up to and well into the nineteenth century Acre was the most important Ottoman port and administrative center on the southern shores of Syria. Administratively, it formed a district center in the province of Saida. Haifa, a nearby and rather small town in the early Ottoman period, did not belong to the district of Acre in spite of their proximity, but to that of Lajjun in the province of Damascus. As mentioned earlier, its port attracted smugglers and pirates who took advantage of the combination of its accessible harbor and lack of either a military force or defending walls. The Ottoman governors tried to bring Haifa under tighter control, but only Dahir al-ʿUmar succeeded in the 1760s. From then on, Haifa gradually grew, and although it was annexed to the province of Saida and became a *nahiye* cen-

---

77; Özkaya 1985, 211). İnalcık mentions this principle regarding the sixteenth century, and Özkaya regarding the eighteenth century, both without a specific reference. I am grateful to Jun Akiba for sharing with me his observations on this issue.

6. For this and other instructions regarding the work of the *shariʿa* judges, see *Düstur* 1, 1: "Bilumum mahakim-i şerʿiye hakkında müceddeden kaleme alınan nizamname," "Nüvvab hakkında nizamname," 17 B 1271/5 IV 1855, 301–24; *Al-Dustur* 1, 1310/1883, 130–41, " ʿUmum al-mahakim al-sharʿiyya," 16 S 1276/14 IX 1859, 147–49; and *Düstur* 1, 2: "Hükkâm-ı şerʿiye nizamnamesi," 13 M 1290/12 III 1873, 721–25. See also Kupferschmidt 1986; Akiba 2000, 3–5, 2003, 2005.

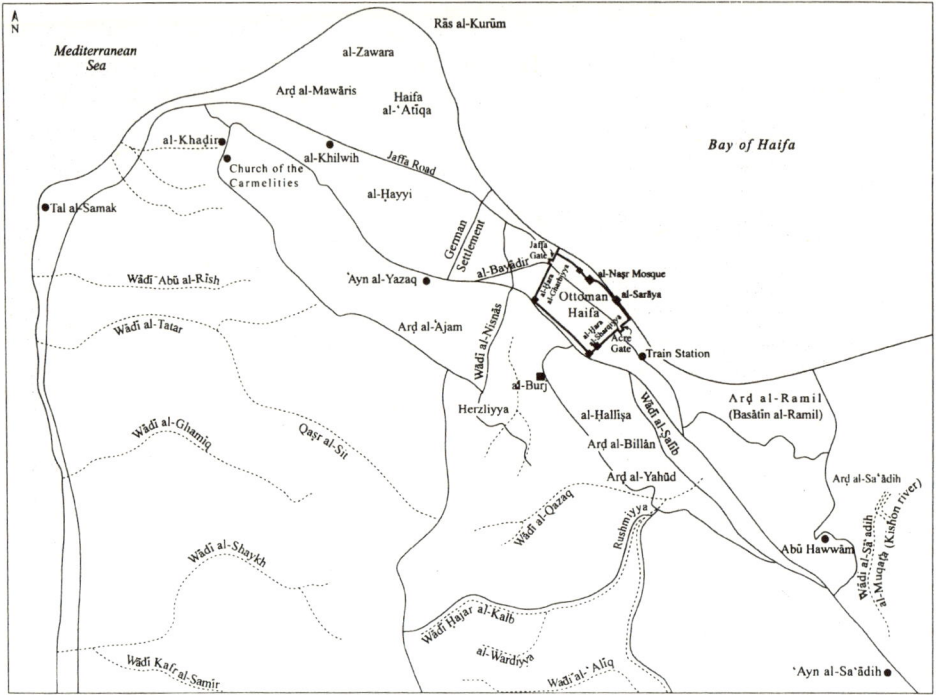

Map 3. Late Ottoman Haifa. From Yazbak 1998, 8. Courtesy of Brill Academic Publishers.

ter, it was ruled directly by a representative of the provincial governor and not by the district governor of Acre, as a means of keeping it firmly under control. Only in the 1840s, after the Ottomans had restored their rule in Syria, was the status of Haifa elevated to that of a subdistrict in the district of Acre (Cohen 1973, 121–22, 137–44; Yazbak 1998, 7–25).

Thus, administratively speaking, only during the Tanzimat era were the links between the two neighboring port cities regulated and strengthened. In 1867, as part of the reorganization of the provinces, the status of Saida as provincial center was abolished, and the district of Acre, with Haifa as one of its subdistricts, was annexed to the province of Damascus. Twenty years later, in 1887, a new province, that of Beirut, was established to cover the district of Acre, including Haifa (Yazbak 1998, 7–25). By that time, the emergence of Haifa and the weakening position of Acre as the main port in the Bay of Acre, the parallel process discussed in the first chapter, were already in motion.

Thus, Jaffa enjoyed a relatively long and uninterrupted period of growth together with Jerusalem, being politically "tutored" by its elite before the Ot-

2. A view of Haifa from the sea, late nineteenth century. From a postcard produced by the studio of Bonfils in Beirut. Courtesy of almashriq.hiof.no.

tomans embarked upon their more intrusive reforms in the provinces. Haifa, in contrast, emerged in response to various governors and rulers' interests and direct involvement, combined with the strong economic stimulation facing many port cities along the Mediterranean shores; in this case, its growth was also at Acre's expense.

The *shariʿa* court in Haifa also developed differently from that in Jaffa. The judicial and other legal and religious positions in Haifa were held by members of a fairly small number of ulama families, mainly al-Khatib, al-Suhayli, al-Bashir al-Zaydani, and al-Nabahani. All were local families; some had immigrated to Haifa from neighboring villages: the al-Suhayli family came from Balad al-Sheikh and the al-Nabahani family from Ijzim. The al-Bashir al-Zaydani family was descended from Dahir al-ʿUmar, whereas both the al-Suhayli and al-Khatib families bore attributes of *ashraf* (descendants of the Prophet Muhammad) (Yazbak 1998, 128–37). In the nineteenth century, few members of these families had even been appointed to legal and other positions in Acre. Until midcentury, judges of local origin were appointed in Haifa, sometimes for long terms. ʿAbd al-Rahman al-Suhayli, for instance, was the presiding judge in Haifa between 1827 and 1845 (Yazbak 1998, 133). Later on, however, appointment of judges of local origin occurred only when a substitute temporarily replaced the judge for a short term, in line with the policy of reform. During that period, members of those families who had acquired a legal education were appointed to courts outside Haifa (SA dos. 2221; SA dos. 2341; Albayrak 1996, 2: 164, 4: 365–66). As in Jaffa, local scribes and interns did serve at the Haifa court, but it appears that they were members of various families and not necessarily the prominent ones listed here (Yazbak 1998, 50–52). Thus, in comparison to Jaffa, the Haifa court appears to have had a shorter history as a subdistrict court, without a continuous dominant source of patronage. In the late nineteenth century, therefore, its legal culture was shaped more intensively than that of Jaffa by the innovations of the Tanzimat.

The Reforms, the Judges, and the Scribes

As an institution, the *shariʿa* court is considered as historically epitomized in the persona of the judge *(qadi* or *kadı)*. Historians often speak and write about "the *qadi* court" instead of the *shariʿa* court, although this terminology is not the one normally used in the historical sources, at least not in those sources produced in the Ottoman *shariʿa* courts. The Weberian concept of "kadi-justice" (see chapter 6)—namely, that the judge's discretion in this court was entirely arbitrary—might be seen as a far-reaching Orientalist twist of this historical representation of the *shariʿa* court. Historically, judges had been conducting legal proceedings at various locations, not necessarily indoors, and they sometimes remained in one position for very long terms, even for a lifetime (Hanna 1995, 50). Thus, the common image of the *shariʿa* judge as an old man sitting under a tree and conducting legal proceedings might be understood as yet another Orientalist interpretation of such historical findings, an image that fits the concept of "kadi-justice."[7]

Even in the late Ottoman period, after great changes had taken place in the work of the *shariʿa* courts, the judge was still identified with the court, as is illustrated by the very first sentence of many case records. A typical and rather

---

7. See, for example, Messick 1993, 167–71; Hallaq 1998, 418–19. Indeed, these scholars should by no means be held responsible for this image; on the contrary, their scholarly works show how futile this image is.

common opening of a record reads: "In the *shariʿa* session [*majlis*], which is set out by me [literally: at me; *ladayya*] in the *shariʿa* court of Jaffa / Haifa, which belongs to the district of Jerusalem/Acre X sued Y." Moreover, it does not seem to be a mere coincidence that in court records from various periods and places, before and after the Tanzimat reforms, there is no mention of the court's specific location. In spite of the profound institutionalization the *shariʿa* court underwent during the Tanzimat, it did not become identified with a location or with a structure built according to a specific style that would symbolize its authority. As I show later, the court's work underwent substantial standardization, resulting in larger court staff and changes in the balance of power between them and in their interaction with litigants. Nevertheless, as shown by the court records, the judge kept his authority and his role as the personification of the court.

The Ottoman government's control over the provincial *shariʿa* courts was rather loose before the Tanzimat. The appointment of deputy judges for Jaffa by their superiors in Jerusalem, typical also of other judicial centers in the provinces, was part of the system of the delegation of authority by the central government to the provinces. Another aspect of the same situation was that judges were paid directly from the court revenues and not by the government (Marcus 1989, 106; Hanna 1995, 47). In this way, each court was maintained like a "self-sufficient economy," which further weakened central control over the appointment of judges, their integrity, and the income that the state derived from the court system. Many new instructions issued by the central government for the *shariʿa* courts, beginning in the 1850s, aimed to change this situation, and many also concentrated on the question of the judges' appointment and status. Thus, the Ottoman reformists apparently also saw the *shariʿa* judges as the embodiment of the court system.

In the 1850s, the government issued several sets of instructions to the courts. The instructions of 1855 reorganized the ranks of the provincial judges and defined them in a hierarchy of five according to various criteria. Their term of service was restricted first to eighteen months (twenty-four in distant regions), and then somewhat later it was extended to twenty-four months (thirty in distant regions). At the same time, the Muallimhane-i Nüvvab, College for Shariʿa Judges, was founded in Istanbul (Akiba 2003). Later waves of instructions in 1859 and then in 1873 included a list of fixed prices that the courts had to charge clients for various legal services. At the same time, the Ministry of Şeyhülislâm, the head of the Ottoman legal system, reformed the methods of recruiting new judges. It gradually cancelled the practice by which senior ulama were leasing 'out judicial positions to juniors and took over the appointment of judges of both the lower and the higher administrative levels. Finally, all judges were put on the government payroll and received fixed salaries according to rank and some other criteria. In addition, as I mentioned earlier, the old norm of not allowing judges to serve in their hometowns was implemented more strictly, and the education of judges was reformed and centralized. Thus, the central government stopped the process that had turned the court into a self-sufficient unit strongly connected to local networks in an effort to regain direct control of both local and provincial forces.

It is clear that all these regulations aimed at the subordination of the judicial system to the center and the weakening of local forces with vested interests in the provincial legal institutions. Shortening judges' term of service, paying them salaries from the Treasury, and making sure that they were not local were all measures aimed at preventing judges from having too deep an involvement with local forces and from cultivating vested interests of their own during their terms of office. A look at some judges' personal dossiers, which the central government had began to record in the Ottoman capital in that period as yet another means of control, indicates the extent of mobility and the instability that this type of career path forced on the judges.[8] Granted, extensive mobility had been part of the elite lifestyle of some high-ranking judges and other officials. This, however, was not always the case with lower-ranking judges. Moving every two or three years to a new location, sometimes far away from the center, from their hometowns, or from their former place of service must have affected the judges' entire course of life. It probably shaped their practical arrangements and developed that certain state of mind typical of frequent travelers. At the same time, it provided them with opportunities for rel-

---

8. From this period, the Ministry of Şeyhülislâm kept records of the curriculum vitae of state employees of the *ilmiye* as part of the policy of making the presence of the state more visible on the provincial scene. These files (SA dos., SA def.) were updated occasionally and are rather illuminating as to the career paths of late Ottoman state employees in the legal system. See also my discussion on this source material in chapter 2 and in Agmon 2004b. The career paths of some of the judges who served in Jaffa and Haifa at some point during this period are presented later in this chapter and in the following chapters, demonstrating their mobility.

atively safe migration at a time of growing mobility. After the restrictions on judges' terms of service were eased in 1913, some remained in Jaffa or Haifa, towns that became very attractive during that period. Their families settled there and joined the many other immigrants in these two cities. Others came alone and married local women, establishing new family households there (Agmon 2004b).

At the same time, the policy dictating short terms of service also affected the court work and the internal balance between the judge and the rest of the staff. Court decisions required not only legal and religious knowledge, but also local knowledge (Geertz 1983; Messick 1993, 182–86). Being an outsider who was replaced every so often, the judge would desperately need some local knowledge when making his decisions, particularly in rapidly changing cities such as Jaffa and Haifa. The regulations for the work of the *shariʿa* courts may have successfully released the judges from their dependency on the local networks for their appointment and income (while integrating them into much wider networks in the capital instead), but in the process the judges were left without much to bargain with on the local scene in exchange for local knowledge. In the later period of the Young Turks, the central government acknowledged some of the disadvantages of the regulations concerning the short terms for *shariʿa* judges, for, as mentioned earlier, in 1913 it abandoned this policy.[9]

Although *shariʿa* judges, both as state employees and state representatives, were brought under tighter direct control of the central government, the rest of the court personnel apparently did not attract so much attention from the government. At subdistrict level, this personnel included the chief scribe *(başkatib),* several other scribes *(katib, zabt katibi, mukayyid),* sometimes a legal intern, and a clerk or another employee in charge of summoning witnesses *(muhzır)* (Yazbak 1998, 51).[10] The changes that did take place in their status

9. *Düstur* 2, 5: "Hükkâm-ı şerʿ-i ve memurin-i şerʿiye hakkında kanun-u muvakkat," 19 Ca 1331/26 IV 1913, 352–61. According to the corrected instructions, a judge would be appointed to serve at a certain court without a final date and would then be moved to another court, either in response to his explicit request to the central authorities or at their own initiative.

10. The list of the court employees in Jaffa in 1911 included, in addition to the judge, a chief scribe, protocol scribe, registrar, manager of the orphan fund, maid, and janitor (SA dos. 3056). In courts of higher administrative level, the personnel included a few other officials. See the list of the court employees at the provincial court of Damascus (*Salname* VS 1318/1900, 107) in comparison to that of the subdistrict of Hama (*Salname* VS, 185).

and functions resulted mainly from instructions regarding the procedures of court work and indirectly from changes in the judge's position. The court personnel were also state employees, but their appointment was left in the judge's hands at the local level, their term of service was rather flexible, and they could be recruited from among the local ulama.[11] Thus, they were likely to be dependent on the judge regarding several aspects of their employment and their career prospects. Furthermore, the judge, although cut off from local networking, gained an alternative source of power; at the subdistrict level, the *naib,* ex officio, also chaired the newly established *nizamiye* court for adjudicating civil and criminal cases of first instance *(bidayet).* In this capacity, he presided over a council that included a number of local notables and was aided by court scribes and other junior officials.[12]

However, the personnel of both the *nizamiye* and the *shariʿa* courts had the very local knowledge that the judge himself lacked, so they were in the best position to help him. Some judges brought with them a skilled relative, a son or nephew, and appointed him as a court scribe under their judgeship. It was probably part of the process of internship and the transmission of the professional and social status within ulama families. In addition, this situation might be seen as an indication of both scribes' advantageous position in these power relations and judges' efforts to improve their own position in the court by placing someone related to them on the local staff. In Jaffa, for instance, two judges from Damascus who served consecutively at the turn of the twentieth century brought their sons and appointed them as court scribes. In 1896, Muhammad Abu al-Nasr Efendi al-Khatib was accompanied by two of his sons, ʿAbd al-Qadir Hikmat and Ahmad Badawi. Both served under his judgeship, and one of them replaced their father as the *naib* of Jaffa in 1902 after his second term there. Murtadazade Sayyid Mahmud Nadim Efendi served between 1898 and 1900 as court scribe under the judgeship of his father, Muhammad Darwish Efendi al-Murtada from Damascus, and stayed in this position when his father was replaced by Abu al-Nasr.

---

11. The dossier of the manager of the orphan fund in Jaffa also includes a correspondence between the court of Jaffa and that of Jerusalem regarding the appointment of a new scribe in Jaffa (SA dos. 3056). See also the discussion on the orphan funds in chapter 5.

12. *Salname* VB 1310/1892, 178–79, and 1318/1900, 288. See also Reid 1981, 81–82, and Agmon 2004a, in particular notes 30 and 31.

In Haifa, Sheikh Ahmad Khayr al-Din from Tripoli was appointed as judge in 1905, and he brought his nephew, Muhyi al-Din al-Mallah, with him as chief scribe (HCR, *Sijill* 6, 10 M 1323/17 III 1905, 1). Muhyi al-Din stayed in Haifa and pursued his legal career there. He became deputy to the judge for conducting legal procedures outside the court, in the town as well as in the villages of the subdistrict of Haifa. In 1909, the presiding judge, ʿAbd al-Muʿta Efendi from Jerusalem (SA dos. 797; SA def. 1, 268), had to leave Haifa before his successor, ʿAbdalla Haqqi Efendi from Aleppo, arrived (SA dos. 819; SA def. 5: 216). Muhyi al-Din was appointed deputy judge and presided over the court for three months late in 1909 (HCR, *Sijill* 8, 16 N 1327/1 X 1909, 115, *Sijill* 8, 17 Z 1327/10 XII 1909, 151). He continued his service as chief scribe and a couple of years later was appointed manager of the orphan fund in town (see chapter 5).

Whatever judges' motivation in bringing relatives and appointing them as scribes may have been, the successive reforms in the *shariʿa* courts and the work of low-ranking judges, which changed their position vis-à-vis both their superiors in Istanbul and the staff of the local courts, affected the balance between judges and local court personnel. The judge lost some of his previous power as he was turned into a short-term outsider on the local scene, but he gained new power from his extended position in the reformed local court system and from his authority over the local staff. The staff also lost some power when the government tightened central control over lower-ranking courts, but gained new influence by virtue of access to local knowledge lacked by the judge and by the reinforcement of recording assignments and legal procedure entailed in the court reforms. The changes that occurred in the interrelations between the judge and the court personnel reshaped the internal balance both in court and in the local legal culture.

A Judge Facing Judgment: The Case and the Court

The dynamics in the reformed courts may be understood better through a microanalysis of a certain case record. This case was deliberated at the Jaffa *shariʿa* court in December 1900. The events that brought this case about and the deliberations in court, according to a straightforward reading of the case record, seem rather simple. A couple of years prior to the trial, Mustafa ibn ʿAbdalla al-Maridi from Lydda had borrowed money from Sheikh Husayn Husni Efendi al-Khatib from Lydda to be returned two years later. To guarantee the payment of the debt the borrower had mortgaged two properties, the value of which was equal to the total sum of the loan plus interest, signing a contract with the lender by which the latter temporarily bought the properties from the borrower. However, Mustafa al-Maridi died before paying his debt, and Sheikh Husayn sued Mustafa's legal heirs—an adult son, a widow, and an attorney representing the late Mustafa's orphans and other heirs, claiming that the heirs ought to pay him the debt. He provided the court with legal proof sustaining his claim, and indeed the judge ruled in his favor (JCR, *Hujaj* 81, 6 Ş–11 N 1318/29 XI 1900–2 I 1901, 97–102, 105–6, 111–12).

When we read this text while looking closely both at the circumstances of the production of the record in court and at the background of the main protagonists—the judge, court scribes, and litigants—this case turns out to be more intricate and telling, one that well fits the purpose of developing a hermeneutic reading of court records and sustaining a reconstruction of the local court arena.

It should be noted that, legally, this was a civil case. It was probably adjudicated in the *shariʿa* court, not in the civil court, because it was linked to inheritance that was legally part of the *shariʿa* family law. However, many civil cases, and not only those relating to inheritance or any other family legal matters, were deliberated at the *shariʿa* court as well. Legally, the dividing lines between the jurisdiction of the *shariʿa* court system and the *nizamiye* court system were clear, but practically, at least at the lower subdistrict level, they were blurred. As I show in the following chapters, the *shariʿa* courts maintained an open-door attitude. Judges and court clerks left it to the litigants to choose where to take their legal problems, and because reform reinforced bureaucratization in all realms of life, the *shariʿa* courts had the advantage of being familiar and hence probably the default court for most of the rank and file who required legal services. In this regard, judicial reform resulted in "legal pluralism" that provided people with the option of "forum shopping"—a wider selection of institutions where, within certain restrictions, they could bring up their legal problems according to their needs.[13]

13. The model of legal pluralism was developed for the analysis of colonial and post-colonial situations in which a number of partially overlapping or contradictory judicial systems or both exist within a single political system. Scholars often use this model to reveal the power relations of colonial and other modern states in which oppression of a variety of subaltern groups (natives, subjects, women, minorities) is inherent and achieved through the fragmentation of

The Plaintiff

A rather striking aspect of this lawsuit is that the plaintiff, Sheikh Husayn Husni Efendi al-Khatib from Lydda, was a *shariʿa* judge himself. In the record, his name was mentioned with the official *ilmiye* title *faziletli* (his honor),[14] and he was described as the former *naib* of Hisn al-Akrad (a subdistrict of the district of Tripoli in the province of Beirut). Sheikh Husayn was born in Lydda in 1859–60. His father, Sheikh ʿUmar, was a preacher (*khatib,* which explains his last name) and imam at the big mosque of Jaffa, to where he had apparently moved with his family. Husayn acquired his legal and religious education first in Jaffa, with a private teacher, and then in Istanbul, where he continued his religious education. He started his career as a teacher in the Ottoman Ruşdiye school system and served in this capacity in several places during the years 1888–93.[15] Then he was appointed as judge in subdistrict *shariʿa* courts. For the next twenty years, he served in several subdistricts in Arabia and Syria. His appointments brought him to Hudayda (Yemen), Qatar, Hisn al-Akrad, ʿAkkar, Nasira, Maʿan, Salimiyya (Hama), and Biqaʿ al-ʿAziz (Syria). During this period, he also took the examinations at the College for Shariʿa Judges in Istanbul, which the government made obligatory for active judges who had not graduated from this school. He served about two years at each court, according to the term regulations mentioned earlier. However, in between terms of service he also had a few periods of unemployment, a common situation in the careers of judges during this period. One of these periods of unemployment lasted for one and one-half years at the turn of the twentieth century, in the course of which Sheikh Husayn went to the court in his hometown and sued the legal heirs of his late debtor (Albayrak 1996, 2: 137–38).[16]

---

prevailing legal systems, invention of local legal traditions, and so on. At the same time, this model is useful for reconstructing the agency of subaltern groups and individuals who conduct forum shopping and benefit from the pluralistic nature of the legal system in question. On legal pluralism, see Merry 1988. See some examples of works on Muslim courts using this model: Christelow 1985; Hirsch 1994, 1998; Shahar 2000b, 2005. See also Agmon 2004a, note 29.

14. On various Ottoman titles, see Hagopian 1907, 457–63. On titles of the Ottoman *ilmiye* and *kalemiye* at the subdistrict level, see Yazbak 1998, 118–19.

15. On the Ottoman state education system, see Fortna 2002, 115–17.

16. Sheikh Husayn's personal record could not be traced at Müftülük. See also Akiba 2000, 4, about periods of unemployment of judges.

The Defendants

The debtor, Mustafa ibn ʿAbdalla al-Maridi from Lydda, had quite a few heirs, the defendants at the trial. Three of them were present at court: the deceased's widow, Fatima bint Jadalla al-Rubaʿi from Lydda; his elder son, Shahada; and Muhammad Najib Efendi, who was the executer *(wasi)* of the will for the deceased's minor sons and the attorney *(wakil daʿawi)* for a few of their adult brothers and sisters (which means that he was a professional jurist representing clients at court, a new phenomenon in *shariʿa* courts that I discuss further in chapters 4 and 6).

The Circumstances of the Case

The transaction that brought the defendants to court about a year after their husband and father had died, with the goal of trying to avoid paying the debt they had allegedly inherited, was the sale of two properties, an olive grove and another piece of land in Lydda. This common procedure was in fact not a land transaction, but rather a loan for which the properties served as mortgage. This procedure of guarantee sale *(bayʿ wafaʾi)* was one of several variations used for regulating money-lending transactions. The late Mustafa al-Maridi sold the two properties to Sheikh Husayn Husni for only a limited period of time, two years in this case. The value of the properties that Sheikh Husayn Husni committed himself to sell back to Mustafa two years later was in fact the sum of money he had lent to Mustafa plus interest. Until the loan and interest were paid back, the land properties were deposited with Sheikh Husayn Husni, and he was entitled to use them and their profits as he saw fit, as any legal owner. In principle, if the debtor failed to pay back the loan, the lender became the permanent legal owner of the properties. However, as this and other cases of similar nature show, the fictitious buyers expected to get their money back because their investment was based on lending the money for interest and not on buying real estate.

The Presiding Judge

Muhammad Abu al-Nasr Efendi ibn Sheikh ʿAbd al-Qadir Efendi al-Khatib from Damascus, the judge who then served at the Jaffa court and handled the case, signed his name on the protocol record of the lawsuit in question. His career path was somewhat unusual compared to that of others in the generation of low-ranking judges whose patterns of recruitment followed the new regulations more strictly (such as Sheikh Husayn Husni, who came to his courtroom as a plaintiff).[17] Muhammad Abu al-Nasr Efendi was born in Damascus in 1834–35 to a family of merchants and artisans that in the course of the nineteenth century established its position among the ranks of the Damascene ulama. When Abu al-Nasr—as he used to sign his name on court records— was about fifteen years old, he was sent to Egypt and studied at al-Azhar, then returned to Damascus and served, like his father, as a *madrasa* teacher. He spent almost thirty years as a teacher in his hometown and at times in neighboring towns and villages. During these years, he went on a pilgrimage to the holy cities and spent some time there studying and associating with respected ulama. In addition, he visited in Istanbul and nurtured some connections there that would later be useful. Also during this period, Abu al-Nasr married two women, who gave birth to at least four sons, two of whom accompanied him later to his judicial appointments. Most of the information about his life in Damascus is derived from biographical dictionaries on Damascene notables. These sources clearly emphasize the male lineage of the respective families, so the wives are mentioned without names, daughters are not mentioned at all, and sons are mentioned without specifying the mother.

In the early 1870s, one of Abu al-Nasr's three brothers won the important position of preacher at the Ummayad mosque in Damascus. From then on, the family adopted the title "al-Khatib." About a decade later, in May 1883, when Abu al-Nasr was almost fifty years old, he began his judicial career. Before he was appointed to Jaffa in June 1896, the last court in his career path, he served in six other subdistrict centers, most of them in Syria, and his first appointment was in Libya. Thus, not only was Abu al-Nasr much older than most of his colleagues, but he also lacked the skills and experience that served at that time as criteria for recruiting judges to the reformed court system. In the pre-Tanzimat system, he could have used his rank as an *ʿalim,* his good connections, and his title as a *madrasa* teacher to get an appointment as judge, and then lease out his term to a younger and poorer judge, who would in prac-

17. The following description is derived from my article "Social Biography of a Late Ottoman *Shariʿa* Judge" (Agmon 2004b), which deals with the social biography of Judge Abu al-Nasr based on the files of *shariʿa* judges at Müftülük (SA dos. and SA def.); the court records of Jaffa; Schilcher 1985; and Al-Hafiz and Abaza 1986.

tice serve as judge at the local courts in question while Abu al-Nasr stayed home. In the late-nineteenth-century reformed system, however, this option no longer existed. Furthermore, it is plausible that, in addition to his above-mentioned merits, the reason he was admitted to the judiciary in spite of being unqualified was his willingness to serve in Libya, one of the frontier regions always short of qualified personnel, although the Ottoman reformers gave it priority (Akiba 2005).[18]

Judge Abu al-Nasr was appointed and served as *naib* (as noted earlier, the regular title for "judge" in this period) of Jaffa twice, between June 1896 and September 1898, and once again between September 1900 and August 1902. He then stayed in Jaffa as a court employee for another two years though his capacity was not specified in his file. His successor at the Jaffa court in August 1902 for about half a year was his son, 'Abd al-Qadir Hikmat. In August 1904, after about twenty years in service, Abu al-Nasr submitted a request to retire to the authorities in Istanbul and returned to Damascus. A couple of years later he died of a heart attack and was buried in his hometown. He had already been older than sixty years of age when he had arrived in Jaffa for his first term and older than seventy at the time he requested to be released from service, explaining that he was old (he wrote that he was eighty years old) and unable to fulfill his duties anymore. In 1910, the Ministry of Şeyhülislâm was informed about his death. His son, 'Abd al-Qadir Hikmat, serving as his father's executor, wrote that his father had died and was survived by two widows and three orphans, a minor son and two daughters to whom the ministry was to pay a pension from a special fund for the dependents of deceased judges that formed part of the orphan funds (Agmon 2004b).[19]

During his twenty years as a subdistrict judge, Abu al-Nasr married another four women in a row. Two of them, Libyans, he apparently married while in service there (he served about two years at his first Libyan assignment, but only for half a year in another Libyan subdistrict from which he resigned). The two Libyan women did not bear any children. He probably divorced them

18. In both his appointments to Libya, Judge Abu al-Nasr earned the highest salaries in his entire career (SA dos. 3720; Agmon 2004b), which demonstrates the Ottoman efforts to tackle the problem by paying higher salaries for service in Libya. On the Ottoman depiction of frontier regions of the empire as colonies, see Makdisi 2002, Deringil 2003, and Kühn 2003.

19. About the orphan funds, see chapter 5.

and married the other two women, who later became his widows. These two wives, the mothers of his two minor daughters, he had apparently married while in service in Jaffa. Alternatively, he may have married one or both of them in Damascus, where it seems he spent the two years between his terms in Jaffa. The mother of his minor son was apparently his slave. In addition, as I mentioned, two of his adult sons from Damascus, ʿAbd al-Qadir Hikmat and Ahmad Badawi, accompanied him and served as court scribes in Jaffa, and the former also replaced him as the Jaffa judge in 1902.

Abu al-Nasr's domestic cycle points to two significant issues. First, it stresses the notion of the patrilineal family. This notion is particularly emphasized by Abu al-Nasr's polygamous family structure. Most of the family structures discussed here, of people from a higher-middle-class or lower-middle-class background in Jaffa and Haifa, are different. Polygamy did exist, but among these strata in most cases it was serial, in which a marriage to a second woman led to divorce from the first wife. Second, and more significant for the current discussion, Abu al-Nasr's family structure illustrates his lifestyle as a traveling judge. This aspect of younger judges' career paths is more difficult to trace because they normally began their judicial wanderings at about the same time that they married for the first time. However, Abu al-Nasr spent most of his adult life in Damascus, where he married two women and had four sons and probably a number of daughters. Had he not decided to begin a new career at the age of fifty, and if he had remained in his hometown instead, his family structure would probably have continued to develop along the same lines as before. Maybe he would have married a third, younger woman, particularly in the event that his first two wives did not survive.

But the extensive marital and reproduction activities during the last twenty years of his life, between the ages of fifty and seventy, can hardly be understood unless his situation as a traveling judge is taken into account. Establishing a new household—or rather, households—along the way probably helped him to cope with his domestic life in the new places, and at the same time it was a means for networking in the local communities. Because he was not a young man to begin with and grew older in service until he finally announced that he could not fulfill his duties anymore, he possibly also needed some special care.

In order to consider the latter plausibility, we should ask what happened between 1898 and 1900, why Abu al-Nasr was not appointed to a new position elsewhere, and why he returned to Jaffa in the summer of 1900 for another term (and more). Abu al-Nasr apparently hoped to become the mufti of Damascus after the presiding mufti, Sheikh Muhammad al-Manini, had died in 1898. However, a member of the al-Qattan family won the position (*Salname* VS 1318/1900, 94). I believe that at this point Abu al-Nasr tried to remain in the judicial system in order either to be eligible for a pension or to improve the one he would have received had he retired in 1898 after serving only fifteen years.[20] Either possibility is suggested by his return to Jaffa, his temporary replacement by his son two years later, and the fact that even then he managed to be considered a court employee for another two years and only then sent in his request to retire and get a pension. This chain of events suggests that he was not well and that his efforts to remain in the system were supported by the authorities in the capital or by his networks in Jaffa or probably by both.[21]

Several details in the case record under observation suggest that when Judge Abu al-Nasr deliberated the lawsuit of his colleague Sheikh Husayn Husni half a year after his last term as a judge had begun, he was not at his best and may have appeared more rarely at court. In fact, the court records from his two terms as a judge in Jaffa include irregularities in comparison to the terms of other judges who served there during that period. In the Jaffa court records from those years, the scribe usually gave the name of the current judge on the opening page of each volume (this page, however, has not always survived in the volumes we have) and recorded the appointment of a new judge in the volume of records at hand. The judge signed the protocols of cases he handled. Sometimes he also signed footnotes that included amendments to case records.[22] For instance, between Abu al-Nasr's first and second terms at the Jaffa court (1898–1900), another Damascene judge, Muhammad Darwish

20. Unfortunately, I have not yet traced the specific rules regarding the pensions for retiring judges.

21. It sometimes happened that the authorities would mention personal reasons, such as a health problem, as a consideration for an appointment or relocation of a certain judge. In Abu al-Nasr's file, no reasons for either his second term in Jaffa or his function in the court after he was replaced by his son were recorded. His letter announcing his own retirement, however, was unusual, as was the mention of the cause (old age). In other judges' files, the date of retirement or death was recorded without any mention of who had announced it and why.

22. I discuss in chapter 4 the nature of this kind of record that was introduced into the *shari'a* courts from the 1870s.

Efendi al-Murtada, was appointed. His signature can be recognized on many protocol records and amendments to the footnotes in volumes that cover his term. His name is also explicitly mentioned as the *naib* of Jaffa on the opening page of a volume of records covering the period between January 1900 and June 1901, during which time he completed his term and was replaced by Abu al-Nasr, who returned for his second term in Jaffa and last term as a judge.[23]

In comparison with Judge Muhammad Darwish and other judges who served in Jaffa during this period, Judge Abu al-Nasr signed protocol records far less frequently, which might mean that he was not present at court in those cases whose records he did not sign. If indeed this was the case, it is possible that in his absence one of the authorized scribes functioned as his deputy without signing the protocols, although no mention was made of this fact in the records. Toward the end of his service, however, his signature appeared more frequently. The fluctuations between periods in which he signed more consistently and periods in which he rarely signed initially led me to think that there was something unusual in his conduct and to look for evidence in order to reconstruct his biography.[24]

When we combine all the hints about him and his career, we can see that Sheikh Abu al-Nasr had a problem, perhaps a health problem, that affected his work. In any case, for the purposes of this discussion we should notice that whereas he did not sign many protocols in the volume that includes the lawsuit I discuss here, which means he did not always attend court sessions, he did

23. Sheikh Murtada's signature appears on many records included in JCR, *Hujaj* 79, B 1316–Za 1318/XI 1898–II 1901. On one of them (p. 10) he signed "Hakim [Judge] Muhamad Darwish"; then his name is specified as the current *naib* on the opening page of JCR, *Hujaj* 83, Ş 1317–S 1319/I 1900–VI 1901. Muhammad Darwish brought his family with him when he came to Jaffa, and they rented a house in Manshiyya, a neighborhood populated by many immigrants on the northern outskirts of Jaffa, outside the (former) old city walls (see chapter 7 and the map of Jaffa in this chapter). As noted, his son, Murtadazadeh Sheikh Mahmud Nadim, served as one of the court scribes under his judgeship and was often authorized to conduct legal proceedings that took place outside the court. See also Agmon 2004b, note 28.

24. Sheikh Abu al-Nasr's signature first appears in a volume of protocol records covering his first term of service. See JCR, *Hujaj* Z 1313–M 1315/VI 1896–VI 1897, 98, 106. His signature also appears on protocol records in a volume covering the period shortly before he completed his second term as a judge; see JCR, *Hujaj* 86, Za 1318–Za 1319/III 1901–III 1902, 162, 163, 172, 173, 179, 181.

sign the latter protocol for this lawsuit. In fact, he signed it twice, in the middle of the record and below the last paragraph that contains the verdict. His presence and conduct of this case were also explicitly referred to in a certain place in the record. I return shortly to the significance I see in this reference and in the fact that he deliberated this case.

The Court Scribes

The chief scribe in this case was a member of the Dajani family. As I noted earlier, this family was constantly represented at the court one way or another during this period, usually in the capacity of chief scribe or of another type of scribe. In addition, at least two of the most active attorneys who represented litigants at court during this period were also members of that family, as was the mufti of Jaffa, whom the plaintiff, Sheikh Husayn, mentioned as one of his potential witnesses. The chief scribe at this time, Muhammad Fawzi al-Dajani, son of the current mufti, held this office for quite long. He was already there when Muhammad Abu al-Nasr was appointed as judge in Jaffa for the first time (1896) and continued in this position throughout the six years of the judgeships of both Abu al-Nasr and Muhammad al-Murtada and also after the former's retirement.

Two other scribes who served at the court were, as noted, Abu al-Nasr's sons. A third scribe was Mahmud Nadim al-Murtada, the son of Muhammad Darwish, the other Damascene judge who served between Abu al-Nasr's two terms. Mahmud Nadim al-Murtada served uninterruptedly as court scribe long after his father had completed his service in Jaffa. Another two scribes, apparently of local origin, served at court during that period; both had been there for a long time and were occasionally authorized to conduct and record legal proceedings outside the court on the judge's behalf. The senior among them was Muhammad Shakir al-Taji, about whom we know little, except that he was the one usually authorized by the judge to replace him outside the court. His service in court began quite some time before Judge Abu al-Nasr's arrival and continued after Abu al-Nasr retired. He apparently conducted many legal proceedings on the judge's behalf and recorded the important parts of Sheikh Husayn's lawsuit. The junior among the scribes was Muhammad Samahan, who was an intern at the court and frequently accompanied his senior colleague to legal proceedings out of court.

Unlike the judges, this group of scribes served for many years at the court and thus were rather dominant in running it and shaping its culture. Although in the period under discussion three of them were the sons of outside judges, they integrated themselves into the local court, at least several of them remaining after their fathers had completed their terms and left. They merged into the local community like many other immigrants. Furthermore, unlike the judge, who was alone in his position, they had local peers at court. Owing to the scribes' long service in court and their local family affiliations and connections, the court as inscribed in its records seems a somewhat intimate institution. Thus, it is not surprising that when a judge was appointed to this court, knowing that he was going to stay there for only a couple of years, he had no reason to use his authority to change the prevailing personnel apart from adding his own relatives. In this regard, Abu al-Nasr was no exception, as he presumably did not know that he would end up spending a longer period, in fact almost the rest of his life, in Jaffa. Keeping the same personnel meant that the judge was able to gain from their local knowledge and experience. Thus, when Abu al-Nasr returned to his post as judge in July 1900, he continued to work with the same personnel, including Mahmud Nadim al-Murtada, the son of his predecessor. In the case of Judge Abu al-Nasr, it was perhaps even more reasonable not to change anything because he already knew most of the personnel from his previous term of judgeship, and his health problem probably made him more dependent on their cooperation. One change, however, did take place: his own son, 'Abd al-Qadir Hikmat, left for what was apparently his first judicial position in Bani Sa'ab (in the district of Nablus), from where he returned later to replace his father as the Jaffa judge (Kupferschmidt 1986, 126).

A Judge Facing Judgment: The Record and the Court Culture

The details of the transaction and the loan deliberated in this case are not the focus of the current discussion. However, a survey of the case record is required in order to look more closely at some of its orthographical and textual features and to place them in the context of the court culture.

As I suggested earlier, the scene at the Jaffa court at the turn of the twentieth century was shaped to a large extent by this group of long-serving scribes, who were in most cases members of local ulama families and thus had variegated connections with and an intimate knowledge of the local community. Under the circumstances resulting from legal reform, the judge, who was usually an outsider, was extremely dependent on the scribes for the management of the court. At the same time, the scribes' professional status and positions as well as the continuity of the court work, which was their source of local power, depended on the current judge's performance. Furthermore, the scribes belonged to the same social level as the judge. Granted, the judge was ranked higher, and his lifestyle as a frequent traveler was entirely different from that of the scribes, whose locality and stability were major aspects of their socioprofessional identity. However, in terms of hierarchy, judges of subdistricts were located rather low professionally and like the scribes had a vested interest in the continuity of the *shariʿa* court system and its accessibility to the provincial communities.[25]

Thus, cooperation was basically in the mutual interest of both the judge and the scribes and especially so in Abu al-Nasr's situation, if indeed he had a problem that prevented him from functioning at full capacity. During his second term of office in Jaffa, he enjoyed more local connections. He probably authorized one of the experienced scribes to conduct legal proceedings in his absence more often than in a court where the judge worked to full capacity. Such absences entailed a bigger workload for the scribes, but also more responsibility, professional experience, and local authority.

The case of Sheikh Husayn, who professionally and socially was a counterpart of both the judge and the scribes, seems helpful in understanding these relationships. Sheikh Husayn's position was deeply rooted in the local ulama. Moreover, he himself was a judge, and this fact was stressed in the record as his main identity. The handling of his lawsuit by the current judge was rather significant for Sheikh Husayn, both symbolically and practically, for achieving an authoritative decision in his favor. However, the judge in question, Abu al-Nasr, was unable to deliberate all the legal proceedings at that time, as he would normally have done. It can be assumed that the fact that the plaintiff was a colleague and a member of a local ulama family well connected to the court was not insignificant in the judge's decision to handle this case personally in spite of his problem.

The record contains no indication of abused judicial discretion. On the contrary, judging by the way the evidence is inscribed in the record, it looks as if Sheikh Husayn possessed all he needed to win his case. At the same time, he

25. On transformations in the local court culture in nineteenth-century Jaffa, see Agmon 2004a.

apparently was not willing to take any risk and used every possible legal procedure to make sure that not only did he win the case, but in the event of a future
appeal no procedural flaw would be found. Perhaps he was not sure how long
he would still be unemployed and be capable of maintaining his business at
home.[26] His professional experience may also have motivated his unwilling-
ness to take any risk. During his career, he may have seen enough cases that
seemed clear-cut and turned out to be long and complicated, resulting in an
unexpected decision. This was particularly the situation under the circumstances of the legal reform that reinforced the procedural aspects of court
work. Various procedures of appeal also constituted an important aspect of
the judicial reform, a fact of which Sheikh Husayn, an experienced judge,
must have been aware. In any event, in order to secure the result he desired, the
cooperation of the court personnel, in particular that of the judge, was essential.[27] In the next section, I summarize and interpret the protocol of the court
sessions in this lawsuit in the chronological order of the legal proceedings.
The format of my summary does not reflect the format of the actual protocol
(see chapter 4 for a discussion of protocol format).

Court Session 1

Scribe: Muhammad Samahan

The protocol of the trial begins with the deposition of the plaintiff followed
by the defendants' response (*dabt al-da'wa,* see chapter 4). The date, Wednesday, 6 Sha'ban 1318 (29 November 1900), was registered, and then the plaintiff was introduced as follows: Faziletli[28] Sheikh[29] Husayn Husni Efendi,[30] the
son of the late Sheikh 'Umar, son of Sayyid[31] Bakr Efendi al-Khatib,[32] adult,

---

26. In retrospect, it took almost another year before he had to travel to his next position,
but he might have been waiting for a new appointment any day or, more plausible, might have
planned to go to Istanbul to take care of his next appointment, as was the normal pattern in
such cases (Albayrak 1996, 2: 137–38; Akiba 2000, 4).

27. I assume that the importance attributed to appeals motivated the introduction of protocol records to the *shari'a* court system because this type of record was meant to give higher
legal authorities the means to check the court procedure at a lower instance (see chapter 4).

28. His Honor (Turkish).

29. The religious title of a learned man, *('alim).*

30. An administrative title of *naib*s and many other state employees (Turkish).

31. A distinguished lineage related to the tribe of the Prophet.

32. Preacher.

sane, Muslim, Ottoman, Ludi,[33] the former *naib* of Hisn al-Akrad, legally identified.[34] A full list of the defendants whom he sued was then given, including
the two heirs and an attorney who were present in the courtroom and those
absent defendants who were represented by the attorney. Witnesses identified
the two heirs in the court, but the attorney was already known to the court.

Two points ought to be highlighted regarding this introduction. The attorney, who seemingly became the main cause of concern for Sheikh Husayn in
the course of the deliberations, was by definition known to the court.[35] This,
however, was not the case regarding the two defendants, who came from outside Jaffa and were unknown. Their names were mentioned without any title.
At the same time, Sheikh Husayn—who, like the defendants, was born in
Lydda but grew up in Jaffa and was connected to its ulama—was introduced
with all his titles and ranks. For a better understanding of the discourse of the
court record, it is important to notice this contrast between a litigant who was
known to the court and mentioned with many titles and litigants who needed
identifying witnesses and were mentioned without any titles. Of course, it is
possible that these defendants bore no titles even in their hometown and community (although it is unlikely because, as we shall see, they signed their deposition with personal seals, a fact that suggests that their social status was not a
lower one). Nevertheless, this example illustrates the extent to which the court
records were written from the point of view of the judge and scribes, who in
writing them re-constituted the society of which they were part, both as ulama
and as members of the local elite.[36]

33. From the town of Lydda. The latter five adjectives reaffirm legal, religious, civic,
and resident status and were fixed terms repeated for every litigant, approving his or her legal
personality.

34. That is, known to the court *(ma'aruf al-dhat)*. Every litigant had to be legally identified
(al-ta'arif al-shar'i) either by the court staff or else by two witnesses through a procedure conducted at court. The identifying witnesses' names were also recorded in the protocol. The law
of procedure required a variety of witnesses who would testify to specific aspects of the proceedings (at least two of each kind). Regular witnesses *(shuhud)*, witnesses approving the reliability of the regular witnesses *(shuhud al-tazkiya)*, and notary witnesses *(shuhud al-hal)* approving
the record were required in addition to the identifying witnesses *(shuhud al-ta'rif)*, as well as a
number of experts who would testify on specific issues.

35. About the professional attorneys, see chapter 6.

36. For a discourse analysis of court records, see al-Qattan 1996.

The second point is that Sheikh Husayn's status as a judge was stressed in the first part of his introduction by the titles *faziletli* and *sheikh,* and then in the last part of his introduction, where his former appointment as judge was explicitly mentioned. In the personal files of judges in the office of Şeyhülislâm, mentioning a former appointment was a common form of identification of a former judge. In the court records, however, mention of the former appointments of people who were still alive was less common. For that reason, this aspect of the case record attracts more attention and was in fact the part that made me read the record more closely to begin with. At first sight, this introduction of Sheikh Husayn, in addition to being informative, looks as if it were intended to show respect to a colleague and hence to the social group to which he and the rest of the court personnel belonged. If we consider it together with the rest of the protocol, however, more seems to be involved. Stressing the plaintiff's professional experience might also have been motivated by a practical line of thinking—namely, the need to convince, in the event of an appeal, any professional reader of this record that the plaintiff was an experienced judge and not likely to make legal mistakes.

The deposition of Sheikh Husayn that follows this introduction includes a fully detailed description of the transaction he had made with the late Mustafa, son of ʿAbdalla al-Maridi from Lydda, preceded by an account of the defendants' responsibility, as the legal heirs of the deceased, to see that the transaction was completed. He mentions the sums of money involved, the exact description of the landed properties, their legal status, and the dates and numbers of the official documents covering the transaction in the Jaffa land-registration office *(tapu)*. Later, a footnote added to the protocol and signed by Sheikh Husayn states that a contract between him and the deceased concerning the transaction was also recorded in a *shariʿa* court document. The existence of a footnote and signature in the margin indicates that the record of the deposition was recited to Sheikh Husayn and that he demanded this amendment (see chapter 4). On this basis, he asked the court to oblige the defendants to pay him the debt, and he signed the record of his deposition.

The defendants' response to his claims was short. The two heirs (the widow and son of the deceased) and the attorney confirmed all the details in the lawsuit related to the death of Mustafa al-Maridi and the list of his heirs, but denied the debt and demanded that Sheikh Husayn be obliged to prove it. All three of them signed this response with their personal seals. This line is the only part of that record written by the scribe Muhammad Shakir al-Taji, not by Muhammad Samahan, who recorded the rest of the protocol of this session. Then the attorney separately signed an additional statement saying that he denied the entire claim and demanding that it legally be proved. In so doing, he apparently was stressing the fact that he worked separately as the orphaned heirs' representative and that he too—not only the plaintiff—was a professional jurist familiar with procedures. Sheikh Husayn was then asked about his proof, and he mentioned a long list of witnesses that he would bring to testify to the truth of his claim at the next session, due to take place four days later. Among these names are some officials of local branches of state departments in Jaffa—such as the *tapu* (land registration), the *awqaf* (religious endowments), and the *vergi* (taxes) departments—and the mufti of Jaffa, Faziletli Sayyid 'Ali Efendi Abu al-Mawahib, a prominent member of the notable al-Dajani family, whose son served at the *shari'a* court as the chief scribe at that time. None of these officials on Sheikh Husayn's list actually testified at the trial. All the actual witnesses were people from Lydda, who testified to the transaction that took place in that town, whereas the details about the properties deposited and their legal status were proved by documents and not by eyewitnesses.

In fact, this case demonstrates rather convincingly the combination of eyewitnesses and official documents that was increasingly though inconsistently used at court as legal proof during this period. Muslim law clearly preferred eyewitnesses and oral testimony to written documents. Scholars often raise the question of the roles played by written documents in legal proceedings in various historical situations (see, e.g., Agmon 2004a, note 38). Nineteenth-century reform, with its strong emphasis on procedures and written records, pursued the use of documents as legal proof in court, although this tendency became apparent in *shari'a* courts only in the post-Ottoman states. In the observed case, the legal debates between the two litigants/jurists were mainly about the procedures for using documents as testimony.

The names of the witnesses mentioned by Sheikh Husayn may give us some idea about his connections and social networks, and although he probably genuinely meant to bring these witnesses to give testimony if necessary, he might also have mentioned their names with the intention of hinting at his extensive connections and to stress the fact that his claim was covered legally. He and two other people signed this part of the protocol, but although these two people bore the name of prominent families, Haykal and Abu Radwan, their capacity and the reason for obtaining their signatures are not clear, for their names are not mentioned anywhere else in the entire record.[37]

Court Session 2

Scribe: Muhammad Shakir al-Taji

At this stage, without stating that it was a new court session taking place a few days later, two testimonies were recorded.[38] The two witnesses from Lydda testified to the truthfulness of Sheikh Husayn's entire claim. The testimony was recorded in detail only once, with only a mention that the second witness was repeating what the first had said, and both witnesses signed their respective testimonies. Considering the meticulousness and many repetitions of evidence typical of the rest of the case record, this shortcut in recording the second testimony stands out. Both the shortcut here and the detailed repetitions later in the record are somewhat exceptional when compared to other records. One of the repetitions includes the full contents of these two testimonies and the signatures of the witnesses in the last session. It is possible that the testimonies were repeated to ensure that there would be no later claim about flaws in the protocol just because the second testimony was not fully recorded. I emphasize this point because it indicates the way the scribes shaped the structure of the court record. The judge, who normally would have dictated the text for the record to the scribe, did deliberate at least part of this case, yet he did not attend all the sessions owing to the problem that prevented him from working at full capacity. Under these circumstances, he might have authorized one of the experienced scribes to replace him at those sessions he was unable to attend. He did, however, handle this particular session and dictated its record, abridging the second testimony; later, either he or the scribes or the plaintiff apparently identified the procedural problem that this shortcut might cause and decided to take precautions.

I return later to the issue of who deliberated and who recorded this case.

---

37. They were possibly officials serving in one of the departments that dealt with landed properties who came to testify and thereby approve the documents brought by the plaintiff. A case record involving a woman from the Abu Radwan family is described in chapter 6. The two families, Haykal and Abu Radwan, were related to one another through marriage (see chapter 7).

38. On the routine of recording protocols that developed somewhat differently in the court of Jaffa from that of Haifa, see chapter 4.

At this point, it is most probable that the court session ended and the deliberations continued at another session, although the record gives no indication of this possibility: after the testimonies were heard, the defendants were asked for their comments. The reason why I suspect that two sessions were in fact recorded as one session (session two) is that other case records show the responses of the parties to the testimonies as being requested in a separate session or sessions. In this case, most of the dispute occurred after the testimonies were heard, so that it is even more plausible that not all of the case took place at one court session.

Whether at the same session or at another session, the two lay defendants responded that they did not know the witnesses. The defendants' attorney, Muhammad Najib Efendi, claimed that the witnesses' testimony should be rejected because they did not specify when the property transaction that led to the loan had taken place. To this claim Sheikh Husayn replied that because the witnesses did mention the *tapu* documents covering the transaction, which recorded the time of the transaction and were available for examination, there was no need for this information to be included in the oral testimony. On this ground, he repeated his request that the court carry out the required legal proceedings. Each of the two litigants, the attorney and Sheikh Husayn, signed the record of his own claim in the matter.

At this point, the recording scribe mentioned that the judge requested the deeds from the plaintiff and Sheikh Husayn handed them to him. The scribe then registered the details that the judge found in the three documents: the first dealt with the transaction relating to the land planted with olives, the second with that of the trees in this grove, and the third with the second piece of land included in this transaction. Sheikh Husayn also signed this part of the record. The attorney still objected, this time on the grounds of another procedural claim that he based on the regulations of the *tapu*. Sheikh Husayn responded by the same token, explaining why, according to these regulations, the documents were valid, hence sustaining his claims. The continuation of the session was then postponed to Sunday, 17 Sha'ban 1318 (10 December 1900).

Court Session 3
  Scribe: al-Taji

On that Sunday, the deliberations were postponed again, this time with Abu al-Nasr's signature next to Sheikh Husayn's, and a reference to the continuation of the record on another page.

Court Session 4
    Scribe: al-Taji

When the next session began on Thursday, 21 Sha'ban (15 December), Sheikh Husayn said that he would bring the rest of his witnesses on the next Wednesday to complete his response.

Court Session 5
    Unidentified Scribe

However, on the next Wednesday, the deliberations were postponed once again, to Saturday, 29 Sha'ban (23 December).

Court Session 6
    Scribe: Samahan

The next session of this case was recorded on another page in that volume of the court protocol. This recording contains a reconstruction of the entire case record up to that point. The record was recited again in front of the parties and the previous witnesses, who signed once more. There was no mention of why the witnesses had been invited again and whether there was any dispute between the parties about testimony that was not recorded and thus caused this very unusual addition. Sheikh Husayn might have initiated this repetition when he noticed the way the second testimony was recorded after the second session. This is one of the components of this record that strengthens my impression that some unusual steps were taken in this case in order to avoid a long trial and unexpected results for Sheikh Husayn. After this reconstruction, a third witness, also from Lydda, testified and repeated the previous testimonies.

Court Session 7
    Scribe: al-Taji

The record of the last session, which took place on 11 Ramadan (2 January 1901) and was written on another page, opens with a statement that the defendants had no objection to the testimony of the three witnesses, who had been checked and approved by public as well as confidential testimonies (as part of the legal procedure of verifying the reliability of witnesses, *tazkiya*). The names of these witnesses, all of them from Lydda, are also mentioned. Then the entire story is repeated in order to clarify that this is the version legalized by the testimonies. In addition, Sheikh Husayn took an oath that the total sum of money had remained as a debt that was still owed to him. This was yet another unexplained legal step. It is the only one in the record that explicitly deviated from *shariʿa* law of procedure. I discuss in more detail the procedure of taking oaths and its function in determining actual court decisions in chapters 5 and 6, but in this case record the oath looks like yet another precaution taken by Sheikh Husayn to leave no doubt that his claim was fully proved. Alternatively, it is possible that more objections on the defendant's side were not recorded, claiming that Sheikh Husayn should have brought proof that the debt had not been paid to him, to which he responded by taking an oath. However, if that was the case, then not recording this exchange was both unusual and inconsistent with the overrecording typical of the rest of this case. In accordance with the content of Sheikh Husayn's oath, it is stated in the record, in the first person, that "I decided [in favor] of the plaintiff," and the record again repeats the details of the debt and the transactions, together with explicit instructions that the defendants would pay the debt from the deceased's inheritance. Judge Abu al-Nasr then signed the protocol.

◆   ◆   ◆

Two scribes recorded the entire protocol (except for a couple of lines in session 5 informing that the court session was postponed, written by a third scribe). Judging from the handwriting, one of them was most probably Muhammad Shakir Efendi al-Taji.[39] As noted, we do not know much about his background from sources other than the court records. He might have been a member of the established family of al-Taji (al-Faruqi) from Ramla. Also, one of the *tazkiya* witnesses from Lydda, who seemed to belong to an ulama family, was called al-Taji. However, I never came across any indication that Muhammad Shakir al-Taji was originally from one of these neighboring towns. The court records provide evidence that he was a senior scribe who had been serving at this court for many years and was frequently authorized by the judge to conduct legal proceedings on his behalf outside the court. I was not able to trace his personal dossier, nor did I trace the dossier of any of the

39. The scribes did not sign the protocol of lawsuits except for those cases that had been recorded out of court. They did sign registrations of cases. See chapter 4 and Agmon 2004a about types of records and scribes' signatures.

scribes in the *Sicill-i Ahval* (SA) at Müftülük. This fact probably testifies to the way the central government constructed the judicial system; for the central authorities, the judges, and not the scribes, epitomized the courts at the lower administrative levels and were the target of the policy of centralization. Thus, the point in the career path of a jurist when he was required to fill in the necessary forms for a personal dossier was after his appointment as judge or to other positions in the system, but not as a scribe. Hence, the career path of a judge for whom the authorities kept a record might have included the information that he had been a court scribe at some point, but the record was apparently written only because he was later promoted to the position of judge. In this case, al-Taji recorded all the sessions in which the main legal struggle took place—the first two testimonies, the submission of the *tapu* documents to the court, and the entire legal debate between the two jurist-litigants about the question of whether the plaintiff's claim had been proved by the documents. He also recorded the last session containing the reasoned court decision.

The second scribe was most likely Muhammad Samahan. He was a junior scribe, a legal intern *(amin al-Shar')*, who frequently accompanied Shakir al-Taji to conduct legal proceedings that took place out of court. He recorded the first court session at which the parties' depositions were obtained and the burden of proof was put on Sheikh Husayn (except for the first short response of the three defendants, which was recorded by Shakir al-Taji). Later in the trial he also recorded the session before the last one, when a third witness was brought to give testimony. As the next section demonstrates, this division of labor between the two scribes points to the possibility that the judge did not attend all the court sessions in this trial.

The Judge and the Local Court

The routine of recording protocols at the Jaffa and Haifa courts is discussed in detail in chapter 4. According to the method developed by the Jaffa court scribes, recording each court session separately was not deemed important, and therefore we only know for sure that a certain session began or ended when the record explicitly mentions it or when the continuation of the record in the volume is interrupted owing to lack of space. However, evidence suggests that there were in fact more sessions in some cases than mentioned explicitly in the case records. For that reason, it is more difficult in the Jaffa court record to keep track of who was present at court during this or that session and who was not than in the Haifa court record (and it is not always an easy task there either). I divided the record of Sheikh Husayn's lawsuit into court sessions partly on the basis of indirect evidence of this sort. This division indicates a plausible picture of the judge's and scribes' presence at the court and of the division of labor among them in handling and recording this case.

If we look again at Judge Abu al-Nasr's signature on protocols in the volume that contains the lawsuit under consideration, we notice that he signed eight times throughout the entire volume, including his two signatures to the protocol of Sheikh Husayn's lawsuit, which were also his last in that volume. His appointment began in September 1900. He signed three protocols in September, another two in November, and then twice in the lawsuit under discussion, and a third signature on a protocol of a case recorded just after this lawsuit, on the very same day he decided Sheikh Husayn's lawsuit (January 1901). His signature does not appear again in this volume, which ends eight months later, in August 1901.

Two aspects of the observed lawsuit suggest that it was not a mere coincidence that Abu al-Nasr signed this particular lawsuit and that his signature reflected the fact that it was the judge himself who conducted this case. First, as noted, his relatively rare presence in court is evident from his inconsistent signatures on records. If it were not for this particular feature of his judgeship, his signature in this case would have been only one example of many. That he was in court while at least two sessions of this lawsuit were deliberated and did not just sign the protocol later on is underlined by the fact that he also signed another protocol record for a case deliberated and decided on the same day. This coincidence confirms my understanding that the protocol was recorded gradually as the deliberations of the case in question progressed (see chapter 4). If that were so, it also supports the assumption that the lack of his signature in many case records testifies to his absence from court during those cases.

The second aspect is the explicit mention of the judge in the record. In other records, the scribe sometimes refers to the presence of the judge, accompanied by the accepted honoraries and socioadministrative titles, but this form was infrequent and usually in the opening lines of a case record. In the Sheikh Husayn lawsuit, "his honor" is referred to in the middle of the protocol, at a point when he requested the plaintiff to present the documents of the official registration of the property transaction, which the plaintiff claimed he had signed together with the late debtor: "thumma talaba fadilat mawlana al-hakim al-shar'i al-qawajin [the title deeds] min al-muda'i" (JCR, *Hujaj* 81, 100).

As noted, Abu al-Nasr signed this protocol twice. His first signature appears in the third court session, below a postponement of a session that was planned for 17 Sha'ban and was rescheduled to 21 Sha'ban. The second was his signature below the verdict at the end of the trial. In the Jaffa court record, unlike that of Haifa, even those judges who attended the court every day usually signed the protocol records only once, at the end of the case. Thus, the signature in the middle of the protocol was an exception. In the context of Abu al-Nasr's inconsistent signing of the case records in that period, which ceased altogether after he signed this lawsuit, the additional signature was probably meant to record his actual presence in court and his handling of the deliberations of this case.

If we examine the sessions for which we have evidence of his presence and compare them to the structure of the entire case record, two sections in this trial were apparently crucial from the plaintiff's point of view: (1) attorney Muhammad Najib Efendi's attempt to refute Sheikh Husayn's proof and (2) the verdict. Judge Abu al-Nasr deliberated most or all of the sessions that belonged to these two categories. No more objections by the defendants were recorded after the judge signed his name for the first time in the middle of the record. Furthermore, the division of labor among the scribes is important here. The account of the crucial sessions, plausibly conducted by the judge, was apparently recorded by the senior scribe, Muhammad Shakir al-Taji, and the rest of the sessions by the junior scribe, Muhammad Samahan. Thus, it is possible that the judge authorized either Muhammad Shakir Efendi or another senior scribe to head the less-crucial sessions, as he probably did in other cases when he could not attend court, although no such authorization was registered in the record, as was usually the procedure for cases handled out of court.

The significance of Judge Abu al-Nasr's attendance and deliberation of this case—or, rather, of its crucial sessions—seems to be multilateral. In the context of Sheikh Husayn's lawsuit as it is inscribed in its record, Abu al-Nasr's presence was apparently emphasized as part of his own and his scribes' effort to support their social counterpart and colleague, the plaintiff, in winning his case. If indeed a problem prevented Abu al-Nasr from functioning at full capacity, then Muhammad Najib, the minor heirs' legal representative and a professional attorney who spent much time at court, must have known about it. Abu al-Nasr's relatively frequent presence at this trial was for Muhammad Najib an indication that in this case endless procedural arguments and playing for time (as professional attorneys did in such situations) were not going to tip the scale in his clients' favor. At the same time, it is also possible that Abu al-Nasr's presence was further emphasized "for the record" should the protocol be examined by higher authorities.

In the context of the Jaffa court culture, the somewhat unusual situation of a *shariʿa* judge on leave requiring the services of the *shariʿa* court in his hometown highlights some of the characteristics of this small community of scribes. The various indications in this record of the support that Sheikh Husayn might have received from the court personnel also suggest a substantial level of cooperation and solidarity among them.

In addition, several indications of a somewhat flexible attitude toward recording standards shown in this record might suggest that the scribes had developed some sense of "ownership" of the local court, or at least of its record. We ought to bear in mind that most of the scribes who served at this court when the protocol was recorded had already been serving there for several years, and some of them also conducted legal proceedings on the judge's behalf. As described earlier, they were used to seeing judges come and go every second year, and at this particular juncture they were working for the second term under a judge who was working only part-time and was the father of two of them. When all is added together, the legal arena of this court was apparently run mainly by this cohesive group of local scribes, whose composition changed rather gradually. This situation enabled a legal culture, which was part and parcel of the Ottoman *shariʿa* court culture and yet also very local in nature, to evolve and develop (Agmon 2004a).

The court's local nature was thus personified in its community of scribes, at least at this relatively lower administrative level, and the scribes worked toward securing the continuity of the court work and toward the epitomization of the court by the judge in spite of the profound change that the *shariʿa* court system had undergone. Within about three decades (between the 1850s and the 1880s), the *shariʿa* court had lost its priority, almost exclusivity, in the official judicial Ottoman system and had become only one court in a multicourt system. The ulama families of small provincial towns, for whom the *shariʿa* court had been a major source of power, had witnessed the emergence of various other institutions with which the *shari'a* court had to share its earlier judicial authority.

Nevertheless, this situation was not always a disadvantage for the local ulama. As I mentioned earlier, in the case of the *nizamiye* courts at the subdistrict level, the *shari'a* judge gained another power base as the ex officio head of this court, which was conducted by a council of local notables and state officers rather than by a single judge. The same can be said about the new institution for the management of orphans' properties (Emval-ı Eytam Nezareti). The supervision of orphans' properties, traditionally the judge's exclusive responsibility, had been extended and divided between the court and this new institution, a development that created new professional opportunities for ulama in the orphan funds (see chapter 5).

In the next chapters, specifically chapter 4, a detailed analysis of Haifa court cases and the somewhat different local culture of the Haifa court complements the picture presented in this chapter. Despite this difference, a substantial similarity between the Jaffa and Haifa courts resulted from legal reform. The regulations concentrated on the judges, cutting them off from the local setting and binding them to a unified central system. Thus, although putting the *shari'a* judges and courts under greater control and restricting their jurisdiction, the reforms reinforced the figure of the judge as the embodiment of central authority in the periphery. A by-product was the enhanced position of the scribes in epitomizing this periphery.

However, the result was not a binary division between center and periphery, state and local setting. In spite of the conditions restricting judges and their resultant lifestyle, so different from that of the scribes and other local court staff, the two groups had much in common. Generally speaking, the background of the judges who had been appointed to subdistrict centers in the Arab provinces was not dissimilar from that of the local scribes. The two groups also shared an interest in the continuation of the work of the *shari'a* court and the preservation of its local authority. As I show later, the court clientele, and in particular certain social groups involved there, formed a third party that shared this interest. Thus, the legal culture reconstructed in these courts combined strong local elements, in spite of the standardization emphasized by the reforms, with universal features resulting from government regulations and the constant movement of the judges from one court to another.

4

Documenting the Family

The Registration *(Sijill)* and the Protocol *(Dabt)*

KEEPING RECORDS of the court proceedings was the scribes' main assignment.[1] In the course of the reforms, this aspect of court activities underwent some significant changes, which ought to be considered at three levels. First, the changed documentation procedures have a direct bearing on our interpretation of the texts that serve as source material. Second, these procedural changes need to be investigated from the point of view of the court's activity, the nature of the tasks that the scribes fulfilled, and the balance between the scribes and the judge. Third, they should also be studied from the perspective of interrelations between the court staff and those who required the court's services.

In this chapter, I compare two prototypes of case records, one old and one new, to explore the innovative late-nineteenth-century recording procedures. I then deal with the implementation of the new procedures, which did not wholly replace the old type, but rather were an addition to the court's recording practices. I discuss this issue against the background of instructions issued by the central government in Istanbul and of certain differences between the Jaffa and Haifa courts in interpreting these instructions. Finally, I pay particular attention to the novelty of reciting the records before the parties involved, followed by the signing of the final version, a practice included in the new

1. This chapter is based on Agmon 2003b. I thank the State University of New York Press for permission to use it.

recording procedure, and consider the plausible implications of this practice for the construction of the family in Jaffa and Haifa.

My point of departure is that the family, as a social practice, was discursively constituted in various spheres. Here, I consider the construction of the family in the legal arena. I show how participants' involvement in the process of authorizing the documents covering their legal affairs may have resulted in an emphasis on the legal notion of family in shaping family construction in Jaffa and Haifa. Each court adopted a different version of the new recording procedures, and the version adopted in Haifa may have had a stronger effect on the legal notion of the family there than the Jaffa version had in Jaffa. In addition, other changes in the courts and communities of those two cities may have exposed members of the lower and middle classes who attended the court to these aspects of legal culture more than were their upper-class counterparts.

As described in the second chapter, the court records of both cities include varied documented legal proceedings. These accounts differ from each other in their structure, literary expressions, legal terminology, and many other features.[2] However, a major division into two types is pertinent to almost all the documents in the Jaffa and Haifa court records. One type is the registration *(sijill)* of a completed court case or official document, a summary recording one of several forms of legal proceedings.[3] The registration is the most common type of document among the surviving Ottoman *shari'a* court records from different periods. The other type is a detailed protocol (Arabic: *dabt,* Turkish: *zabt)* of legal proceedings according to court sessions. The development of this type into an authorized official record was one of the innovations in the late-nineteenth-century *shari'a* courts, and it is this form that serves as the focus of the following analysis.

The registration type of record *(sijill)* is a summary of a completed court case (or an official document that arrived at the court), which was by definition registered after the case was decided, no matter how many court sessions had been conducted or how long the deliberations had lasted. Thus, simple procedures, such as giving power of attorney *(wikala)* or the details of complicated

2. I discuss these differences in my dissertation (Agmon 1995, 36–56).

3. Some of the legal forms documented in the court records as registrations are *hujja* (deed), *i'lam* (court decision), *waqfiyya* (endowment), and *wikala* (power of attorney).

disputes could be summarized laconically in the same manner and take up similar space in the record.[4]

The raison d'être of the registration is clear from the form and legal narration of the documents of this sort: the court decision was their climax. The registration was to supply the court with a legal reference to the decision reached and the litigants with a formal document that they could use in any future related business in or out of court.[5] In other words, it ensured the legal work of the court and sustained its function of creating and preserving the public record. Recorded after the legal deliberations were over, these documents obviously leave out many details, including legal exchanges in the courtroom.[6] Social historians who read them may sometimes feel rather frustrated, for the registrations are laconic and formulaic, tending to conceal more than they reveal, and mainly covering aspects that may seem trivial and insignificant.[7]

The protocol *(dabt),* in contrast, represents a different type of record altogether. A court case recorded this way may include an account of each court session, its proceedings chronologically listed and recorded shortly after it was conducted, before the decision was reached and even before any further session took place.[8] The record of a court session includes a full description of

4. The three registrations given in figure 1—case 497, case 595, and case 630—relate to the lawsuit unfolded in this chapter. The first two records summarize procedures of giving power of attorney, each requiring a short court session, whereas the third summarizes a four-court-session case.

5. See references made by the court in one case record to other records in a volume of registrations (fig. 2, case 83, session 1, lines 4 and 7). The aim of the registration type of record is explicitly mentioned in the instructions issued in 1874, requiring the scribes to ensure that the record was legible and written clearly (*Düstur* 1, 4: 83, "Sicillat-ı şerʿiye ve zabt-ı dâva-ı cerideleri hakkında talimat," 15 Z 1290/3 II 1874, Article 3). I discuss these instructions later in this chapter.

6. This assumption relies mainly on ethnographies of contemporary *shariʿa* courts (Shahar 2000a, 2000b, 56–57, 2005).

7. However, these characteristics have challenged social historians to read between the lines of these legal texts and tell some fascinating stories that contribute to a much better understanding of past realities. Among these reconstructions, I find Leslie Peirce's "Le dilemme de Fatma" (1998a) to be exceptionally thrilling. See also her recent monograph (2003), which includes Fatma's story as its last chapter.

8. The records of the four court sessions appear in figure 2 on the same page, but in the volume of protocols they were recorded on different pages in chronological order. See also the case of Sheikh Husayn in chapter 3.

its legal content. The participants in the session signed the record under titles that stated their legal capacities (plaintiff, defendant, witness, and so on). Sometimes the text of the record was slightly changed, certain words or lines were erased, or missing details were added in a footnote. At the end of the text of each session record, the page number of the record of the next session was reported, and that next record began with a reference to the previous session's record. The judge (or the scribe on his behalf) often added a comment regarding the legal agenda of the following session.

The focus of the protocol recording procedure was entirely different from that of the registration. Its climax was not the final decision in the case, but rather the exact details of the deliberations, molded into legal vocabulary and signed by the participants. The details of the legal deliberations recorded in protocols obviously render these documents a historical gold mine when compared to some of the registration-type documents, and their textual and orthographical features add further "thickness" to their "description" (Geertz 1973).

The Protocol: From a Draft to an Authorized Record

The first official volume of Jaffa court protocols that survived is dated 1293–94 A.H. (1876–77 C.E.) and is entitled *Hujaj* (deeds, records) like most of the earlier volumes of registrations in that court. On the first page of this volume, however, the scribe explicitly states that "this register contains protocols of lawsuits" (" 'utukhidhat hadhihi al-jarida li-dabt al-da'awi," JCR, *Hujaj* 47, 8 M 1293–3 S 1294/1876–77), not registrations. The earliest surviving volumes from the Haifa court date to as late as 1870, and several volumes covering a full decade (1291–1301/1874–84) are missing.[9] Thus, the first volume of protocols *(Jaridat al-dabt),* preserved as part of the Haifa court record, is dated 1308 (1890). The earliest volumes of protocols found in the courts of Damascus and Aleppo date to the late 1880s, and those from Istanbul to somewhat earlier.[10] However, in an article dealing with earlier changes in the

9. Scholars who have worked at the Nablus *shari'a* court claim that these volumes are kept there. I have also heard rumors about earlier volumes from Haifa in private possession. So far I have not been able to verify these rumors.

10. HCR, *Jaridat al-dabt* 1308/1890; Marino and Okawara 1999, 54–55. As I mentioned in chapter 2, a small number of scholarly works drawing on late-nineteenth-century court records have appeared so far. I am not aware of the existence of protocols preserved in other court records, but I hope that future research projects will uncover further volumes.

recording procedures at the court of Jaffa (Agmon 2004a), I show that at least a decade before the first official volume of protocols was recorded, the scribes there had already recorded initial proceedings of court cases (depositions) using new methods. In fact, the instruction to prepare depositions had been issued as early as 1840, but deposition records in the Jaffa courts may be found only since the mid-1860s. These depositions gradually developed into full protocol records.

Two sets of instructions issued in Istanbul in 1874 and 1879 specify the routine of recording protocols and preparing court records.[11] Therefore, the new recording procedure should be seen as part of the innovations introduced to the *shari'a* courts from the 1850s onward, when, as described in chapter 3, the Ottomans embarked on reforming the *shari'a* court system. Moreover, it should be seen in relation to the Ottoman reformers' efforts to rationalize (according to the reformers' ideology) the judicial system by developing a multicourt system, each court specializing in a certain legal field. The *shari'a* court formed part of this system and its reform—rather than being, as sometimes presented in the literature on legal reform, an untouched residue of premodernity that coexisted with the *nizamiye* courts in a dualistic judicial system. For instance, the second set of instructions to prepare detailed accounts of legal proceedings was issued to the *shari'a* courts in April 1879. A couple of months later a new law of procedure inspired by French law was promulgated for the *nizamiye* courts. The recording procedures in this code were rather similar to those included in the regulations issued to the *shari'a* courts.[12]

The logic behind these regulations is clear: similar to reforms in other institutions and to those regulating the work of *shari'a* judges, the regulations for the innovative recording procedures aimed at centralizing the *shari'a* court system and bringing its personnel under tighter state control. The introduction of the protocol—accompanied by detailed instructions for authorizing the records by affixing stamps and seals, numbering pages and cases, and maintaining the court records in a way that would allow their supervision by the central authorities—was a step in the same direction. The protocol was meant to enable the authorities to keep track of judges and scribes and to check the

11. *Düstur* 1, 4: "Sicillat-ı şer'iye ve zabt-ı dâva-ı cerideleri hakkında talimat," 15 Z 1290/3 II, 1874, 83–85; "Bilâ beiyyne mazmunuyle amel ve hükm caiz olabilecek surette senedat-ı şer'iyenin tanzimine dair talimat-ı seniye," 4 Ca 1296/26 IV 1879, 78–82. See also note 17.

12. See discussion and references in Agmon 2004a, especially notes 27–29.

legal procedures undertaken by the courts in deliberating specific cases that were the focus of complaints about misconduct or appeals submitted to higher legal instances.[13]

At the same time, owing to the new procedures, the production of the records became more professional and time consuming and hence was considered more important, giving the scribes a relatively stronger position in court. Their improved position also involved greater responsibility and unavoidable sanctions in cases of misconduct.[14] Furthermore, in the late nineteenth century the populations in Jaffa and Haifa grew so quickly that probably even the scribes could not be personally acquainted with all those who attended the court and their interrelationships, let alone an outside judge. As the case of Sheikh Husayn (chapter 3) demonstrated, the judges were increasingly dependent on the scribes for both local knowledge and for producing records that showed that the legal proceedings were handled as required.[15]

Clearly, the protocol type of record would have been most helpful in up-

13. Complaints and petitions about the misconduct of officers of the state constituted an important aspect of Ottoman political culture (Jennings 1979, 152–54, 182–84; Zarinebaf-Shahr 1996, 85–89). Legal reform reinforced this aspect by structuring the *nizamiye* court system as a hierarchy of legal instances and court of appeal. The *nizamiye* courts are currently the focus of a timely investigation by Avi Rubin at Harvard University, which I hope will provide us with a much better understanding of judicial reform and the interrelations between the different court systems. Various instructions to the *shari'a* courts included articles on procedures for complaining about the misconduct of judges and other court officials and for transferring records to the Ministry of Şeyhülislâm in order to check them. See, for example, *Düstur* 1, 2: "Hükâm-ı ser'iye nizamnamesi," 13 M 1290/13 III 1873, 725, Article 16; *Düstur* 1, 3: "Molla tayin-i hakkında nizamnamedir," 14 Ca 1291/29 VI 1874, 156–57, Articles 5–7.

14. *Düstur* 1, 4: "Sicillat-ı şer'iye . . . ," 1874, 83–84, Articles 7, 9, 10. Doumani presents a similar argument regarding the position of the chief scribe vis-à-vis the judge at the court of Jerusalem during the sixteenth to eighteenth centuries (1985, 158). He interprets the changes that took place in the nineteenth-century *shari'a* courts, whereby the responsibility for appointing judges for Nablus was transferred to the center, as an indication of the growing importance of Nablus in comparison to Jerusalem (1985, 164). This conclusion ignores the fact that the same policy was implemented in the rest of the districts as well and reflected the efforts at centralizing the legal system. However, his conclusion should be seen in the context of the mid-1980s research on reforms in the provinces: Doumani studied the Palestinian court records for his 1985 article at a time when many of the prominent provincial histories (including Doumani's own in 1995) had not yet been published. For discussion of the notions behind some of the legal reforms, see Messick 1993, 54–66, and Deringil 1998, 44–46, 50–52.

15. See also Messick 1993, 178.

dating the judge, although there is no indication to suggest that this possible advantage motivated the introduction of the new practice. In this respect, it should be noted that the protocol very much resembled the *mahdar,* one of the major types of register that the *shariʿa* judge was instructed to maintain in his record *(diwan al-qadi)* according to various pre-Ottoman Islamic manuals. The main purpose of the *diwan,* as described by Wael Hallaq, was to ensure the continuity of justice. In the pre-Ottoman court, literally the personification of the judge, who could maintain his post for many years, the *mahdar* was not intended for keeping new judges up to date. Its purpose was presumably rather similar to that of the Ottoman deposition before it was reformed from the 1870s. It provided the scribe with accounts of former cases that would serve as a basis for the preparation of summaries, to be compiled in the *diwan* in the event of the appointment of a new judge (Hallaq 1998, 418–22).

In contrast, the protocol record was yet another step toward the further institutionalization of the court within the local setting (in addition to being part and parcel of the broader endeavor of creating a multicourt system). The problem of continuity at this court was, in a way, opposite to the one described by Hallaq regarding earlier Islamic courts. Whereas in the latter the continuity represented by *diwan al-qadi* was useful to a judge who held his position for very long and had to run the local judiciary system almost single-handedly, in late Ottoman *shariʿa* courts the problem facing judges was a lack of information owing to short periods of service in a complicated court system and a fast-growing community. True, at face value, the pre- and late Ottoman court records were rather similar. Nevertheless, the protocol type, primarily an authorized court document registered for preservation and state inspection, was apparently not a continuation of the old *mahdar.*

Hallaq has argued that the *shariʿa* court records are not a unique Ottoman phenomenon, but rather a more recent link in a much longer chain of Muslim court records. He considers as only circumstantial the fact that they were preserved, even though earlier *shariʿa* court records were not. However, after considering the concepts behind both the Ottoman protocol and *diwan al-qadi,* I believe that the logic of the protocol fitted the prevailing recording procedures at the Ottoman *shariʿa* courts and differed essentially from the logic of the pre-Ottoman court records. In other words, although it is true that the Ottoman court records were a continuation of a prolonged Muslim court tradition, the very fact that they have been preserved also points to a unique Ottoman contribution to this tradition—namely, the bureaucratic culture of keeping records, which transcended the purpose of continuity. Pre-Ottoman court records were probably not prepared for centuries-long survival, but merely to aid newly appointed judges during the initial period of their appointment and to support the work of the current judge until he was replaced. When such replacement occurred, the old documents, used for preparing a copy of the *diwan* for the new *qadi,* were not required anymore, so they were not preserved. The documents in the Ottoman *shariʿa* court, in contrast, served some requirements of the state, local community, and daily work of the courts long before legal reform. Their preservation was both a prerequisite for the fulfillment of these tasks and an indication of the Ottomanization of the *shariʿa* courts.[16]

Although it is true that the protocol, as an official record, was part of a broader concept of state control adopted from European legal systems, the way it was implemented and even the name of its recording practice, *zabt* (Arabic: *dabt*), stemmed from both *shariʿa* court practice and the Ottoman bureaucratic culture. The English lexicon of the Ottoman language published in that period gives six meanings for this noun, the last two being "taking down in writing" and "fixing the orthography and vocalization of a word by a verbal description" (Redhouse 1890, 1206). As I show later, the instructions regarding the recitation of the protocol and their implementation in the Jaffa and Haifa courts were in keeping with the literal meaning of this term. Moreover, if we look at the period from the 1840s to the 1870s, when an early version of the procedure was officially introduced, a gradual development can be discerned. The scribes' practice of taking notes for the sake of both assisting the judge in the process of decision making and recording the official verdict evolved into a formalization of these notes into authorized documents that were preserved for the sake of the government's new agenda.[17]

16. Hallaq's main concern is to show that the recording of legal proceedings was already an institutionalized tradition in the pre-Ottoman *shariʿa* courts and not an Ottoman innovation. He substantiates this claim rather convincingly (1998, 417, 434–35). However, I detect some confusion over the issue of the preservation of the records, seen as a mere coincidence, not as an indication of different kinds of documentation culture. My argument is that, under the circumstances that Hallaq describes, long-range preservation of the record was unnecessary for the institutionalization process typical of that period, whereas it was a typical feature of the institutionalization of the Ottoman court record. See also Hanna 1995, 49; Findley 1980, 8–12, 51–57, 86–87.

17. The first step in this direction was taken when instructions issued as early as 1840 used the term *zabt* to refer to note taking by the scribes while listening to the litigants' claims (depo-

A Domestic Dispute

A domestic dispute deliberated and recorded in the Haifa *shariʿa* court illustrates some of the points discussed so far and raises several other issues. The record of this case includes four legal accounts: two registrations of powers of attorney given separately by the disputing husband and wife to their legal representatives (fig. 1, cases 497 and 595), the protocol of the trial (fig. 2), and, finally, the registration of the verdict (fig. 1, case 630). The entire proceedings took about four months, from October 1913, when Amina bint ʿUthman al-Sabʿ Aʿyun from Saida gave power of attorney to Ibrahim Edhem Efendi Şalcı to represent her in court and to sue her husband, Salim ibn Nimr Qaraman al-Nabulsi, until February 1914, when Judge Abdülhalim Efendi decided Amina's lawsuit against her husband, Salim, in support of her marital rights, apparently on the basis of a compromise reached between the parties out of court.[18]

---

sitions) at the beginning of a legal proceeding. These instructions were probably based on the scribes' existing practices in the *shariʿa* courts. See my analysis of the development of the depositions into full protocols in the Jaffa court before and after the circulation of the 1870s regulations (Agmon 2004a).

18. HCR, *Sijill* L 1331–Ca 1332/IX 1913–IV 1914, 35, 79, 99, cases 497, 595, 630; *Jaridat al-Dabt* 5, L 1331–R 1332/IX 1913–III 1914, 110–11, 120, 124, 131, case 83 (see figs. 1 and 2). All four accounts of this case were recorded in two corresponding volumes of protocols and registrations in the Haifa court record. Both volumes cover about six months, September 1913 to March 1914. The volume of protocols (*Jaridat al-Dabt* 5) includes mainly protocols of lawsuits (sing. *dabt al-daʿawi*). The summaries of about one-third of these protocols (twenty-one out of sixty-one) are recorded in the corresponding volume of registrations. The latter includes registrations of many other court cases, the protocols of which are recorded in volumes that did not survive. The recording of the same cases as both protocols and registrations in separate (various) volumes is indicated by the reference given at the end of every registration to the exact volume where its protocol may be found (fig. 1). At the same time, the other forty protocols of lawsuits in the volume we do have and that are not summarized in this volume of registrations were apparently summarized in volumes that did not survive. According to the references in the volume of registrations, at least five volumes of protocols were recorded at the court simultaneously, covering the legal procedures that took place during the same six or seven months. At least one of them includes only powers of attorney (in addition to the surviving volume "specializing" in lawsuits). Thus, the scribes apparently maintained several protocol volumes, each one containing records of a specific legal procedure according to instructions from Istanbul (*Düstur* 1, 4: "Sicillat şerʿiye . . ." 1874, 78, Article 2).

The registration of the power
of attorney given by Amina to
Ibrahim Efendi Edhem Şalcı

The registration of the power
of attorney given by Salim to
Sheikh ʿAbd al-Hafiz Efendi

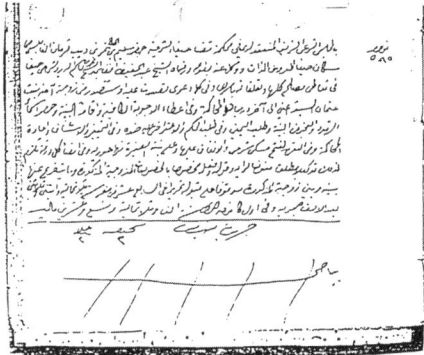

The registration of the verdict in the case of Amina vs. Salim

Figure 1. Samples of registrations. HCR, *Sijill* 1913–14, 35, case 497; 79, case 595; 99, case 630.

The records of this case, like many of these court records, tell a multilayered story, many aspects of which had bearing on the construction of the family under the changing realities of late Ottoman Haifa, which I discuss in chapter 7. Here I focus mainly on two aspects of this domestic dispute: what the two different types of record (registration and protocol) tell us about the event and the production of its records; and how the people who participated in the legal proceedings experienced the court routine as inscribed in these records.

Protocols of the 4 sessions of the lawsuit of Amina vs. Salim

(from right to left)

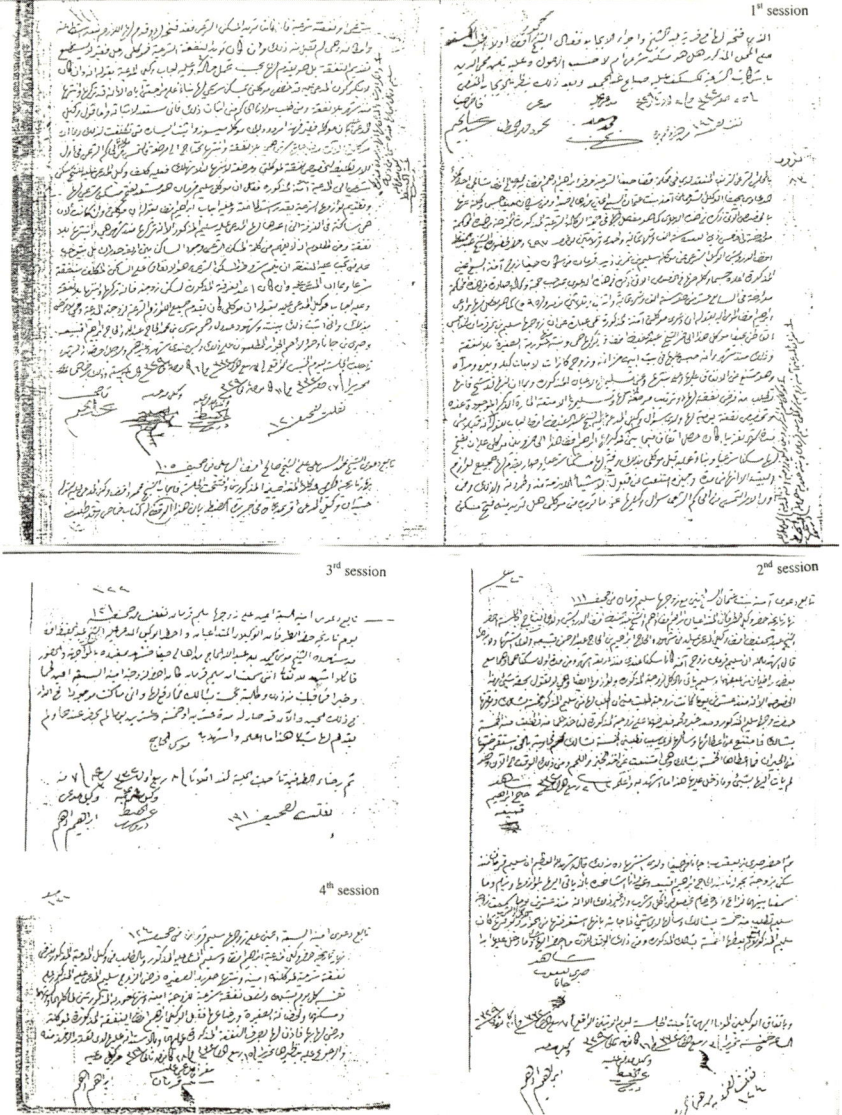

Figure 2. Samples of protocols. HCR, *Jaridat al-Dabt* 5, 110–11, 120, 124, 131, case 83.

The Court and the Case

The judge, Abdülhalim Efendi, was an experienced judge in his late forties who at the time of the trial had already served for about twenty years in subdistrict courts. He was of Bulgarian origin, from the district of Sultanyeri, a graduate of the College for Shariʿa Judges in Istanbul. He was about to complete his two-year term in Haifa in 1913 when the new instruction for longer terms was issued. He stayed on in Haifa, and when he deliberated Amina's lawsuit against Salim, he had already been there for a third year. He spent the years of the First World War there and returned to Istanbul only after the entire region had been conquered by the Entente armies, thus becoming the last Ottoman *shariʿa* judge in Haifa. Most of his career as a *shariʿa* judge was spent in Turkish-speaking regions, but according to his dossier he knew Arabic. His signature can be easily recognized on the left side at the end of each and every court session protocol, under the title "Qadi Haifa" (as noted in chapter 3, in 1913 the title *naib* was again replaced by *qadi*).[19]

The chief scribe, Muhyi al-Din al-Mallah, recorded one protocol session (fig. 2, session 3). As I mentioned in the previous chapter, he had come to Haifa from Tripoli with his uncle, Sheikh Khayr al-Din, about eight years earlier, when the latter was appointed as judge in Haifa. Muhyi al-Din continued his service in court under the judgeship of his uncle's successors and served as their deputy in legal proceedings that took place out of court. In addition, he became manager of the local orphan fund.

The scribe registering most of the protocol sessions of this case, summarizing its verdict, and noting the two powers of attorney given by the litigants (fig. 1; fig. 2, sessions 1, 2, 4) was yet another immigrant, Muhammad Hasan al-Badran, originally from Nablus. In Haifa, Badran, an al-Azhar graduate, also taught another immigrant from Nablus, young ʿAbd al-Raʾuf Karaman, who later on became his son-in-law.[20]

Thus, this Haifa court scene reflected the constant immigration to Haifa more than the Jaffa court reflected the immigration to Jaffa, in spite of the fact

19. SA def. 3, 193; Albayrak 1996, 1: 121–22; *İlmiye Salnamesi,* 224; *Düstur* 2, 5: "Hükkâm-ı şerʿi ve memurin-i şerʿiye . . ." 1913, 352–61. See Abdülhalim's signatures in figure 2. In comparison to those of Jaffa, the protocol records in Haifa are structured more systematically according to court sessions, and the judge's signature appears at the bottom of many of these session records. The differences between the protocols of the two courts are discussed in detail later in this chapter.

20. Privately communicated by members of the Karaman family, Ibtin, 9 April and 26 December 2000. The Karaman family became one of the most successful families in Haifa during the Mandate period. It is not clear to me if and how the defendant in this case, Salim Qaraman, was related to this family.

that Jaffa attracted immigrants in even larger numbers than Haifa. As noted, the two courts developed somewhat differently as part of the administrative history of their respective subdistricts, and it is possible that this different development was also reflected in the composition of their personnel, with newcomers being appointed more easily as scribes at the Haifa court and becoming more prominent on its staff. Moreover, as the court of Haifa included a smaller number of scribes, two or three compared to five or six in Jaffa, the court culture in Haifa might have also been less "local" in nature compared to that of Jaffa. Hence, the instructions that came from Istanbul were implemented more strictly and systematically in Haifa, serving the scribes there as the main source for shaping innovative methods and routines, whereas in Jaffa the scribes leaned more on their local legal culture (Agmon 2004a), as I show later regarding the adoption of the protocol.[21]

The Case. In the power of attorney given by the plaintiff, Amina, to her attorney, the latter was specifically assigned to represent her in court regarding her marital relations with her husband, Salim. It took three months before Salim also commissioned an attorney to respond to his wife's claim (fig. 1, cases 497 and 595). The trial began ten days later, on 27 Safar 1332 (25 January 1913), and was concluded after about three weeks and four court sessions, on 15 Rabi' al-Awwal (11 February 1913). The attorneys represented the husband and wife in court during all four sessions of this trial. Amina and Salim did not appear in court until the last session. Salim attended this session and

21. Furthermore, several times during the first decade of the twentieth century there was a gap of a few months between the end of one judge's term in Haifa and the beginning of his successor's term. In these situations, the current *başkatib,* or a judge from Haifa awaiting at home for an appointment elsewhere, filled the gap as a deputy judge (HCR, *Sijill* 5, 19 § 1322/29 X 1904, 385; *Sijill* 6, 10 M 1323/17 III 1905, 1; *Sijill* 7, 10 C 1325/21 VII 1907, 74; *Sijill* 7, B 1325/17 VIII 1907, 78; *Sijill* 8, 16 N 1327/1 X 1909, 115; *Sijill* 8, 17 Z 1327/10 XII 1909, 151). Apparently, a similar solution was also adopted in Jaffa when Judge Abu al-Nasr was replaced by his son, 'Abd al-Qadir Hikmat, in the summer of 1902 (see chapter 3). See also Yazbak 1998, 137–38. Yazbak does not make a distinction in his analysis between judges who served regular terms (about two years each) and substitutes, such as Muhyi al-Din al-Mallah, who were appointed temporarily for a couple of months. Thus, his description of the court as dominated by the al-Mallah family is somewhat exaggerated, ignoring the judges who served regular terms in Haifa, such as 'Abd al-Mu'ta Efendi from Jerusalem, who served between August 1907 and October 1909 (SA dos. 797; SA def. 1, 268); 'Abdalla Haqqi Efendi from Aleppo, who served between December 1909 and October 1911 (SA dos. 819; SA def. 5, 216), and, finally, Judge Abdülhalim, who served for eight years, from October 1911 to June 1919 (SA def. 3, 193).

signed the verdict, which looks like a compromise reached out of court and then legally confirmed.

According to the protocol (fig. 2), Amina's attorney claimed that Salim had left her and their minor daughter, Huriyya, without support for about a month and demanded that he be forced to pay daily maintenance *(nafaqa)* for Amina and to hire a wet nurse for Huriyya. Amina's attorney also claimed that Salim had locked up her furniture in his father's house and refused to return it. In response to a demand by Amina's attorney, Salim's attorney stated that his client had arranged a conjugal dwelling *(maskan shar'i)* for both Amina and Huriyya and had provided them with their necessities, but that Amina had refused to accept these provisions and had expelled Salim. He was willing to support the two of them, but could not afford to pay maintenance. After a dispute between the two attorneys about the meaning of the term *maskan shar'i*, in which Amina's attorney stressed that it did not mean that "its resident dwells within only a four-walled room," the burden of proof was left with Salim's attorney.

The latter brought three witnesses: the man who had rented the room to the couple in his house and two of their neighbors. All three testified that Amina and Salim had lived peacefully together in that room for four months; then some twenty-five days before the trial Amina had borrowed the sum of 5 beşlik (then about 17 kuruş) from her neighbors. When Salim had come home and brought her bread and meat, she had asked him to return her loan. He had asked her why she had taken the money, and she had said that it was for buying food. He refused to pay, and she had reacted by refusing to take the food from him. Since that day, he had not returned, nor had he slept with her. For the last session, Salim came to court with Amina's attorney and agreed to pay daily maintenance and child support of 1.5 beşlik (about 5 kuruş, a medium sum of daily support compared to other cases) and Amina's attorney agreed. Both of them signed the protocol.

In the summary of this case recorded in the volume of registrations (fig. 1, case 630), the account of the last session was more or less repeated with the additional condition that Salim was obliged to pay maintenance and child support to his wife and daughter until he arranged a conjugal dwelling for them. Meanwhile, Amina was permitted to borrow money up to the total sum of her maintenance.[22]

22. The legal terms mentioned in this case record are rather common in the vocabulary of *shari'a* family law. Because the focus of this discussion is not the legal content of this terminol-

A Note on Money and Daily Conditions

Amina and Salim's socioeconomic position as inscribed in the court record requires some elaboration before we turn to the way their case record was produced. The following brief discussion on coinage, rates of exchange, costs of living, and incomes serves both for the reconstruction of Amina and Salim's situation and as an initial description of the conditions prevailing in the port cities.

When a bimetal monetary system was adopted in the Ottoman Empire in the 1840s, the golden Ottoman lira comprised of 100 silver kuruş. The government did not eliminate the old beşlik and altılık coins (literally, 5 and 6 kuruş respectively) that had been minted in the late 1820s, and they remained in circulation until the First World War. Their value, however, decreased in the course of the century, reflecting the changes in the rates of gold and silver and local fluctuations in the rates of exchange of Ottoman and foreign currency (Pamuk 2000, 206–11, 218–22).[23]

In the Jaffa and Haifa court records, most of the prices of daily payments—such as maintenance, alimony, child support, and some of the real-estate prices—are mentioned in either kuruş or beşlik. The actual rate of the latter in this period was about 3.5 kuruş. In addition, larger sums of money, such as dowers or real-estate prices, are given in lira fransawi (LF), equal to 1 French golden Napoleon (20 francs), the local value of which was about 109 kuruş (in other words, 5.5 kuruş were equal to 1 franc). The Ottoman lira was sometime also used in determining dowers and real-estate values. It was equal in that period to 124 kuruş (which was also the approximate rate of exchange for the English pound). The sums of money mentioned in the

---

ogy, I mention the meaning of these terms only briefly, but I do use them in later chapters. According to *shari'a* family law, the husband's duty is to provide his wife and minor children with their basic necessities—food, clothing, and housing. *Nafaqa* is the sum of money paid by the husband to his wife for buying these necessities, either as part of an agreement between them or following a court decision in the matter. *Maskan shar'i* is the dwelling that the husband is required to arrange for his wife and children. It should meet certain conditions set by *shari'a* law. See a broader discussion of the legal notion of the family in chapter 5.

23. The following description is based on Agmon 1995, 179–88, where I present economic data drawing on Jaffa and Haifa court records, British and French consular reports on the two cities, and newspapers. See also Yazbak 1998, 199–201, on the rise in the prices of basic products.

court records as maintenance, alimony, and child support cannot testify to the exact economic position of the people involved, but they provide a general picture: the judge's decision in these matters was based on testimonies about the husband's or father's (or other male relative's) financial ability. When the various sums decided in court over the years are examined, a structure comprised of three levels emerges. High sums of daily support were about 2 beşlik a day per capita, medium sums were around 1 beşlik, and low sums around 1 to 1.5 kuruş. It seems, therefore, that the judge would make his decision in these general terms, defining which of the three levels fitted the testimony relating to the financial position of the person in question. A somewhat more accurate picture of the situation of husbands paying and of wives or ex-wives receiving these sums of money depends on other indications of their economic situation—such as their dowers, descriptions and evaluation of their household items, or properties they possessed. I use this sort of evidence to establish the position of the protagonists in the legal cases unfolded in this and the following chapters.

For the purpose of the current discussion, it suffices to note the medium-level sum of money Amina received (1.5 beşlik). In this case, however, the sum did not represent a court decision based on a testimony about Salim's economic position. Rather, it represented both husband's and wife's bargaining positions, which most probably involved other aspects in addition to the financial and later received court approval. In order to get an idea of what Amina could buy for the money she received from Salim (150–60 kuruş per month), we need some relevant prices. The rent for her room would be around 30 kuruş per month. Food basics: one kilo of bread, a little more than 1 kuruş; one liter of milk, 1.5 kuruş; four eggs, about 0.5 kuruş; one kilo of oil, about 0.75 kuruş; one kilo of meat, about 6 kuruş; one chicken, about 5.5 kuruş. On the basis of these prices, she could spend about 80 kuruş a month on food for herself, and she would still have between 40 and 50 kuruş left for clothes and a wet nurse for her baby daughter. Moreover, it should be noted that both Amina and Salim hired attorneys. This choice testifies to both financial ability and a somewhat higher social status, or aspirations to that status (as discussed in more detail in chapter 6).

Integrating the Protocol, Constructing the Family

Through a synthesis of the material presented so far with a discussion of the Ottoman authorities' instructions to the courts, I now turn to examine how

Amina's lawsuit against Salim developed and how it was recorded at a time when recording protocols already formed part of the routine at the courts of Jaffa and Haifa.

The Protocol and Registration in Practice

Prior to appearing before the judge, litigants had to apply to the court, register, and pay court fees according to the nature of their case. Amina and Salim came separately to the court in Haifa, each with an attorney *(wakil da'awi)* and authorized the attorneys in court to represent them. Amina initiated the lawsuit. She hired an attorney while—according to the husband's witnesses—the couple were still living together peacefully in their rented room. Obviously, that was not the case: she had authorized Ibrahim Edhem Efendi Şalcı, an attorney of Turkish origin who appeared frequently in court on behalf of litigants, to represent her regarding her marital relations. Salim apparently had authorized an attorney only after the court notified him about Amina's lawsuit against him. The trial protocol also indicates that some time after Amina hired an attorney and before she initiated her lawsuit, her attorney raised the issue of Amina's residence with Salim.

The information provided in the protocol and recorded during the deliberations, when compared with its registration recorded after the case was decided, illustrates the substantial gap between these two types of record in terms of the details they provide and their different goals. A study of the registration of the court decision alone (fig. 1, case 630) does not give any indication of the rather complicated legal exchange in court (fig. 2), let alone the even more intricate domestic dispute that brought about this case. In fact, reading the registration alone does not indicate whether a dispute or a lawsuit preceded the verdict.

From the protocol, it appears, however, that the couple eventually settled the matter out of court. The judge then legalized this settlement at the fourth court session. Several indications in the protocol point in this direction. For instance, after the witnesses were heard, there is no record of the procedure of verification of their credibility *(tazkiya)* as usually was the case; the end result was not based on the content of their testimony, nor was it mentioned in the record explicitly as a decision made by the judge, as in other cases. In fact, there is no continuity between the third and the fourth sessions. However, whereas in the protocol of this case the records of all the sessions were kept, in the registration of the case, even after a compromise had been reached, only the compromise approved by the judge was deemed important owing to the nature of this type of record.[24]

Although the description given in the protocol is extensive in comparison to the registration, we cannot assume that it provides more than one layer of this multifaceted family affair; more precisely, we are shown only the legal framework within which the case was deliberated in court, and even these deliberations were not recorded in their entirety (Ze'evi 1998). What was behind this dispute between Amina and Salim? Was it really about the limits of her independence in running their tiny household, as the testimonies indicate? Was Amina's attorney's complaint about her residence connected to its location in a house of nonrelatives, the nature of the neighbors, or the fact that it was small and crowded? Was the difference in origin and perhaps also in social background between Amina and Salim the true reason behind their dispute? Or was it about an entirely different issue not exposed at all by the record and molded by the attorneys into a matter involving one of the most widespread conventions of *shariʿa* family law: conjugal dwelling? At this point, I leave these questions open. After considering more aspects of the court and the family in the following chapters, I turn to consider some of the plausible scenarios in this affair and connect them to family structures in highly populated and growing towns such as Haifa and Jaffa.

What this protocol illustrates in terms of the current discussion is the interaction that took place in court between the litigants who brought their family business to court and the legal discourse on the family. Amina and Salim were not actually part of this interaction because they authorized legal representatives to take care of their affairs in court, joining a growing group of people in these communities who detached themselves from the court during that period—a phenomenon whose relevance to the current discussion I explain later. Nevertheless, many other people still came to court and participated in the legal process that remolded their family relations in legal terms.

The recording of protocols was indeed an innovation, and the access his-

---

24. See also Agmon 1995, 42–43, where I point to several cases of alimony in which the registrations indicate no previous dispute or lawsuit and suggest that this does not mean that such a dispute did not precede the verdict. At that point, I was not yet aware of the official difference between the registration and the protocol.

torians have consequently gained to a detailed account of court cases has been new as well. However, for the people who came to court and were involved in the interaction, it was, to a large extent, not a new experience; in principle, it was typical of hundreds of years of *shari'a* court work. Historians who have explored court records of varied periods and places have been impressed by the extent to which people who came to court seemed to possess enough knowledge of its concepts and procedures and thereby were able to make rather efficient use of the system for their own benefit.[25] At the same time, this long-standing acquaintance of lay people with legal concepts is in part what leads me to my major point: that the new type of record contributed to the intensification of the interaction between lay people and the legal notion of the family.

Recording the Depositions

After the litigants had been legally identified in court and had presented their claims or requests, the scribe prepared a protocol of this preliminary session. When it was the litigants' turn to enter, they approached the judge together with the scribe. The latter recited the depositions (in a lawsuit like the one analyzed here, the deposition included the plaintiff's claim and the defendant's response), amended them if necessary, and the litigants and the judge signed this record. The court scribes kept several volumes of protocols and registrations and recorded the protocol of the session in the relevant volume.

Article 6 of the second set of instructions issued in Istanbul in April 1879 included specific orders as to how to record protocols. Apparently, most of the official volumes of protocols known to historians were registered in *shari'a* courts after these instructions were issued.[26]

25. See, for example, Marcus 1989, 112–13; Agmon 1998, 488–90; Meriwether 1999, 210; Peirce 2003, 372–73. Ze'evi raises the idea that women might have received some sort of education that qualified them to function efficiently in the economic and legal realms of their lives (1995, 167–68). See also Zarinebaf-Shahr 1996, 85–89, about women as petitioners.

26. One exception is the first volume of protocols from Jaffa, which was registered after the issuing of the first set of instructions in 1874. As I mentioned earlier, the court record of Jaffa also includes early versions of protocols (depositions) from about a decade before the first set of instructions was issued (Agmon 2004a). The second set was much more detailed than the first (which, apart from its title, mentioned the recording of *zabt* in only one of its articles, number 16). See notes 5 and 11 in this chapter.

After the protocol of the case [*dâva-ı zabt*] has been recorded, the recording clerk enters with the two parties before the official adjunct [*müsteşar*], in courts that have adjuncts, or before the judge [*hakim*] or *naib*, in courts that do not have adjuncts, and reads the protocol [*zabt*] to him. After the reading, the adjunct (or judge, or *naib*) asks the parties, separately, whether their statements conform to the text of the protocol. If each one of the parties so does, [the protocol is] immediately recorded in the protocol register. If, [however], they do not [so] affirm (either because a mistake or omission had occurred, or because a required question and answer [regarding] some issues had not been recorded by the court), it becomes necessary to correct the protocol. Having been amended, the text of the protocol is to be recorded in the court's protocol register. Once the parties have signed at the bottom [of that protocol] and the seal [is affixed to it], no erasing or rubbing out is [allowed] to occur. (*Düstur* 1, 4: "Bilâ beyyine . . . ," 1879, 79, Article 6)

Articles 4 to 11 suggest that these specific instructions referred only to protocols of litigants' initial claims (depositions) in a lawsuit. Apparently, the record of the first session of Amina's lawsuit against her husband (fig. 2, session 1) includes an account of this sort of preliminary session, which both attorneys, Ibrahim Edhem Efendi Şalcı and Sheikh 'Abd al-Hafiz Efendi al-Darwish, attended.[27] The scribe Muhammad Hasan al-Badran conducted this session, prepared the protocol, and then read it out to the attorneys in the presence of Judge Abdülhalim Efendi. During the recitation, an amendment was requested and made in a footnote, signed by Sheikh Darwish, Salim's attorney. This footnote shows that the instructions to recite the record were implemented and illustrates the role of the recitation.

In this footnote, Salim's attorney acknowledged that his client was indeed Amina's husband and Huriyya's father. Legally, this sort of acknowledgment should have been included in a husband's response to any claim by his wife relating to their marital relations and offspring. The record of the entire session was seemingly written without interruption. Verbal expressions were omitted, and legal formulas were used instead. Either the judge dictated the claims to the scribe, or the latter skillfully recorded them this way. The text of the footnote,

27. Sheik al-Darwish was the son of a rural notable from the neighboring village of Ijzim. He moved to Haifa, acquired religious education in town, and became an attorney at the local *shariʿa* court (Yazbak 1998, 155–56).

however, is phrased as the direct speech of Salim's attorney in response to an unrecorded question. He said: "Yes, the plaintiff Amina is my client, Salim's wife, and his daughter Huriyya is hers." Apparently, when Judge Abdülhalim noticed that these basic legal details were missing from the record, he stopped Hasan al-Badran's recitation and asked Salim's attorney whether he acknowledged his client's marriage to Amina and his fatherhood of Huriyya. When the attorney responded, Badran wrote his exact words in the footnote without rephrasing them because this exchange took place in the course of the overall recitation of the protocol.[28]

In the same volume of protocols, one case record was registered in Ottoman (HCR, *Jaridat al-Dabt* 5, 9 Za 1331/9 X 1913, 6–7, case 51). This protocol uncovers another domestic dispute and illustrates my point regarding the recitation. Both the husband and wife, as well as the witnesses and the ad hoc attorney,[29] the same Ibrahim Edhem Efendi who represented Amina, were from the Turkish-speaking community in Haifa. The husband was a clerk at the Hijaz railway station; his brother-in-law, who testified as his sister's witness, worked at the customs office, as did her other witness, her brother's colleague. They had come to Haifa from Edirne. At first, I was curious why this record was registered in Ottoman. Of course, both Abdülhalim Efendi, the Bulgarian judge who had acquired his legal education in Istanbul and served most of his judicial career in Turkish-speaking towns before being appointed to Haifa, and Muhyi al-Din al-Mallah, the chief scribe from an ulama family in Tripoli who recorded this case, knew Turkish. Therefore, most probably the participants were allowed to present their claims in their mother tongue. These litigants and witnesses, or some of them, were probably not fluent in Arabic. But why did the judge not dictate the material, molded into legal formulas, in Arabic as in the other records? My understanding is that the record was prepared for recitation to the same Turkish-speaking audience.

The second point that the footnote in the protocol record of Amina and

28. See Peirce 1998b, where she discusses the circumstances under which the litigants and witnesses were recorded in verbatim summaries of divorce cases in sixteenth-century Anatolian *shari'a* court records. See also Peirce 2003, 352–56.

29. *Wakil musakhkhar:* a court-appointed representative of an absent party. See my discussion on the attorneys in chapter 6.

Salim's case illustrates is the way the recitation intensified the interaction between lay people and the legal discourse. Salim's acknowledgment of his marital relations with Amina and of his fatherhood of Huriyya was legally
essential. It is true that in this particular case, those directly involved, Amina
and Salim, were not even in the courtroom when the recitation took place.
However, litigants often did attend the deliberation of their cases. We may also
assume that people other than the litigants—such as relatives, witnesses, or
other litigants awaiting their cases—were among the audience. They heard the
legal exchanges, clarifying for them that those details they considered to be so
obvious were indeed important in court and therefore required explicit acknowledgment, and consequently in the process they may have reinterpreted
their understanding of their own family affairs.

Another such exchange was the debate between the two attorneys about
the standard of the conjugal dwelling that Salim was required to provide for
Amina. When Amina's attorney claimed that the meaning of conjugal dwelling *(maskan shar'i)* was not just four walls (fig. 2, session 1), he presented a
much broader interpretation of this otherwise rather technical term. His interpretation may be understood as stressing the husband's legal obligation to
provide his wife with all her necessities, not just a roof over her head. At the
same time, *maskan shar'i* can be understood in this context to mean that a marital residence should not become the wife's prison. Whatever the interpretation (and for the current discussion the term's importance lies less in how the
attorney defined it and more in what the audience understood it to mean), the
point is the courtroom audience's exposure to this type of legal exchange, intensified by the process of authorizing the protocol record.

Completing the Protocol

According to the instructions received from the center about the protocol,
the court scribes were to keep two sets of protocol registers. One would contain drafts of the original claims, where the scribes would make the required
amendments and obtain the parties' signatures, and which the judge would
then use during the trial. The other would include the official register of protocols to which the scribe would copy amended claims and testimonies and finally add the verdict. All would then be signed and sealed, authorized by the
judge, and kept in a safe place. The main difference between the actual recording procedure, as inscribed in the court records under observation, and the

Ottoman instructions is that both the Haifa and Jaffa courts kept only one set of records, which seems to have been a combination of drafts of protocols and their authorized versions. Furthermore, both courts registered protocols of various types of cases and not only of lawsuits, although the instructions explicitly related only to lawsuit protocols.

The differences between the Jaffa and Haifa court records are at this point more important than the similarities. Obvious differences between the volumes covering earlier and later years reflect the process of adjustment to the new regulations and the stylistic variations shown by the scribes. Generally speaking, after about three decades of protocols being recorded,[30] the protocol volumes of Jaffa looked more like final records, whereas those of Haifa looked more consistently like a combination between the drafts and the final records.

The instructions did not refer to court sessions. In fact, except for the Article 6 description of recording the first session, to be conducted by the scribe before the judge began to deliberate the case (*Düstur* 1, 4: "Bilâ beyyine . . . ," 1879, 78–79, Article 6), no explicit instructions were given as to how the rest of each case ought to be recorded. Rather, there were explanations of how the content of the continuation of each case should be added later to the authorized protocol. This lacuna in the instructions might have caused the difference in interpretation between the two courts. With this lacuna in mind, it is possible to follow the logic of the two different interpretations. Apparently, in both courts the scribes continued to record draft protocols for the entire proceeding, not just the claims presented in the preliminary session. It was impossible to record everything in the clean copy of the register after the case was over without taking notes during deliberations. Furthermore, taking notes was a familiar practice also used for preparing registrations.

However, the scribes in Jaffa generally continued with the former method of taking notes, and if they did keep drafts of the initial depositions according to the instructions, these drafts did not survive. Alternatively, as I show elsewhere (Agmon 2004a), because the scribes developed the recording method typical of the early-twentieth-century protocols from Jaffa over many years, they became skillful enough to record the protocols directly in the authorized

---

30. For Jaffa, there is enough evidence to suggest that the development of this practice began much earlier. In Haifa, earlier records did not survive (Agmon 2004a).

volume.[31] In this volume, the scribe allocated a certain space for each case in advance and registered session records there as the case was pursued (without always noting the beginning and end of each session). When the case was over, the scribe completed this protocol, amended it, and obtained the required signatures and seals. If the space allocated in advance was not sufficient, he continued somewhere else in the volume, as shown in the description of Sheikh Husayn's lawsuit (chapter 3); if the space was excessive, he crossed out the empty pages or left them to be filled by other protocols for which the allocated space did not suffice.[32]

In Haifa, at the same time, the scribes followed the new instructions about recording the initial claims and applied them to the rest of the court sessions. They did not allocate a certain space for each case in advance, but rather treated each court session as a separate unit. When a court session was over, the scribe wrote it up in the same volume of protocols where the earlier sessions of this case had been recorded, but not on the same page. He recorded them in chronological order (fig. 2). Then he noted the date and the hour of the next session of that trial—if a decision had not yet been reached—and prepared the titles for the signatures of the participants. Later on, perhaps at the beginning of the following session, he read out this protocol. If anyone commented about missing or redundant information in the record, the scribe would correct the text, crossing out words or adding a footnote. The party that requested the amendment would sign the footnote (see fig. 2, session 1). Then all the participants, including the judge, signed with their names or seals or fingerprints under their respective titles. In Amina and Salim's case, two of the witnesses signed their testimonies by fingerprints (fig. 2, session 2), as did Salim himself when the compromise reached by the parties received the

31. When the scribes in Jaffa developed this method through trial and error, they used the first and last pages in a volume of depositions (the early version of protocols) for drafts. It is possible that this practice continued, but that these pages were eliminated after the volume was completed.

32. As a result, these records, when compared with those of Haifa, contain a smaller number of amendments, which were officially allowed in the clean register provided their number was limited (*Düstur* 1, 4: "Sicillat şer'iye . . ." 1874, 85, Article 16; *Düstur* 1, 4: "Bilâ beyyine . . . ," 1879, 80, Article 12). See some examples of crossed-out pages illustrating the method of allocating a space in advance for each case record in JCR, *Hujaj* 139, Z 1329–R 1332/XII 1911–III 1914, 10, 14, 17, 22, 25–27, 57–58, 110–11, 203, 210, 224.

judge's approval (fig. 2, session 4). It appears that some time after a session record was prepared and before the next session, the judge read the new protocols and in the margins added some professional considerations on how to pursue the case. This register became the authorized version, and here, too, if drafts were made, they did not survive.

The difference between the two interpretations of the center's instructions may be defined in terms of their focus. In the Jaffa version, the completion of the protocol record in the official register was deemed more important. In this respect, this version was closer to the raison d'être of the familiar registration type of records. The form used in Haifa, in contrast, concentrated on the process of amending the protocols according to the participants' comments and on keeping a record of this process. Its focus represents a more visible departure from the concept of the old registration, perhaps a bigger change than originally demanded by the central government. I return to the significance of this difference for the construction of the family in the latter part of this chapter.[33]

Finally, when completed case records had accumulated in the volumes of protocols, the scribes would register the summaries twice—in one of the volumes of registrations with reference to the original protocol in the volume of protocols and as a separate authorized document given to the participants. When a volume of protocols came to an end, the chief scribe edited it: he added a serial number to each case record; below the text of every recorded session that was not the last of that court case, he wrote the page number where the protocol continued (fig. 2; in Jaffa, the latter practice was less consistently adhered to). The pages were apparently numbered in advance in both the volumes of protocols and the registrations, judging by the cross-references

---

33. In the earliest volume of protocols that survived in Haifa (HCR, *Jaridat al-dabt,* 1308/ 1890), a strange page was recently found that does not belong there. It contains what seems to be a raw draft of one of the protocols that is recorded, session by session, in the pages just before and after it. It is probably the notes that the scribe took during the sessions as a basis for the final protocol and apparently was then forgotten. Its existence points to the process of preparing a protocol in the earliest years for which we have protocols in Haifa. It may also testify to the tradition of taking notes that the scribes followed when only summaries of cases were officially registered in the court records. I am grateful to Mahmoud Yazbak, who found this rough draft among the protocols of that volume and, after reading an earlier version of this chapter, realized the nature of that strange page and gave me a copy.

and explicit instructions in the matter (*Düstur* 1, 4: "Bilâ beyyine . . . ," 1879, 83–85, Articles 1 and 16).

Family and Court Culture

The routine of protocol recording developed in the Jaffa and Haifa courts during this period highlights the issue of the construction of the family in the legal arena. I suggest that the entire experience in court, in particular the recitation and validation of the record in the presence of the parties and other participants—professional jurists together with lay people—should be understood as a significant contact between the participants and the legal concepts of the family. Lay people, both litigants and witnesses, participated in the deliberations and listened to exchanges between the judge, the attorneys, and the scribes, exchanges by which their family ties and relations were molded in legal terms. Being the audience at these exchanges was not a new phenomenon, as I mentioned earlier, but two features of the reformed court intensified this contact. One was the emergence of professional attorneys in the *shariʿa* courts, and the other was the recitation of the protocols to and the signing of them by the participants.

The emergence of professional attorneys in the *shariʿa* courts is discussed in chapter 6, so here I only briefly mention the points relevant to this chapter. Unlike the long-standing legal representative *(wakil)*, or a layman who represented one of the parties free of charge in court, the *wakil daʿawi* was a professional attorney. The involvement of such attorneys in court, although widespread and institutionalized in the late nineteenth century, was a new phenomenon that came with the reforms,[34] together with several economic, social, and cultural implications inside and outside the courtroom. Professional attorneys' involvement resulted in longer trials and an intensive use of legal terminology, a point illustrated by Amina and Salim's case record. In such cases, lay people in court thus had more exposure to legal terminology on the family than in earlier periods.

At the same time, the very presence and involvement of professional jurists with their own court agenda tended to emphasize the procedural aspects of the court culture. The growing population in the port cities and the judges'

---

34. İnalcık points to evidence of the activities of professional attorneys much earlier in some Ottoman cities. The authorities objected to this activity and prevented it (1991, 5).

short terms of service combined to strengthen this tendency. Thus, although lay people were becoming more involved in the legal culture, that culture was undergoing profound changes, with the deliberations becoming more legalistic. Although it is true that the litigants represented by attorneys did not usually come to court themselves, other participants—witnesses of various kinds and sometimes even represented litigants, such as Salim—did appear. In some cases, only one party was represented by an attorney, whereas the other participated in all sessions. Some litigants would come to court accompanied by their relatives, who also became part of the audience, and, as several legal proceedings were usually scheduled for a single day, some of those who came to court for their own proceedings heard other cases while waiting.[35]

Finally, there was the recitation itself. In addition to the court session, the participants were requested to sign the record soon after it was prepared. Whereas during the session they only inadvertently became an audience, the recitation specifically and officially gave them that role. It was not meant to be a lesson in Muslim jurisprudence, and most probably did not become one, but it nonetheless was not only a multilayered meeting between professional jurists and lay people, but also an interaction between the educated and the illiterate, the elite and the lower strata, and, last but not least, the state and its humble subjects. States have many different ways of demonstrating their authority within and outside the courtroom, and the Ottoman rulers, like any other state rulers, had exhausted most methods during their centuries-long rule. The protocol record, with all its symbols of state authority—seals, stamps, and styled signatures—was clearly one of them. However, involving the people in the process of authorizing these documents by their own signatures, and in this way confirming the symbol of domination, appears to have been a brand new concept.

In the context of the formation of the modern Ottoman state, requiring people—in particular the illiterate, who constituted the majority in court—

---

35. The presence in the court audience of litigants and witnesses who awaited their turn in court and of litigants' relatives and acquaintances is evident from the names and signatures of identifying witnesses *(shuhud al-taʿarif)*. The names and signatures of the notaries, witnesses of the record *(shuhud al-hal)*, were frequently those of litigants and witnesses whose case records appear just before or just after the record that they signed as witnesses. On the variety of witnesses, see chapter 3, note 34.

to sign legal documents in which they themselves were concerned and that in most cases they could not independently read and comprehend, or could not refuse to read and sign, represented an intrusion of the state into these people's lives. However, in the context of the current discussion, the focus is somewhat different. The parties and their witnesses certainly held their own ideas about their family ties and relations, but in court they witnessed the scribe reciting these ties in legal terms, interrupted frequently by the judge or the attorneys demanding clarifications or amendments of the record. In many cases, people presumably did not understand most of the terms, yet they were standing there, and their cooperation was vital for the completion of the procedure. Some may have taken part more actively, asking for their own amendments, and when the recitation was over, the record was handed to them, and they signed it. Some signatures, judging by the handwriting, were clearly of people who could hardly write, but who insisted on signing with their names and not their fingerprints. Thus, it may be concluded that at least some of the lay people in court were becoming more familiar with the legal jargon and the current court culture and had their own ways of interpreting it. At the end of the day, their understanding of the legal concept of the family, in relation to other perceptions that shaped its construction, must have been strengthened.[36]

Two points mentioned earlier are relevant here. First, the slight difference in the application of recording procedures between the courts of Jaffa and Haifa indicates that people in Haifa were exposed more intensely to the recitation than were people in Jaffa because only in Haifa was the recitation held after each court session. Second, some litigants' inclination to hire professional attorneys suggests another division among the clientele of the court and their involvement in the new procedure—a division according to class affiliation. Because hiring professional attorneys became widespread, particularly among litigants of upper-class or successful middle-class families who were upwardly mobile, mainly litigants of this social background, such as Amina and Salim, were not present in court and hence lacked the sort of exposure experienced by their lower-class and lower-middle-class counterparts.

36. On the intrusive practices of modern states, see Foucault 1979, 135–69; Mitchell 1991, 91–95; Messick 1993, 231–50; Fahmy 1997, 195–98. On a new notion of "civic Ottomanism" in other arenas in late Ottoman Palestine, see Campos 2003.

Dialectically, then, the reforms that substantially reduced the jurisdiction of the *shariʿa* court and the *shariʿa* law as a source of jurisprudence at the same time contributed to reshape and reproduce *shariʿa* notions of the family. The legal reforms turned the *shariʿa* court into a "family court" by default. In parallel, they inadvertently provided this official change with a specific social and cultural content. This chapter has demonstrated one aspect of this content— namely, how the interaction in court between laymen and learned people of *shariʿa* law sustained the construction and the reproduction of both family and court culture in Jaffa and Haifa. The next two chapters focus on the analysis of both topics: the legal notion of the family is the main theme of chapter 5, and the court culture is further discussed in chapter 6.

Part Three

◆   ◆   ◆

Negotiating Versions

5

Gender and Family

IN THE PREVIOUS CHAPTER, I suggested that the new recording procedures emphasized the legal notion in the construction of the family among middle- and lower-class families in Jaffa and Haifa. In the first part of this chapter, I argue that the concepts of gender and social justice were intertwined with that of the family and underpinned the family's patrilineal structure. I discuss the overlap of the two notions, gender and social justice, within the legal construction of the family and the way they sustained the patrilineal structure. Furthermore, I show that the judge understood this family form as a framework for his decisions, thus contributing to the reproduction of these notions in court.

I dedicate the second part of the chapter to the question of family-state relations in the age of Ottoman judicial reform. I show that some aspects of reform in the *shari'a* courts meant in effect that the state took over certain domains of the family, mainly the responsibility for orphan properties. In so doing, the ruling elite inadvertently introduced some changes in family relations that reinforced the notion of the simple family, particularly among the urban upper and higher-middle classes. At the same time, this state intervention did not affect most people and did not change their prevailing concept of the family, so that the position of children, in particular girls, remained extremely vulnerable.

Family and the Gendered Division of Labor

The summary of a registration of a divorce agreement, selected at random, serves as a starting point for the presentation of the main principles of the concept of gender in the legal discourse.

In May 1900, Hajar Abu Tabikha, originally from Beirut, came to the *shariʿa* court in Jaffa together with her husband, Muhammad Ibn ʿAbd al-Nabi ʿInad, a sailor from Jaffa. In the judge's presence, she announced that she was willing to release her husband from the payment of her deferred *(muʾajjal)* dower of 1 LF and her alimony of another 100 kuruş for the waiting period *(ʿidda)*, on the condition that he would divorce her. The husband then announced the divorce by calling *talaq* three times. He also paid her a sum of 600 kuruş for the maintenance of *his* minor son (the emphasis is mine), then five years and four months old, for the rest of the period that the child would remain in his mother's custody *(hadana)*. At this point, the judge declared the couple legally divorced (JCR, *Hujaj* 83, 30 M 1318/30 V 1900, 86, case 1147).

This quite unexceptional record documents a divorce case of renunciation *(ibraʾ)*, whereby the wife gives up some or all her financial rights as divorcée in exchange for her husband's consent to divorce her. A regular divorce required that the husband loudly declaim the divorce declaration *(talaq)* three times, and then he was obliged to pay alimony to his wife for about three additional months, during which period she was not permitted to remarry *(ʿidda)*. In addition, according to the Hanafi school that was dominant in the Ottoman Empire, the children, boys under seven years old and girls under nine, were to be in their mother's custody *(hadana)*. A registration type of record, this summary provides us with no information about the reasons behind the termination of the marriage, not even a clue as to whether a lawsuit preceded the verdict. However, as a highly normal case documented in the court records, it illustrates some of the basic values of the concept of gender.

Although the details are not stated explicitly in this case, we may safely assume that when Muhammad first married Hajar, he took it upon himself to pay her a dower *(mahr)*, in part immediately and in part later.[1] The prompt dower, as implied by the meaning of the legal term *muʿajjal*,[2] was supposed

---

1. See, for example, HCR, *Sijill* 1287–91/1870–74. In this volume of registrations from the court of Haifa from the early 1870s, the scribe designed a format for the registration of marriage contracts. At the top, he entitled the contract as "setting the marriage [*ʿaqd nikah*] between [X] and [Y]." Next to the title, on the right, he wrote "prompt" and registered the sum of the prompt dower. On the left side, he wrote "deferred," then specified the sum, or "without deferred dower." He underlined the title, divided sums of dowers, and wrote the text of the contract below them.

2. With ʿayn, as opposed to *muʾajjal* (deferred), with hamza.

to be paid prior to consummation of the marriage. In practice, it was often not paid or only partially paid, as can be learned from many records of domestic disputes in which the wife demanded her unpaid prompt dower.[3] Apparently, Muhammad did pay it, which is why this detail is not mentioned in the couple's divorce agreement. Hajar gave up the deferred dower *(mu'ajjal)*, which was one of the husband's financial obligations to his wife that was to be paid only in the case of divorce or the husband's death, in order to get her husband's consent to the divorce. She also gave up her lawful alimony for the waiting period *('idda)*. Legally, he was obliged to pay this and the other sums of money because as her husband he was also her provider. This responsibility included the period immediately after the divorce, during which she was prevented from remarrying and when he therefore still had to provide for her. With the termination of this period, she was to become financially dependent either on her natal family or on a new husband in the event that she remarried.

Hajar gave up her financial rights as a divorcée owing to the fact that although a husband was entitled to initiate divorce without his wife's (or, for that matter, anyone else's) consent, the wife needed her husband's consent if she wanted him to divorce her. In the latter cases, consent was usually given in return for the husband's exemption from his financial obligations to his wife. The only payment Muhammad still owed Hajar after she released him was child support. She had no right to exempt him from this obligation because it was not hers to give up. It was his responsibility for his children to begin with; legally, the mother had to take care of minor children, and the father had to provide for them.[4]

The only direct information about Muhammad and Hajar provided by this record relates to their socioeconomic position. The sums of money men-

3. See the case of domestic dispute between Husun and Muhammad discussed later in this chapter and two other cases of domestic dispute in chapter 6. See also Agmon 1995, 106–12, about the custom of avoiding the payment of the prompt dower, or part of it, and the way in which women who wanted to bring their marital disputes to court took advantage of this custom. The extent to which the sums of dowers indicated the socioeconomic position of the families involved is also discussed there.

4. See chapter 6 for the discussion of a case of renunciation divorce in which the wife gave up her minor son's maintenance and the court cancelled this part of the divorce agreement, obliging the husband to pay his ex-wife alimony on behalf of their son. See also Zilfi 1997.

tioned in this case—according to the currency, rates of exchange, and prices mentioned in chapter 4 ("A Note on Money and Daily Conditions")—show that Muhammad belonged to the lowest of the court's three-level system of payments of daily support. He was to pay only 1 kuruş per day for child support (600 kuruş in twenty months). Had he initiated the divorce and had he paid Hajar all her financial rights, the sum he would have paid her for the waiting period would also have equalled approximately 1 kuruş a day (100 kuruş for about three months). The value of the deferred dower (1 LF) that Hajar gave up was also of a similar value (the LF was equal to 109 kuruş). It was a relatively small dower (in comparison, the deferred dower of Khadaja, a woman from a well-to-do family whose dual lawsuit against her husband is analyzed in the next chapter, was ten times higher). As a sailor *(bahri),* Muhammad probably belonged to the lower-middle social level of Jaffa. However, he could afford to pay Hajar the sum of child support, 600 kuruş, for the remaining period of custody in one payment, which suggests that although he was of modest background, he was nevertheless able to recruit this sum. Hajar was from Beirut (where Muhammad, the sailor, had probably met her and then married her), and she may have intended to return to her natal family there after the divorce; getting the entire sum of child support in advance would have enabled her to leave without being dependent on Muhammad's payments. Court decisions on child support usually defined sums of daily or monthly payments, and the age of the minor child was not determined so accurately as in this case, which means that there was no need to calculate the total sum to be paid in one installment. By leaving Jaffa, however, Hajar would have jeopardized her rights to custody of her minor son because his father, being his legal guardian, could demand that he remain near him. However, if Hajar stayed in Jaffa without a family to fall back on, she would have to remarry, and unless her new husband was her son's close agnate, which was very unlikely under circumstances of divorce, her son would be taken from her anyway on the grounds of another rule of *shari'a* family law. This rule and its implications for women and children of a modest background are discussed in detail both in this chapter and in chapter 7.

The philosophy behind the rules of family law may be described in terms of a division of labor between men and women in the family. This division assigned the men the burden of providing for the women and the responsibility for their moral behavior, whereas women were not expected to provide for anyone, not even for themselves.[5] Their assignment was to bear children and rear them *(hadana)* when they were very young and to obey their husbands or their legal guardians (always a man from among their patrikin). The rest of the rights and duties followed the same logic, by which those of men were defined very differently from those of women: men were conceived of as responsible not only for themselves but also for their entire family, which belonged to them to begin with. Women, in contrast, were conceived of as creatures who needed guidance, protection, and supervision—in other words, not responsible or "incomplete" human beings.[6]

The difference in the construction of the categories of man and woman can be detected in the *shari'a* inheritance law, which consistently allocated to women half of the share allocated to men who were related to the deceased to the same degree (although, historically, the difference between the share received by men and women in the inheritance is considered an improvement on the situation of women who did not inherit at all in pre-Islamic tribal societies). According to the *shari'a* law of evidence, two reliable women were considered to equal one man for giving testimony *(Mecelle,* Article 1685). In this regard, it is also interesting to notice that when the court scribes in Jaffa began to ask litigants to sign the protocols of their respective cases, only men's

5. About the gendered "division of labor" between the parents, see also Tucker 1998, 146–47. This principle did not mean that women were not allowed to own property, to buy and sell, and to make profits, but only that they were not expected to support anyone. They were also entitled to keep any property they might have owned before their marriage or acquired during their marriage. Such property neither belonged to their husbands nor became communal property. All the studies on the role of women in economic activities in different eras and in different parts of the Ottoman Empire show that this practice was followed and that women owned properties and were highly involved in all spheres of the economy. See, for example, Gerber 1980; Marcus 1983; Agmon 1995, 188–212; Ze'evi 1996, 183–85; Doumani 1998; Meriwether 1999, 117–18, 167–68. Baber Johansen mentions that "[O]nly if the father is unable to fulfill his duties toward his children can the mother be compelled to take in these responsibilities" (1981, 292). I did not come across any such case in the Jaffa and Haifa court records.

6. See, for example, Sonbol 1996c, 278. See also an illustration of this concept in Rosen 1978. Male and female sexualities were also constructed as being entirely different from each other. Although Fatima Mernissi (2000) interprets this notion of sexuality as much more ambivalent and less dichotomous, her bottom line concedes that the two sexualities are seen as being polarized. This attitude constitutes the main justification for male dominance and women's seclusion.

signatures were required, not women's (JCR, *Hujaj* 47, 1293–94/1876–77).
Women's signatures appeared only in later volumes, after specific instructions
were issued to recite the protocol and allocate all parties' signatures, and the
concept of authorizing the protocols with these signatures was implemented
more meticulously (Agmon 2004a).

The division of labor between men and women in the family and the construction of the categories of man and woman stemmed from the patriarchal
structure of the society. The family in this structure was a male's family. Females joined it as wives, but they belonged to their natal patrilineal family, and
as divorcees or widows they often returned to the household of one of their
male relatives. The children born to them, however, belonged to the father's
family, as emphasized by the description of the minor boy in the previously
described case record as "his" (the father's) rather than as "their" (both parents') son. Except for the few years when the children were in their mother's
custody, they remained in their father's household in cases in which he divorced their mother. Moreover, as explained earlier regarding the choices
open to Hajar, even during the period of the mother's custody, she was subject
to certain restrictions that might have led to her losing that right.[7]

The structure of the protocol of a case involving debt, claimed on February 1876 by a group of heirs from a man to whom the deceased had lent
money before his death, illustrates the patrilineal construction of the family.
This record consists of two protocols, a power of attorney and a lawsuit that
were recorded as one single case. The case was recorded in the first official volume of protocols in Jaffa, before the explicit instructions to maintain a separate volume of documents of powers of attorney had been issued (see chapter
4). The original protocol is registered continuously without any emphases.
Here, I have restructured it to illustrate the construction of family relations as
inscribed in the text (the breakdown and emphases are mine).

> **A power** of attorney was given to Sayyid Salih Aswar by *his wife,* Saliha bint
> Ahmad ibn Radwan al-Bir
> **and** by *her two daughters,* Amina and Latifa, *the daughters of* the late Hajj Muham-
> mad ibn Hajj Ahmad Musa
> **to** represent them in cases that relate to the inheritance of Ahmad ibn Hajj
> Muhammad ibn Hajj Ahmad Musa, who died while on military service in
> Yemen.

7. On contemporary legislation undermining the patrilineal family, see Layish 2000.

Later came ʿAbdalla and *his full brother* [*shaqiq*] Musa, *the sons of* Hajj Muham-mad ibn Hajj Ahmad Musa, and both of them gave power of attorney to Sayyid Salih Aswar to represent them in whatever related to the inheritance of the late Ahmad mentioned above.

According to the recorded power of attorney, Sayyid Salih Aswar sued the debtor [his name and the details of the debt].

He stated that Ahmad had died and bequeathed his inheritance to *his mother,* the woman mentioned above,

and *his two full brothers,* ʿAbdalla and Musa,

and to *Amina* and *Latifa.* (JCR, *Hujaj* 47, 27 M 1293/22 II 1876)[8]

The rest of the record includes the lawsuit itself, which is irrelevant to my point here.

One might need to read this record in its original form several times in order to figure out the family relations: a (late) husband and wife, their two daughters and three sons, of whom one was the deceased whose debtor had been sued in this case. In other words, the group of people mentioned in this record was a simple family. In addition, all the living members of this family (the mother and her two daughters and two sons) had authorized the mother's new husband to represent them at court in this lawsuit.

Deciphering this case reveals the difference between the family construc-tion held by the outside reader (namely, by me) and that held by the author of this court text.[9] The way this text was structured by its author highlights two aspects of the notion of patrilineal family: these people's identity, embodied by their patrilineal pedigrees, and how they related to the inheritance, or to the deceased. The combination of the two elements enables us to figure out how they were related to each other and to reconstruct the recorded simple family. For instance, nowhere does the record mention the fact that Saliha was the mother of ʿAbdalla and Musa, in addition to being that of Amina and Latifa and the deceased soldier, Ahmad. This relation can be deduced from the fact that ʿAbdalla and Musa were mentioned as full brothers of the deceased in order to establish their share in the inheritance; the fact that all three men were

---

8. In that period, the pages and cases were not yet numbered (see Agmon 2004a).

9. This gap demonstrates the difference between the emic (phonemic) and etic (phonetic) perspectives in anthropology. The former is focused on the language as spoken by the native speaker and thus is the perspective of its practitioners. The latter is focused on the language as heard by an outside observer. See, for example, Tilly 1987.

identified by the same pedigree is not sufficient to conclude that they also had the same mother, for she was not part of their pedigree. The fact that the deceased was her son was mentioned only in the later part of the protocol, where the claims about the inheritance were recorded. Up to that point, we are explicitly informed only that the two other women were her daughters.

Other important rules of the *shariʿa* family law should also be understood against the background of the patriarchal structure. However, the patriarchal structure should be seen as a general framework that constituted the rules of the game. For the interpretation of the notions within this game, as it was played in the courts of late Ottoman Jaffa and Haifa, an understanding of certain concepts of social justice is helpful.

The Family and Social Justice

In October 1913, two men came to the *shariʿa* court in Haifa. One of them, Muhammad ibn Qasim Hasun al-Sharut, sued the other, his son Qasim. He claimed that he himself was blind, had no income or profession, could hardly obtain work, but nevertheless supported a wife and four minor children, and that his son, Qasim, was a professional construction worker who earned 15 kuruş a day. Thus, he requested that the court order his son to pay him sufficient maintenance *(nafaqa)*.[10] Qasim answered his father's claim by saying that his salary was hardly sufficient to support his own family, including his mother, a divorcée for twenty years, and that his father's income was higher than his own because he was a property owner and also engaged in some buying and selling. He thus requested that the court reject his father's claim that he (the father) had no income of his own and his demand that his son provide for him. It took Judge Abdülhalim six court sessions and about two months to give his verdict in this case. During this time, the manager of the *tapu* (land-registration) office in Haifa confirmed to the court that Muhammad was the

---

10. The term *nafaqa* (literally, expenditure) is normally used with regard to the support that men are expected to provide for their wives and minor children. It is an articulation of the gendered division of labor in the family and a common legal issue in court. Men, however, were also expected to provide for their needy parents (Ibn ʿAbidin n.d., 2: 671–74), although in the court records one comes across such situations mainly when it is mentioned incidentally that a woman lives in her adult son's household, as in the case of the defendant Qasim. A father suing his son in demand of *nafaqa* is extremely rare.

owner of a one-room house in the neighborhood of Wadi al-Nisnas in Haifa, the value of which was 2,000 kuruş. Four more witnesses brought by Qasim testified that Muhammad, his father, had enlarged this house, which now had three rooms and an additional place for animals. They were also able to tell the court that Muhammad owned a donkey, which he would ride through the streets, selling vegetables and earning between 5 and 7 beşlik a day (17–25 kuruş, which was more than his son's alleged salary). They said that Muhammad and his family lived in that house in Wadi al-Nisnas and that he stored the vegetables in one of the extra rooms, kept the donkey in the area designated for animals, and even rented out the third room. After the witnesses' credibility was confirmed, the judge decided in favor of the son, Qasim, and rejected the father's claim for daily support (HCR, *Jaridat al-Dabt* 5, 12 Za 1331–17 M 1332/X–XI 1913, 7,18, 20–22, 26–27, 55, 72, case 52).

This record reveals several aspects of family ties and relations as well as household structures, among them the concepts of economic dependence and social justice. When Muhammad demanded support from his son for himself as well as for his wife and minor children on the grounds that he was unable to provide for them, his son, Qasim, thwarted a verdict that would have made him share his income with his father, proving that his father was in fact better off than he was. Muhammad had divorced Qasim's mother years earlier and at the time of the trial was married to another woman with whom he had four children. Qasim at that time had a wife and children of his own, and his mother also lived in his household. Thus, at the beginning of the trial, Muhammad and Qasim, two adults, were each providing for a wife and minor children, but Qasim also provided for his mother, for whom his father, after divorcing her, no longer served as provider.

The verdict of this trial did not change the situation. Its protocol illustrates the division among family members between providers, who were always adult men, and those who were supported by them—their adult female relatives and their minor children of both sexes. However, Muhammad, by raising his claim, and Qasim, by responding to it in the way he did, exposed the possibility that sometimes adult men could join the women and children in the supported group. Thus, although the gendered division of labor was similar to the division into providers and their dependents, the two divisions did not entirely overlap because age and health were also relevant issues. This points to yet another layer of the concept of social justice—namely, that the framework within which it was to materialize was the patrilineal family and that this family was looked on as a sort of small-scale welfare economy in which members in dire straits, including men and their dependents, would get some help from other male family members who were better off. This was not the resolution of the case between Muhammad and his son because apparently Muhammad was not in dire straits, at least no more so than his son. However, the way this case and others of similar nature were dealt with in court suggests that such issues were considered within a framework of welfare.

Placing the responsibility for providing for needy dependents on their male relatives, in the absence of the natural provider, meant that if there was more than one such relative, the burden was divided among the new providers. When, for instance, Niʿma al-Abiad came to the court in Jaffa and claimed that she was a poor woman with neither money nor the capacity to provide for herself, she named her four adult sons, two from each one of her former husbands, whom she claimed could afford to provide for her by paying 1 kuruş a day each. Then two of them came to the court with her and announced that they would cover her daily expenses by paying 2 kuruş, and she asked the court to inform her other two sons about the maintenance. Apparently, this decision reached at least one of these sons, who came about a month later to court and registered his willingness to pay his share.[11] Cases like this also show that the court both functioned and was depicted as a guardian of Muslim social justice and as an arena for social negotiations, a point discussed further in the following section.

When we look at the two concepts, gender and social justice, we see that not only did they resemble each other in their logic and content, but that gender in this context is part of the construction of social justice, and neither can be properly understood outside the discourse on the family. The patrilineal family was represented in this discourse as comprising two groups: the providers and their dependents. The division of labor between men and women in the family echoes the division of labor between providers, who are adult males only (but not all of them), and dependents, who include the rest of the family members—all the adult females, minor children, and disabled adults

11. JCR, *Hujaj* 129, 21 N 1329/15 IX 1911, 5 Z 1329/28 X 1911, 321, case 89. For further examples, see JCR: *Hujaj* 83, 24 L 1317/25 II 1900, 12, case 1027; 7 M 1318/7 V 1900, 79, case 1136; *Hujaj* 152, 26 Z 1331/25 XI 1913, 84, case 37. Also, HCR, *Sijill* 7, 10 S 1325/25 III 1907, 12, case 16; HCR, *Jaridat al-Dabt* 32, 29 M 1332/28 XII 1913, 85–86, case 77.

of both sexes. The first group consists of adult men, who were deemed more accomplished than the rest. Hence, they bore full responsibility for the family's maintenance, well-being, and position and reputation in society. The providers' rights and duties followed this logic. Dependents also took on certain responsibilities and were entitled accordingly to specified rights, the implementation of which in principle was supervised by members of the first group—namely, the *shariʿa* judges.

The Court and Social Justice

How and when did the *shariʿa* court become involved, as a supervisor as well as a significant participant, in the reproduction of the legal notions of gender, social justice, and family? How did judges and scribes implement these notions in court? How did they interpret them, and what role did the court play in the reproduction of these notions outside the courtroom? And what can be learned by looking closely at the records, particularly at interjections from and decisions taken by judges?

At first glance, the judge's function was nothing more than making sure that the legal procedure was conducted according to *shariʿa* law: in cases of dispute, he would see that the plaintiff bore the burden of proof and that the case would be decided accordingly; and in cases of a request for the legal confirmation of an action, he would dictate the description of the action to the scribe in legal terms and confirm it.[12] A second, more profound reading, however, reveals that the judge's role was much more complex. From the perspective under consideration here, it seems that he understood the role of the court as being a kind of guardian of social equilibrium, whose duty was to recognize situations of extreme distress among people who sought remedy at court. The social unit considered responsible for carrying this burden of social equilibrium in such cases was the patrilineal family. It was not expected to maintain equality, but rather to keep some kind of balance among its members according to the concepts of gender and social justice described earlier. The case record given in the next section illustrates this interpretation.

Deputy Judge Tawfiq Resolves a Domestic Dispute

In the summer of 1911, for a period of about four months, there was no judge at the Jaffa court. The court decisions were taken by a deputy judge, Qusay

---

12. On the image of the *shariʿa* judge as a negligible figure in legal history, see chapter 6.

Tawfiq Efendi. His predecessor, Judge Abdülaziz Efendi of Istanbul, a man in his early forties at the time, had served a relatively short term in Jaffa, from February 1910 to June 1911, for reasons that are not mentioned in the official record of his curriculum vitae. He was not appointed to another subdistrict right away, nor was he dismissed or forced to retire. About half a year later, he was promoted to a higher rank, and his successful career continued elsewhere (SA def. 5, 148; Albayrak 1996, 1: 111–12). While in Jaffa, he seems to have been rather active; he signed all the protocols, often more than once. However, his successor, Mehmet Sadık Efendi from Alaʿiye (in Antalya), was appointed only in October and arrived in Jaffa in November 1911 (SA dos. 1095). In the meantime, Deputy Judge Qusay Tawfiq conducted the legal proceedings. His signature, with either his two names or only one of them, usually "Tawfiq," under the title "Wakil Naib Yafa," began to appear on protocols in April 1911, a couple of months before Judge Abdülaziz left. For about a month in the course of this period, the two of them conducted legal proceedings alternately, so this arrangement was apparently intentional, to give Tawfiq a short internship period under the guidance of Judge Abdülaziz.[13]

It sometimes happened that the arrival of a new judge was delayed, in which case his predecessor would remain in his position or would be replaced temporarily by a junior jurist until the appointed judge arrived. As noted, in Haifa several such situations occurred during the period in question. In March 1905, Judge Ahmad Khayr al-Din Efendi from Tripoli arrived in Haifa to begin his two-year service there. He replaced the *başkatib* at the court of Haifa, Sheikh Mahmud ʿAla al-Din, who for about half a year had served as deputy judge after the previous judge left and before he himself was promoted to the office of subdistrict judge in the Hijaz. After Judge Ahmad Khayr al-Din Efendi had completed two years of office, in February 1907, he was replaced

13. The signatures of Judge Abdülaziz can be seen on the first 150 pages of the volume of protocols of 1910–11 on almost every page. Then the deputy judge began to sign intermittently with the judge (JCR, *Hujaj* 1328–29/1910–11, 16 R 1329/16 IV 1911, 144). The chief scribe, Sheikh Ahmad Raghib al-Dajani, also signed several times under the title *serkatib.* Judge Abdülaziz's last signature appeared in that volume in late May (JCR, *Hujaj* 1328–29/1910–11, 22 Ca 1329/21 V 1911, 183). Deputy Judge Tawfiq continued to sign the protocols in the next volumes that covered the later part of the year 1329/1911, until the new judge began to sign his name, Sadık, under the title "Yafa Naibi" in November (JCR, *Hujaj* 129, 12 Za 1329/4 XI 1911, 328, case 92). About Judge Sadık's term in Jaffa, see chapter 6.

by Muhammad Kamal Efendi from Aleppo. The latter, for some reason, served only half a year and left his office in Haifa on 21 July 1907. His successor, ʿAbd al-Muʿta Efendi from Jerusalem, arrived a month later, on 17 August. In the meantime, Yunis Efendi, from the established al-Khatib family in Haifa, was appointed deputy judge. Yunis Efendi had completed his legal education and passed the exams of the College for Shariʿa Judges in Istanbul only a year earlier. Within a few months (January 1908), he was to be appointed to his first position as judge in the subdistrict of Zebdani (in Syria). He was probably at home in Haifa, waiting for the beginning of his first term as judge, and therefore was available for service as a stand-in deputy there. A similar situation occurred in Haifa in 1909, when the *başkatib* Muhyi al-Din was temporarily appointed for two months.[14]

Thus, Abdülaziz's shorter term in Jaffa may indicate that he had to leave before his successor's appointment. Under these circumstances, Deputy Judge Qusay Tawfiq was appointed temporarily. No information about his background can be traced. From the information about similar cases in Haifa it may be deduced that he was a senior scribe, a judge of a lower rank, or an intern who had not yet completed all the official requirements for the rank of subdistrict judge at the time his service in Jaffa was required and hence was appointed only as stand-in deputy, entitled "deputy judge."

When Deputy Judge Tawfiq was in office, the following case of domestic dispute was brought up in court. A man claimed that his wife, whom he had recently divorced, unlawfully demanded both maintenance from him for the two and one-half months during which they were separated a year before the divorce and her prompt dower, which, according to him, he had paid her. The wife brought a court decision regarding her maintenance during their temporary separation and demanded her financial rights as divorcée and child support in addition to this sum and the prompt dower. The husband was requested to bring proof in support of his version and failed. Then she declared under oath that her version was true, and the judge decided in her favor.

14. HCR, *Sijill* 6, 10 M 1323/17 III 1905, 1; *Sijill* 5, 19 Ş 1322/29 X 1904, 385; *Sijill* 7, 10 C 1325/21 VII 1907, 74; *Sijill* 7, 7 B 1325/17 VIII 1907, 78; *Sijill* 8, 16 N 1327/1 X 1909, 115; *Sijill* 8, 27 Z 1327/10 XII 1909, 151. Also: SA dos. 797, dos. 819; SA def. 1, 268, 363, def. 5, 216; Albyrak 1996, 1: 74, 147, 4: 365–66. See also chapters 3 and 4 and the discussion on the orphan funds in this chapter.

The record of this case demonstrates how the judge understood the court's social role. That this particular judge was a novice makes this case more interesting because it illustrates the attitude of an inexperienced judge fresh from his studies and internship. The deputy judge decided this case in August 1911 in the course of two court sessions. The record begins with the husband, Muhammad Qashta, suing his ex-wife, Husun Abu Assurayij, originally from Ramla. From his version, it appears that about a year earlier, when still married, they had quarreled, and Husun had gone to court and demanded maintenance and child support for their minor daughter, Halima. The court had decided in her favor, but then Muhammad was reconciled with her, and she had returned to live with him until he divorced her. She then brought up her claim for the payment that he still owed her for the period of their previous temporary separation. Muhammad asked the court to reject her demand, claiming that during the alleged separation period, he had taken care of her and their daughter, providing them with a conjugal dwelling *(maskan shar'i)*.

Husun responded by mentioning the previous court decision regarding the alimony and child support and promised to produce the relevant document within two days. At this point in the record, another scribe replaced the one who recorded the first part containing the husband's claim. He began with a comment that the earlier court decision referred to by Husun was submitted as an *istid'a* (a request to carry out a previous verdict), which does not require further decision. Husun was then asked about her version of the case. She mentioned the exact dates of the previous court decision and the couple's reconciliation, claiming that Muhammad still owed her maintenance of 3 kuruş a day (1.5 kuruş each for the mother and the daughter) for the interim period, which had lasted two and one-half months. In addition, she claimed that according to their marriage contract, Muhammad took it upon himself to pay her a prompt dower of 5 LF and 1 LF for the deferred dower. Because he had divorced her recently—the record continues—he should also pay her this sum of 6 LF, as well as alimony for her *'idda* period and child support for her daughter, Halima. It should be noted that all the sums mentioned in this case record point to Muhammad and Husun's moderate to low economic position; the maintenance was slightly higher than the sum that the sailor Muhammad was ordered to pay to Hajar from Beirut in the renunciation divorce case opening this chapter; it fits on the lowest level of daily support presented in chapter 4).

In this part of the record—the wife's claim, recorded by a second scribe (and not by the scribe who recorded the husband's claim)—Muhammad, the plaintiff, was referred to as the defendant. When Muhammad was requested to respond to Husun's claims, he was referred to as the plaintiff, and the scribe's confusion is revealed by the fact that he wrote the term *defendant (muda'a 'alayhi)* first and then changed it to *plaintiff (muda'i)* by erasing the word *'alayhi*. Muhammad was only willing to acknowledge the divorce and his obligation to pay the deferred dower of 1 LE, the alimony for the *'idda* period, and daily child support, claiming that he had already paid the prompt dower and that there had been no time lag between the previous court decision and their reconciliation. Husun denied his version, and the rest of the case was postponed to another day. The last line in the record of this first session reveals the scribe's confusion once again: he first wrote that "the plaintiff denied Muhammad's claim," then erased "the plaintiff" and wrote her name, Husun, instead, apparently in order to avoid the use of either term, *plaintiff* or *defendant*.

At the beginning of the second session of this trial, recorded by the first scribe, Muhammad was referred to as the defendant and the burden of proof was imposed on him. Because this is one of the main procedural turning points of the case, where the intervention of the judge might have made a difference, I offer an interpretation of this decision after I describe the case in full. Muhammad replied that because he had no witness to the payment of the prompt dower, he requested that Husun take an oath in the matter; regarding the reconciliation, he named a long list of witnesses. The record then cites the testimony given separately by four witnesses, each testimony consisting of partial information about the couple's reconciliation. After the fourth testimony, Muhammad, who this time was referred to as the plaintiff, said that he was unable to produce more witnesses. At this point, Deputy Judge Tawfiq (or a third scribe on his behalf) noted the legal flaws he found in each of the four testimonies, which he then rejected, signing with his first name.

The same scribe or the deputy judge continued the record, adding that, following the rejection of the testimonies, Muhammad had asked that Husun take an oath regarding her version of the reconciliation, and she had done so. The deputy judge ordered Muhammad to pay her maintenance for the two and one-half months of separation in the previous year. Then Husun repeated her claim for the prompt dower. The deputy judge declared that she was divorced from Muhammad on the grounds that he had uttered the *talaq* and instructed Muhammad to pay the deferred dower and to prove that he had already paid the prompt dower, again calling him "the defendant." Muhammad, now referred to as "the plaintiff" in the record, said that he could not prove it and asked that Husun should swear to this claim, too. When she did, the deputy judge ordered Muhammad to pay her the prompt dower as well. The verdict was recorded by a fourth scribe, and Deputy Judge Tawfiq signed his name and affixed his seal at the end of the record (JCR, *Hujaj* 131, 21 Ş 1329, 5 N 1329/VIII 1911, 10, 32–34, case 6).

Deputy Judge Tawfiq's Discretion

The alternate use of the terms *plaintiff* and *defendant* requires some consideration. Legally, the parties did not change roles, even when the burden of proof was imposed on the defendant. The law of procedure instructed the judge to impose this burden on the plaintiff, unless the defendant's version was not a mere denial of the plaintiff's version, but a counterclaim, in which case the defendant had to provide witnesses (*Mecelle,* Articles 1631, 1816, 1817, 1823). My assumption is that the confusion between the two legal terms *muda'i* (plaintiff) and *muda'a 'alayhi* (defendant) had something to do with the decision taken by the deputy judge regarding the burden of proof and was not an innocent slip of the pen. Cases where the parties' legal roles were changed in the record were very rare, in spite of the similarity between the two terms in Arabic. In fact, I can recall only one such case in the Haifa court record, and in that case there was a similar situation, where Judge Abdülhalim apparently used his discretion with regard to the party who would carry the burden of proof in a way that might have influenced the outcome of the trial (which also ended in a way similar to the ending of Muhammad and Husun's trial), but this fluctuation apparently confused the scribe with regard to the legal terminology.[15]

The judge, after hearing the opposing versions, had to make two legal decisions: defining the disputed issues that required proof and deciding which party would carry the burden of proof. In cases of only one version, the plaintiff's, denied by the defendant, the judge's discretion was very limited: he had to place the burden of proof on the plaintiff. In our case, however, Husun, the defendant, responded to her husband's claim by a counterclaim and hence was

15. HCR, *Jaridat al-Dabt* 5, 8–19 M 1332/7–18 XII 1913, 60, 68–69, 72–75, case 72. See also Agmon 1996, 1998, 487–89.

supposed to carry the burden of proof. Yet the deputy judge imposed this burden on Muhammad, the plaintiff. Legally, this decision may be explained by the fact that according to the protocol, after Husun's version was heard, Muhammad responded to it with a counterclaim of his own. But as I demonstrated in chapter 4, the record, even when it was a protocol and not a registration, did not necessarily coincide with every oral exchange that took place in the courtroom. Rather, it is more likely that the order of things was as follows: the parties laid their claims in their own words and probably argued with each other while the scribe, according to the instructions for preparing the protocol, took notes of the claims. The judge then summarized the two versions in legal terms, and the scribe recorded this summary. Thus, the record as we have it—with claim, counterclaim, and another counterclaim—may reflect a decision in advance by the judge to put the burden of proof on Muhammad and was thus not in itself the reason for his decision to do so. We may recall that the scribe who recorded the first session was replaced by a colleague during the process, which might have caused further confusion in the record regarding the litigants' proper legal titles.

In order to understand the meaning of Deputy Judge Tawfiq's discretion regarding the burden of proof, we need to be aware of the possible legal scenarios of which he was also cognizant. The party that was assigned to bring proof would either declare that he or she was unable to bring witnesses or state their names. In the first scenario, the party that failed to bring witnesses would ask that the other party should swear to the truth of his or her version, and this oath would be considered as decisive proof in the verdict. In the second scenario, the witnesses would testify under oath; the judge would make sure that their testimonies pertained to the claim for which they were testifying; their credibility would be checked and confirmed in a special procedure *(tazkiya)* involving additional witnesses; and if the testimonies passed all these barriers successfully, the judge would decide in favor of the party who had brought them (*Mecelle,* Articles 1632, 1706, 1716–18, 1720, 1742, 1817–20, 1823).

These legal procedures indeed emphasize how much the verdict depended on who was to bear the burden of proof. They also reveal a clear imbalance between the two competitive forms of proof, the eyewitness and the oath. In the first case, the party was dependent on other people for proof, and the procedure was quite complicated and exposed to various legal flaws, whereas in the case of an oath the party testified that his or her version was true, and no credibility check was undertaken.[16]

The deputy judge's decision to place the burden of proof on Muhammad rather than on Husun, in addition to the way in which he dealt with the testimony given by Muhammad's four witnesses (legally, two witnesses sufficed), suggests that the deputy judge might have intended to help Husun. Carrying the burden of proof was not necessarily a disadvantage in a trial: in many cases, it was an advantage for the party on which it was imposed. However, in domestic disputes of this nature—or disputes that had started a long time back and were private—it was sometimes not so easy to find eyewitnesses, even under the prevailing living conditions of close proximity among neighbors (see chapter 7). In fact, Muhammad encountered this difficulty when he tried to prove his version. Had the deputy judge been indifferent to the consequences of the trial, he could have placed the burden of proof on Husun, a legally correct placement in the case of a defendant addressing the plaintiff with a counterclaim, and then most probably the trial would have developed quite differently. The deputy judge's putting the burden of proof on Muhammad and then using his discretion strictly with regard to the quality of the testimony given seem strongly to suggest that his acts were intentional and in any case were far from being merely technical.

What motivated the deputy judge, Tawfiq, in this particular case is impossible to ascertain. Maybe his interjections had nothing to do with gender, social justice, the family, or any combination thereof. It is also impossible to substantiate a direct connection between his lack of judicial experience and the way in which he deliberated this case. If at all, a conformist approach in handling trials was to be expected as a result of the fact that he was inexperienced and of a lower rank. Indeed, as I show in the following chapter, the results of this case were not exceptional. The only somewhat outstanding aspect of the case was that the deputy judge seemed to make no significant use of arbitration, a feature that was usually essential in the judge's work. However, the absence of arbitration might have been the result of the deputy judge's inexperience.

Be the reasons for the development of this case as they may, it illustrates my argument about reading the court records from the judge's perspective and

16. See chapter 6 on the case of Khadaja and Hasan.

according to the way he used his discretion. The reading of many more cases has led me to see a certain line of action running through them with regard to the judge's vantage point. He usually used his discretion in order to ensure that people who were in distress would not leave the courtroom empty-handed, provided that the end result was in line with *shari'a* law. These people, in many cases, belonged to the dependent group, not to the provider group, and frequently were women of a low or middling socioeconomic level.[17] Moreover, the way the judge's discretion is inscribed in the court records suggests that the procedural sphere of the law, which is often dealt with only as a technical aspect, ought to be considered much more seriously. I propose that judges understood this field of the law as one that invites interpretation, flexibility, and responsiveness to local conditions, so that they were active participants in legal interpretation more than we tend to think.[18] This question is discussed further in the next chapter.

State, Family, and Social Justice

Another vulnerable group of dependents that requires consideration is that of minor children, in particular orphans. In the court vocabulary, the term *yatim/a* (orphan) was employed to describe a child whose father had died, no matter whether his or her mother was still alive.[19] Used this way, the term simultaneously emphasized three aspects of the child's status. The first was the child's pedigree, his or her patrilineal family. The adjective *yatim/a* also replaced the expression "son/daughter of" *(ibn/bint)* in the pedigree. The sec-

17. Several studies on court and gender have shown that, genderwise, *shari'a* courts functioned as a tool of "corrective discrimination." See Tucker 1998, 146–47, and Peirce 1998a.

18. This observation is a major theme in Shahar 2005. Ido Shahar was working on his dissertation, an ethnography of the *shari'a* court of Jerusalem, while I was writing the present monograph. We often exchanged ideas, and time and again the similarities (the observation here included) between "our" courts and the continuity they represented, despite different historical contexts, astonished us. I thank Ido for his insights on this and many other issues in the present study.

19. It should be noted that the legal vocabulary included a specific term, *latim,* for the exact translation of the term *orphan*—namely, a child whose parents had died (Shaham 2001). I did not come across any case that used this term in practice. Because the situations relevant to this discussion are those in which minor children lost only their father, and in the absence of an exact translation for *yatim,* I use the term *orphan* in translation.

ond aspect was the child's legal minority. In many cases, adults whose fathers had died were mentioned in the records, yet they were not described as orphans, but rather as "the son/daughter of the late so and so," even when the death of their father was the topic of the recorded case. The third aspect stems from the first two—that is, the child's status as a dependent for whom support needed to be organized. Thus, the three dimensions of the term *orphan/yatim* provide yet another expression of the legal concepts of gender and social justice.

The assignment of providers for orphans and the supervision of the implementation of their legal rights were duties of the *shariʿa* courts. As the sole legal system dealing with family law, the *shariʿa* courts also remained in charge of these responsibilities after the legal reforms of the nineteenth century, although the reforms included the introduction of some innovations to this sphere of activity. Historians often present *shariʿa* family law as remaining untouched by the Tanzimat leadership and consider the Ottoman Family Law of 1917 to be the first reform related to this law (Findley 1991, 6; Starr 1992, 39–41). I argue, however, that the procedural innovations discussed in the previous chapters ought to be considered at least as indirect reform of *shariʿa* family law because of their repercussions on the *shariʿa* courts and on the construction of the family in the observed societies. Moreover, I believe that the Emval-ı Eytam Nezareti (Authority for the Supervision of Orphan Properties) and its funds (Eytam Sandıkları), which had been established gradually since the 1850s constituted a direct reform that went unnoticed, apparently because it did not change the letter of the law, but was introduced as yet another set of administrative instructions.

A minor child's becoming an orphan—that is, a dependent who remained without a legal male provider and guardian—raised three problems that might have required court intervention (in the event that the late father had not left instructions): the appointment of a general guardian *(wali)* for the orphan; the appointment of an executor *(wasi)* to take care of the orphan's share in the inheritance; and the imposition of daily child support for the orphan on his or her closest male agnates in cases where there was no inheritance. Later on, the judge's approval was necessary for any transaction made by the guardians in connection with the orphan's property. Thus, it was basically the court's duty to make sure that the family protected and served the orphans' legal rights and interests. In most cases, the responsibility for ensuring these rights and interests was divided within the family between the orphan's mother and his or her agnatic male relatives, and sometimes the judge or one of the local notables would also be appointed as a guardian.[20] The instructions about orphans, issued in Istanbul and gradually implemented in the provinces during the Tanzimat, introduced changes to this situation.

In the division of labor between providers and dependents described earlier, the family was responsible for its orphans as well as for other dependents who had lost their direct providers or become disabled, and the court served as a general supervisor and mediator whenever the need arose. The foundation of a new authority to supervise the management of orphan properties introduced more bureaucratization into procedures related to these properties and, most important, a direct control of orphans' money; it restricted the free hand some adult family members had in dealing with this property. The result was that the state retained a clear say in matters of family domain, in which, de jure, the way was always open to interference by the court, but de facto this interference was only slight.

The significance of the change represented by the foundation of a new organ directly in charge of orphans' properties may be understood better if we look at the concepts of poverty, charity, and benevolence in Muslim societies and at some of the transformations that took place in these concepts vis-à-vis the formation of modern states. As shown by recent studies on these issues, historically the needy and the poor were considered the responsibility of the family, the community, and the ruler in Muslim societies. Earlier I demonstrated the nature of the responsibility that this notion of welfare posed for the family. With regard to the two other parties, the community and the ruler, charity and benevolence were the means for achieving Muslim social justice because they were, first and foremost, religious principles followed in a wide range of societies whose main common denominator was that they were composed mostly of Muslim believers. Charity and benevolence, good deeds highly valued by the Muslim religion, were seen as private and personal en-

20. See the breakdown of the appointments of executors of wills in Agmon 1995, 51, note 43. See also a discussion of the role of women as executors in Ottoman Aleppo in Meriwether 1996, 226–35. Emil Tyan mentions that in the past a special official, *amin al-hukm,* functioned as manager of orphan properties, but by the fifteenth century this office became practically ineffective (1955, 255–56).

deavors. The most important enterprises of charity undertaken by rulers or members of certain communities, mostly in the form of pious endowments (sing. *waqf*), were private (Hoexter 1998; Singer 2002; Ginio 2003).[21] The concept of the state's responsibility for needy people is a modern concept. Mine Ener (2003) shows how in Egypt the state took over the treatment of the poor in the course of the nineteenth and twentieth centuries, a process that resulted in a move from the notion of "the poor" to a greater emphasis on the politics of poverty. Against this background, the operation of the orphan funds in the Ottoman Empire of the late nineteenth century might have indicated a step in a similar direction and affected both the work of the court as state representative and its relations with its clientele.

On 31 December 1851, the Ottoman government issued a decree announcing the foundation of an authority for orphan properties, Emval-ı Eytâm Nezareti, in the Ministry of Şeyhülislâm, specifying its responsibilities and regulating its work (*Düstur* 1, 1: "Eytam Nizamnamesi," 7 Ra 1268/31 XII 1851, 270–75). According to the decree, this authority was to supervise closely the management of properties and money that orphans inherited. It was to be involved in every step, beginning with the death of the parent of a minor who was left an inheritance and ending when the minor heir reached maturity and was legally responsible for his or her own affairs. It specified regulations for inspection of the registration of any inheritance of the minor heirs in the *shari'a* court and the auction of the contents of the inheritance; the management of the orphan's money, kept in a special fund; regulations for borrowing money from the orphan's account in the fund and returning the loan; and finally, the procedure for transferring the assets to orphans who reached maturity.

Some twenty years later another decree was issued, specifying more detailed regulations for the management of the orphan funds throughout the empire and applying them to the mentally disabled and insane, as well as to absent heirs.[22] As in the case of the two sets of instructions issued for recording protocols in the *shari'a* courts (chapter 4), the later instructions for managing orphan funds were more detailed than the earlier ones and deal with practical

21. On the *waqf,* see also chapter 2, note 8, and chapter 7, note 18.

22. *Düstur* 1, 1: "Eytam Sandıklarının Surret İdaresi hakkında Nizamname ve-Zilleri," 16 Za 1286/17 II 1870, 5 Z 1288/15 II 1872, 276–81.

means for implementing the former regulations throughout the empire. For instance, the seventh article of the decree of 1872 instructed that each sub-district center maintain an orphan fund and keep its money in a safe place, together with the Treasury, and that this fund be opened and closed, according to a specific routine, in the presence of certain officials. Each orphan's money was to be kept separately, and the fund would lend that money according to fixed procedures against guarantee and guarantors. Other articles of the decree deal with the regular reports on the funds, periodic checking of their content and management, the allocation of daily maintenance for orphans, charity payments, marriage expenses, the requisite conditions for merchants to borrow money from the funds, restrictions on government officials and departments' access to the money, and other similar issues.

Uncle Khalil and His Late Brother's Orphaned Children

These instructions were apparently not implemented in Jaffa or Haifa before the turn of the century. Until the early 1900s, the orphan fund is not mentioned in records of transactions in orphans' properties and of loans borrowed by relatives and guardians from the money orphans inherited. For example, in the 1876 volume in Jaffa, the judge appointed a man as executor *(wasi)* for his orphaned nephew and two nieces and authorized him to manage their inherited properties. No mention was made in the record of the existence of an orphan fund that according to the instructions should be involved in such a case (JCR, *Hujaj* 47, 25 R 1293/20 V 1876). Years later, in February 1900, another uncle was appointed by the court as executor for his five orphaned nephews and nieces, still without any mention of the orphan fund (JCR, *Hujaj* 83, 14 L 1317/15 II 1900, 2, case 1011).[23]

The first official manager of the orphan fund in Jaffa, Hafiz Hilmi Efendi, was appointed in early 1906. Case records from Haifa indicate that an orphan fund began to operate there only in 1910, when Sheikh Mahmud Efendi

---

23. See also HCR, *Sijill* 1309–12/1892–94, 181, 25 Z 1309/21 VII 1892, case 217; HCR, *Jaridat al-Dabt* 14, 28 R 1319/7 VIII 1901, 7–9, case 5; HCR, *Sijill* 6, 21 M 1323/28 III 1905, 3–4, case 4; HCR, *Sijill* 8, 13 L 1327/28 X 1909, 121–22, case 6. In the last case, a notable's widow had authorized a legal and business representative to sell part of the property she and her minor daughter had inherited. Some of the higher-ranking officials in the Haifa administration were present as witnesses of the proceedings, yet there was no mention of the orphan fund.

al-Khatib was appointed manager of the fund (HCR, *Sijill* 8, 241–43, registration of case 298 of Meclis-i idare, Hayfa, 13 Temmuz 1326/5 VIII 1910). Later on he was replaced by the *başkatib* of the court, Muhyi al-Din al-Mallah (chapter 4). An example of how the latter functioned in this capacity is to be found in a case where Judge Abdülhalim appointed him as executor and legal representative *(wakil shar'i)* for the child of an official in the Department of Forests *(ma'mur al-'orman)* in Acre, who did not return the money he had borrowed from the account of his minor son in the orphan fund. Apparently, the son inherited the money from his mother, for in addition to the fact that his father borrowed his money, the son was not entitled *yatim* (orphan) in the record (HCR, *Sijill* 1331–32/1913–14, 29 Za 1331/29 X 1913, 41–42, case 530). It seems likely that before the orphan funds began to operate, such loans were not always registered in the court to begin with because the court, as the long-term supervisor of orphans' properties, had no direct control over these properties and its involvement depended on application of people to the court voluntarily.

The changes resulting from the operation of the orphan funds are illustrated by the following affair. (See fig. 3 for a presentation of all the data mentioned in this case.) On 2 May 1908, a man named Khalil ibn Muhammad al-Samhudi Abu Sana came to the court in Jaffa. He took it upon himself to pay Maryam bint Ahmad al-Yafi, the mother and custodian of Nazira and Tahir, the orphans of his late brother Ibrahim, 2 kuruş a day for their basic needs. In addition, it was stated in the record that because this sum was not sufficient for the mother's expenses, she would also be paid 1 kuruş more from her children's money, kept in the orphan fund (JCR, *Hujaj* 108, 30 Ra 1326/2 V 1908, 192). Three days passed, and Khalil returned to the court, accompanied by the manager of the orphan fund in Jaffa, Hafiz Hilmi Efendi ibn Sheikh Muhammad Efendi Zu'aytar, a man of medium height and black eyes in his early forties, originally a school teacher from Nablus (SA dos. 3056). Khalil declared that he had borrowed the total sum of 2,290 kuruş and 20 para (half kuruş) from his minor nephew and niece and their sister Farida,[24] which

---

24. Farida was probably more than nine years old, so her mother was not entitled to take care of her, or at least not to receive child support on her behalf, which may explain why her name was not mentioned in the first record dealing with the expenses of her sister and brother. At the same time, if she had not reached legal maturity, her property would still be kept in the orphan fund, and therefore the payment of her uncle's loan was taken from her account as well.

he intended to spend on his own needs. In addition, from them he had bought a volume of the *Mecelle,* the Ottoman civil code prepared during the 1870s for use in the civil and *shari'a* court systems (Findley 1991, 6), for 618 kuruş and 10 para, for which payment was postponed for three years. The judge; the manager of the orphan fund, Hafiz Hilmi Efendi; Khalil himself; and the three

Uncle Khalil's Loans

1. May 1908

	kuruş	para
loan (for 3 years)	2,290	20
interest	618	10
total	2,908	30

2. September 1911

a. Breakdown of debt according to orphans' accounts

orphan's name	kuruş	para
Tahir	1,454	15
Nazira	727	10
Farida	727	10 (sic)

b. Khalil pays back 1,500 kurus.
   This sum covers all the debt to Nazira and part of the debt to Tahir.

c. The rest of the debt turns into a new loan

	kuruş	para
debt	1,408	30
taxes	30	20
total new loan	1,378	10

d. The portion borrowed from Tahir

	kuruş	para
loan (for 7 months)	666	25
interest	35	
total	721	25
monthly payments 7 x	100	10

e. The portion borrowed from Farida

	kuruş	para
loan (for 2 years)	711	25
interest	128	
total	839	25

Interest: ca. 8.3%

Figure 3. Uncle Khalil's loans.

guarantors whom Khalil brought with him, as required by the regulations of the orphan funds, approved the record of the loan with their signatures (JCR, *Hujaj* 108, 3 R 1326/5 V 1908, 193). On the day after Khalil had borrowed the money, he came to the court once again, this time alone, and stated that a couple of days earlier he had volunteered to allocate *(tabarruʿ)* 2 kuruş a day to support his orphaned nephew and niece, but in fact he was unable to commit himself to pay the entire sum. Thus, he reduced the sum he was willing to pay to 60 para (1.5 kuruş) a day, and the sum that the mother of the minor children was therefore entitled to take from their accounts in the orphan fund was raised to a total of 60 para (1.5 instead of only 1 kuruş).

Three years passed. On September 1911, Khalil came to the court again, declaring that a couple of weeks earlier he had returned half of the loan to the orphan fund and requesting a postponement of payment of the other half, which he was as yet unable to return and which was registered as a new loan guaranteed by the same three guarantors. When the story of his first loan was told in the record of the second loan, it became clear that when Khalil had ostensibly bought the *Mecelle* from his nephew and nieces, the purpose of the transaction had been to add interest to the loan, in this case 8.3 percent a year. Hence, the fictitious sale of the book was not even mentioned. Instead, the calculation began by stating the sum of 2,908 kuruş and 30 para (namely, the total sum of the loan and the price of the book) as the sum Khalil had originally borrowed.

This information indicates that alleged sales like this, or the one conducted when Sheikh Husayn lent money to the late Mustafa al-Maridi in Lydda (chapter 3), did not aim at concealing the fact that interest had been charged for the loan. Historically, such transactions had probably been developed in response to the religious reservation about lending money for interest. However, there is no sign in the court records of any effort to hide the fact that money was lent for interest, and in the imperial decrees in the matter (see note 22) it was stated openly as part of the instructions regarding loans from orphans' accounts. Thus, it seems more accurate to interpret alleged sales of this sort as a ceremony that was part of the procedure of lending and borrowing than as some kind of conspiracy against religious concepts.

In Uncle Khalil's case, after the total sum of the first loan was mentioned in the record, the debt was divided into three uneven sums; the sum that Khalil owed to the boy, Tahir, was twice the sum he owed to Tahir's two sisters, Farida and Nazira. The decrees regarding the management of the orphan funds instructed that each and every orphan's account be kept and managed separately, and they did not mention keeping to the rate of two to one for the money borrowed from male and female orphans, a rate that was typical of the *shari'a* inheritance law. Apparently, this rate was a reflection of the legal construction of gender that the management of the orphan funds, functioning as part of the local *shari'a* court, had inadvertently reproduced.[25]

When, according to the record, Khalil was able to pay back 1,500 kuruş of the original loan, this sum covered all his debt to Nazira and part of his debt to Tahir. The rest was listed as two new loans taken from the accounts of Tahir and Farida, after a tax reduction of 30 kuruş and 20 para. Khalil's new debt to Tahir was to be paid monthly in seven equal payments, and for the interest he ostensibly bought from Tahir another copy of the *Mecelle* for the sum of 35 kuruş. His debt to Farida was postponed for two years, and for the interest he bought yet another copy of the *Mecelle,* this time for 128 kuruş. Calculating these sums as interest for the loans show that approximately the same interest was paid for all three loans.[26]

The Troubles of the Fortunate

Uncle Khalil's case illustrates the procedural change at court that resulted from the foundation of the orphan funds and its implications for the court culture and the construction of the family. The court records from the time

25. According to the instructions of the central government, the new Authority for Orphan Properties was part of the Ministry of Şeyhülislâm, like the *shari'a* courts. However, it was not part of the *shari'a* court system, but rather a separate department in the ministry. In practical terms, however, it was seen as one unit, at least as far as officials at the subdistrict level were concerned. Hence, correspondence between the *shari'a* court at Jaffa, the subdistrict office of Jaffa, and the district center in Jerusalem about the appointment of court scribes and the salaries of the court personnel gives the list of the court staff and includes the manager of the orphan fund as one of its employees (AS dos. 3056).

26. The *Mecelle* was sold in other such fictitious transactions as well (see, for example, JCR, *Hujaj* 83, 28 L 1317/1 III 1900, 17, case 1040). When the Ottoman reformers initiated the codification of the *shari'a* civil law in the late 1860s, they probably did not imagine that this pioneering book would end up being used in *shari'a* courts for fictitious transactions. However, my assumption is that the reason for using the *Mecelle* in this way was that it was frequently used in the *shari'a* courts for its original purpose—namely, as a statute—so it was handy whenever loans were registered.

before the orphan funds began to operate include some registrations of loans taken from orphans that the court had approved, requests made by executors to receive court approval for future transactions in the real estate of their protégés in order to support the latter, and some lawsuits by adult orphans against their previous guardians for maltreatment of their properties or for not returning loans taken from their money. These lawsuits, not sustained by court registration of the money borrowed, indicate that loans were sometimes taken without the court's approval and that orphans' relatives, guardians, and executors had easy access to their properties.[27]

Thus, although the court was in charge of inspecting any transaction in orphans' properties, in practice before the orphan funds began to operate and the money inherited by orphans was deposited there, the court's control over guardians and executors was limited, particularly with regard to cash and liquid assets. This meant that orphans almost exclusively depended on their relatives' goodwill for the management of their properties. The introduction of the fund, a new state institution that operated like a deposit bank and actually took over the orphans' money, was an expression par excellence of direct state intrusion into a family sphere. As noted, recorded transactions of money belonging to orphans were rare in the court records before the orphan funds began operating, presumably not because this money remained untouched in the hands of the guardians or other members of their family, but rather because it was fairly easy to use—and frequently abuse—without interference. Furthermore, the few complaints made by orphans against their previous guardians in the matter documented in the records probably indicate a more widespread phenomenon, for family relationships did not always allow weaker family members to bring to justice their stronger counterparts for such abuse or for any form of abuse.[28]

A look between the lines in the records of Khalil's loan offers hints about

27. See, for example, JCR, *Hujaj* 86, 218; HCR, *Jaridat al-Dabt* 13, 5, 6, 71, *Jaridat al-Dabt* 14, 7–9, 14–15.

28. Studies on the formation of modern states in the Middle East (and elsewhere) tend to stress the oppressive nature of the growing state intervention in people's lives typical of modern states (see, for instance, the citations listed in chapter 4, note 36). See also Sonbol 1996b, 11–17. In this case, however, the state's intervention was in defense of a vulnerable group, minor children, against the oppression by their stronger agnates. I owe this observation to Ehud Toledano.

his family and the relations between its members. I suggest that the loan transaction might be read as part of a package deal: Khalil needed money but had no access to his nephew and nieces' money as it was kept in the orphan fund; in return for borrowing their money, he had to oblige himself to pay daily child support to their mother, who apparently was the orphans' executor in addition to being the custodian of two of them. As I pointed out earlier, when orphans did not inherit anything, their support was normally imposed on their close male agnates, usually adult brothers or uncles such as Khalil. The record of such cases would state that the orphans' mother, serving as their custodian, came to court, claimed that her minor children had been left without support or inheritance, and demanded that the court impose this burden on the late father's brothers or other relatives. The judge would check the latter individuals' economic resources and decide on the daily sum to be paid.[29] The principle of imposing the support of orphans on their agnates was not meant to establish equality between providers and dependents, but rather to avoid leaving dependents in dire straits by appointing providers from among the patrilineal family and making them allocate some of their money to their needy relatives.[30]

In this case, however, Khalil volunteered to pay child support to the mother of his late brother's orphaned children, although they had their own money from which the mother was to cover the rest of the their expenses. Thus, by getting part of their expenses paid by their uncle, they may have spent less of their inherited money, which in the meantime was lent to him at interest. Khalil arranged this only three days before he came to the court to ask for the loan, which gives me the impression that the two separate legal proceedings were in fact interconnected. Furthermore, the day after he borrowed the money, he changed his mind and reduced his daily support for the children. Apparently, he was able to do this because the payment had not been imposed on him by the court in the first place. In addition, one of his guarantors for the loan, judging by his name and pedigree, was his brother, another uncle

29. See, for example, the case of a mother of four, three of them still at an age requiring child support, who came to the court in Haifa after her husband died, leaving her nothing; the judge forced her two brothers-in-law to pay for the orphans, each according to his financial ability (HCR, *Jaridat al-Dabt* 5, 29 M 1332/28 XII 1913, 85–86, case 77).

30. See the references in note 11.

of the orphans, who did not share the burden of child support with Khalil, as in other cases of this nature. Thus, this was not the regular case of an uncle obliged by the court to replace his late brother as provider for his needy orphans, but something rather different.

That Khalil agreed to pay child support in order to get the loan is only one plausible interpretation of the circumstances. However, the loan and its financial conditions are less a matter of interpretation. Furthermore, the follow-up by the court and the orphan fund on the payment of the loan over several years seems to have been rather meticulous. Thus, whatever the circumstances behind the records of this case and other such cases, had the orphans' money not been deposited in the fund, most probably Khalil and similar relatives of wealthy orphans would have had much easier access to it, and the orphans' mothers would have been in a worse bargaining position in their capacity as custodians. Granted, it is possible that Maryam, the mother of the orphans in this case, in spite of what seemed an independent and assertive appearance in court, was in fact instructed by some interested male relative of hers—a father, brother, or elder son (presumably, the relative to whose household she moved after the death of her husband)—on how to negotiate with her brother-in-law. In the case record, nothing indicates which one of the interpretations is more plausible. However, the conclusion we can come to about the way the orphan fund affected family relations remains the same either way: the intrusion of the fund into the family domain caused some change in the power relations between providers and dependents in the family, more precisely in the families of the middle and upper classes, in favor of the dependents. Whether Maryam took the initiative to lean on the support of the fund and to bargain for better financial conditions for her minor children (and consequently also for herself), or she was just following the order of her male patron in so doing, her minor children nonetheless benefited from this move and from the existence of the orphan fund. In terms of the notion of the family, the support provided to orphans by the fund meant the reinforcement of the position of the wife and children—namely, the simple-family unit—instead of that of uncles and other agnates, the patrilineal family.

The Weakest Link

The contribution that the orphan fund may have made to the protection of minor children's financial interests highlights a broader question about the situation of minors in the family and the notion of social justice. The Ottoman government's motivation in establishing the authority for the orphans has not been explored in this study. Considering the Emval-ı Eytam Nezareti's constitution as the sole state intrusion into a family sphere before 1917[31] and the economic nature of this authority, the money rather than the orphans' vulnerable position in the family apparently motivated the reformist government. In other words, the reformers were most likely mainly interested in turning the orphans' money into accessible capital for loans and investment and found a procedural way of transferring this particular family responsibility to the state. The reformists achieved two other aims by setting up the funds: orphans' money deposited in the funds was seen as a loan borrowed from the Ottoman Treasury, and hence the Treasury had its own share in that money; the funds also functioned as social security for retired ulama and the support of their dependents after their death.[32]

However, with regard to other aspects of the position of orphans and minors in the family, the motivation for intrusion into the family domain in issues involving the *shariʿa* court was not so strong. It might have been more salient in legal spheres where the reformist state was more dominant to begin with, spheres that had been pulled out of the jurisdiction of the *shariʿa* court system from an early stage of legal reform, such as criminal law, and replaced by codes borrowed from the continental law.[33] Alan Duben and Cem Behar portray a

31. The Ottoman Family Law, which constituted an official reform in family *shariʿa* law, was promulgated as late as 1917. Some specific changes in the conditions of marriage and divorce preceded this reform (1915). See Esposito 1982, 53; Findley 1991, 6; Starr 1992, 38–41.

32. *Düstur* 1, 3: "Infakı muhtacın eytam ve eramili-yi ilmiye nizamnamesi," 12 Ş 1291/24 IX 1874, 552–54; *Düstur* 1, 6: "Infakı eytam ve eramili ricali ilmiye nizamnamesinin tashih olunan on dokuzuncu maddesi," 12 Ş 1306/13 IV 1889, 1179; *Düstur* 1, 6: "Infakı eytam ve eramili ricali ilmiye nizamnamesinin, 12 Şaban 1306 tarihli 19 uncu madde-i musahhahasına müzeyyel fıkra-i nizamiye," 14 S 1307/10 X 1889, 457; *Düstur* 1, 7: "Infakı eytam ve eramili ricali ilmiye nizamnamesine müzeyyel 14 Safer 1307 tarihli fıkrai nizmaiyenin tariki ilmiye tekaüd nizmanamesine zeylen ibkayı mer'iyeti hakkında iradei seniye," 19 B 1319/1 XI 1901, 722. On the support of widows and orphans of deceased judges, see the case of Judge Abu al-Nasr in chapter 3.

33. I hope that the nature of changes in the criminal law and their actual implementation will become clearer with the completion of a timely Ph.D. dissertation on the *nizamiye* court system currently being written by Avi Rubin at Harvard University. See also Miller 2003.

significant change in the notion of children and childhood in late Ottoman Istanbul, mainly among elite and middle-class families. They point to a growing tendency to adopt European values with regard to the position of children in the family and to the investment in their rearing and education (1991, 226–38). Their study undoubtedly represents a landmark in family history in the Middle East not only in that it is one of the first studies in the field, but also in the efforts the authors made to combine their discussion of household structures and formation with findings regarding family values, ties, and emotions.[34]

The foundation of an authority for orphans next to the *shari'a* court was apparently motivated, as noted, first and foremost by the political elite's economic considerations (the interests of the *ilmiye* included). At the same time, in retrospective, the bureaucratic elite's state of mind prepared in this way the ground for reconsidering relations between the state and the family. Although the change that the authority for orphans caused in family relations was restricted by definition to affluent families and took place only in the economic realm, its significance lies in the fact that it indicates a broader transformation that apparently had begun to influence the concept of childhood in middle- and upper-class families in the observed period.[35]

So far the discussion on social justice has emphasized the economic aspect of the operation of the orphan funds. This facet was also predominant in court cases dealing with the relations between providers and dependents in the family in general. Presumably, it was so partly because of what might be called the "legal bias": when a complex of family power relations is brought under the jurisdiction of an official legal institution, it is to be expected that many of these relations, which are also highly emotional, will be transformed, in many cases reduced, into material terms with which the legal formulas can

34. Duben and Behar are aware of the fact that although the people of Istanbul depicted the changes they experienced as a linear passage from "traditional" to "modern," these transformations were in fact much more complicated. Nevertheless, as noted in chapter 2, the authors also tend to describe these changes in binary terms. They attribute, for instance, certain practices to Western culture and hence assume that westernization characterized mainly the literate upper and middle classes. Thus, in their conclusion they find no explanation for the fact that demographic trends sustaining such "westernization" were found among all social levels, including the urban lower class (1991, 246).

35. A broader discussion of these concepts and how they changed in the twentieth century exceeds the scope of the current study.

more easily cope. However, because I am investigating the re-constitution of the family in the sociolegal arena, the question of social justice ought to be discussed beyond the legal bias. What kind of social justice was it? How did it defend the weak? What was considered a violation of the position of weak family members, besides the violation of their financial rights, that would have required the court's intervention? What was required to ensure the well-being of weaker family members?

The legal concept of social justice included aspects that clearly went beyond the economic burden of providing for the family's dependent members. One such aspect can be detected in the principle of the custody of minor children *(hadana)*: in most cases of separation or divorce, custody was given to the mother. This principle was, as I showed earlier, part of the gendered division of labor. The assumption behind it was that minor children would be better off with their mother during their early years. This period was significant for the mother, too, not only because she was able to take care of her small children and nourish her emotional bonds with them, but also because in this way her position in their father's family grew stronger, whether she remained married to him or not, and particularly so if she had male children. In addition, her emotional bonds with her children, her sons in particular, were significant for her future; in the event that she became a divorcée or widow, she often joined the household of one of her adult sons.[36]

That the custody of minor children was a significant right of the mother is demonstrated by the many disputes in court among separated and divorced couples over the age of the children, the criterion for determining which of the two parents would be entitled to custody. But in these disputes the economic significance of being the custodian was always the only aspect documented owing to the legal structure of the records, so that other considerations, if they existed and were raised in court, were silenced by the record. The *shari'a* family law includes, however, a certain limitation on the mother's custody of minor children. A discussion of this restriction and its practical implications for women and children would perhaps bring us closer to some of the emotional layers dealt with in court. In the event that a mother of minor children divorced

---

36. In the case of Muhammad and Qasim, the father and son discussed earlier, Qasim's mother lived with him while his father was married to another wife. This aspect of women's lives is further discussed in chapter 7.

or became a widow and then married a man who was legally defined as a stranger *(ajnabi)*—that is, not from among a certain group of agnates of the children from her previous marriage, their uncle, for instance—she lost her right to custody (Ibn 'Abidin n.d., 2: 633).

Ibn 'Abidin, the influential Damascene mufti of the late eighteenth and early nineteenth centuries, mentions as requisite for a woman to get custody of her minor children (corroborated by Sheikh Khayr al-Din al-Ramli, the important seventeenth-century mufti) that she must be a free *(hurra)*, adult *(baligha)*, sane *('akila)*, trustworthy *(amina)*, and capable *(qadira)* woman who is not married to a stranger *(takhlu min zawj ajnabi)*. He also mentions that the same demands apply to a male custodian, except for the last condition. He explains the term *ajnabi* as *ghayr mahram*, "permissable" or "not forbidden" (n.d., 2: 634)—that is, a man who is not legally prohibited from marriage with his wife's minor children from her previous marriage for reasons of kinship. The prohibitions on marriage constitute a separate chapter in Muslim jurisdiction (2: 276–95). For instance, a man is forbidden to marry the children of his brother. Hence, if a widow marries her brother-in-law, her new husband—the agnate uncle of her children, who is defined *mahram* with regard to her children—would not be considered a stranger, so she would not lose the custody of her children.[37] A case that deals with a woman who married a stranger husband and lost custody of her minor daughter is unraveled in chapter 7. The point relevant to this discussion is that, at face value, the legal notion of the family deemed it more important that minor children live in a household headed by one of their agnates than with their mother if she married a "stranger."

Put this way, the rule of the "stranger husband" may be seen simply as reflecting a set of priorities that identified the minor children's well-being pri-

37. Motzki explains the sometimes contradictory relations between the mother's right to rear her minor children and the father's right of guardianship, which was given preference according to the definition of the "stranger husband" (1996, 131–33, 135). His explanation demonstrates that here, too, the patrilineal family served as the basic framework within which these rights were defined: a closer look at the idea of the children's best interest shows that it was identical to the interest of the children's patrilineal family. About the meaning of this rule in terms of women's divided family loyalties, see Agmon 1998, 484–85. Meriwether inaccurately mentions that one of the conditions required for a woman to retain custody of her children after divorce was that she remain unmarried altogether (1996, 225).

marily with that of the patrilineal family. However, a second glance reveals a somewhat deeper conflict of values behind this rule. Normally, the custody of minor children was lawfully given to their mother, and even in the situation just mentioned, when custody was taken from the mother, another female relative from the mother's family was preferred for this duty, and the father was only the last choice. Thus, custody was considered by the same legal set of values as a feminine, preferably maternal right. Against this background, the rule of taking the right from the mother ought to be seen as a sanction against marriage outside the family. According to the gendered division of labor in the family, a woman required a man's support. As long as she was married to him, this duty was her husband's. The termination of her marriage was a turning point at which she had to become the responsibility of another male: a father, brother, adult son, or a new husband. This was a sensitive juncture, and as I show in chapter 7, it was particularly so for women of modest background or small family—not a rare situation in immigrant towns such as Jaffa and Haifa. At this juncture, the "stranger husband" rule put pressure on a woman who opted for remarriage to avoid marriage to someone outside her ex-husband's family (which sometimes also formed part of her own extended family). However, the rule would have been useless as a sanction had rearing young children by their mother not been conceived of as very significant for the well-being of both the mother and the children. Hence, this rule points to an emotional layer in the legal notion of social justice, wherein the very well-being of both minor children and women is sacrificed in order to reinforce the patrilineal family.

The situation of married young girls also illustrates the precarious well-being of both women and children. Married women in general were entitled to legal support against violence and maltreatment by their husbands and other relatives. Married young girls whose marriage guardian was not their father or grandfather had the right to request cancellation of their marriage as soon as they reached puberty *(khiyar al-bulugh)*, as their consent had not been required at the time of marriage because of their minority. However, in court, judges were not in a hurry to implement these rules. As far as this situation is documented in the records, my impression is that wives' claims against domestic violence did not get in-court treatment as consistently as did their claims against violation of their financial rights.

A domestic dispute brought to the Jaffa court and discussed more fully in chapter 6 reveals a complicated marital relationship. The wife, Khadaja Abu

Radwan, who had run away from her husband, Hasan al-Basumi, demanded her financial rights and a conjugal dwelling separate from his family household. Her husband denied her demands and allegations and demanded that she be forced to obey him *(ta'a)*. In the course of the deliberations, it was mentioned incidentally that she had been a minor when the marriage took place a couple of years earlier. Violence and neglect by the husband and his family were the reasons her attorney gave for the fact that she had left his house and demanded a separate conjugal dwelling. The case was not decided in court. However, the deliberations tended to be systematic as far as her financial rights and conjugal dwelling were concerned, and basically her version in this regard was accepted, whereas her claims about violence were dealt with inconsistently: they were raised and recorded every so often, but the judge was reluctant to turn them into issues requiring testimony. He apparently was in favor of forcing the girl to return to her husband as soon as a conjugal dwelling was ready, without insisting on a thorough inquiry into the issue of violence and maltreatment (JCR, *Hujaj* 152, 2 Za 1331–5 C 1332/3 XI 1913–1 V 1914, 3–4, 9, 14, 29, 251, 254, 257, 275, case 2).

In Haifa, in a clear case of resisting marriage on reaching puberty, the girl, Tamam—an orphan whose guardian, her uncle, had married her off while she was still a minor—demanded the cancellation of her marriage. According to her claim, she had been through all the torments of hell in her marriage to an impotent man who had treated her with cruelty, did not pay her dower, and had tried to kill her after not being able to have intercourse with her, causing her to run away and wait until she finally menstruated and attained puberty. Then she came to court to demand the cancellation of her marriage (*faskh al-nikah*). The husband claimed that she had not been a minor when the marriage took place, that he had paid the dower in kind, that she had never entered his house, and therefore that the marriage had not been consummated (not because of his disability).[38] The burden of proof was imposed on him, and he was instructed to prove that she had not been a minor at the time of the marriage and that she had given her consent. He provided witnesses, but they failed to testify on these issues. However, Tamam was not asked to take an oath on her version, a lawful procedure in a legal scenario of this sort, which, as I demonstrated earlier, would have guaranteed an immediate decision in her

---

38. A minor's unconsummated marriage was in itself legal justification for annulment.

favor.[39] Rather, she was requested to prove her claim that she only recently had reached puberty. Only after she provided two witnesses, one of them a sheikh who testified that a couple of days before the trial Tamam had showed him the blood of her first menstruation in the presence of his mother, the judge eventually announced that her marriage was null and void.[40]

In her discussion on women as executors for children in early-modern Aleppo, Margaret Meriwether (1996) describes the development of the history of children in the Middle East. She points to the contribution of Avner Giladi's study *Children of Islam: Concepts of Childhood in Medieval Muslim Society* (1992) to our knowledge about the large body of medieval Islamic literature that deals with children, and she shows that childhood was conceived of as a special period in human life. "How these views of children and childhood reflected and influenced the realities of children's lives is the next step toward a history of childhood in the Middle East," continues Meriwether (1996, 222). Achievement of this history entails drawing on empirical sources that relate to a specific time and place. In the situation under discussion, in which the prevailing notion of social justice reinforced the patrilineal family and the court sustained this prioritization, children, especially female children, constituted the weakest link.[41]

39. Procedurally, the demand that she take an oath should have been initiated by her adversary after he failed to bring proof. See the earlier discussion of Muhammad and Husun's case. However, we may recall that in Sheikh Husayn's lawsuit (chapter 3), at the end of the recording procedure he took an oath as to the truthfulness of his claim without being requested to do so by the defendants.

40. HCR, *Jaridat al-Dabt* 13, M 1318/V 1900, 16–17, 19, 60. The right of a girl married off while still a minor to cancel her marriage was valid only immediately after she reached puberty. If the girl did not demand the cancellation then, she would lose the right. Judging by this record, it seems that Tamam, or someone who guided her, was well informed about these conditions. About legal opinions on the marriage of minor girls and on the practice itself, see Motzki 1996, 129–30.

41. A major aspect of this situation was the killing of women and girls by their own male relatives for what was entitled "violation of the honor of the family," a deep-rooted tradition of which the *shari'a* law officially disapproved. Historians have been able to show that the court records include a considerable number of cases of ostensibly accidental deaths of women and young girls; by documenting the deaths in this way, the court in fact allowed the continuation of this norm. See, for example, Ze'evi 1996, 177–78. This topic is not discussed here because, after the legal reforms, criminal offenses were deliberated according to a new penal code in the

The superiority of the patrilineal family determined this structure of power relations. The *shariʿa* court system, as the gatekeeper to this structure, implemented and reproduced it. By virtue of both their class and their gender affiliations, the court personnel had no reason to question this set of values and indeed maintained social order along these lines. This order of things did not allocate much power to women and children to begin with. However, women could develop strategies to cope with their inherent inferiority, employing whatever means the process of their socialization afforded them and—most important—asserting their basic legal right to be heard in court (Agmon 1998), whereas children by virtue of their sociolegal position were deprived of both options. By focusing on the material aspect of dependents' well-being, the court, while serving as defender of this group, nonetheless contributed to silencing further the voices of children whose well-being was so vulnerable and hence so difficult to reduce to material values. The state's interference in defense of propertied orphans reinforced the aspect of class differences in this situation of inferiority based on age and gender.

The combination of notions of class, age, and gender emphasizes the question of the links between the formation of the modern Ottoman state and the emergence and reinforcement of the middle class. When assessing the interaction between the court and its clientele from this perspective, we need to bear in mind that both the reformists in Istanbul and the court personnel at all provincial levels constituted "the state." Thus, both the court's notion of social justice, which reinforced the patrilineal family, and its implementation of state-mandated institutions that defended orphans, which undermined the patrilineal family, came from the same source, an agent of the state. The contradiction between two notions of the family, the simple conjugal family and

---

niẓamiye courts. Thus, such murders were no longer reported in *shariʿa* court records, apparently not even as accidents. Sonbol (1996c) claims that, in spite of legal reform and legislation that was meant to reduce violence against women in Egypt, women became more vulnerable in the modern period. These questions are currently being further explored by Liat Kozma at New York University. Sonbol (1996a) also points to a "dark side" of modern legislation that sets a minimum age of marriage in defense of minors, especially girls: expansion of the period during which youngsters are controlled by guardians paves the way for the latter's abuse of their power. As to the position of children in general, they historically were and still are today the weakest link in many societies, including some in which they are given primary importance on the surface. See, for example, Coontz 1992, 4–5.

the patrilineal, can also be understood as a reflection of the changing power base in the Ottoman elite, a process in which the ulama, who constituted the personnel of the *shariʿa* court system, were ultimately losing power.

At the same time, this contradiction, which most probably was not discerned at the time as a contradiction because of the restricted form of intervention by the orphan funds, allows us to watch a mechanism of change at work: as I showed earlier, because of the way the orphan fund was structured, state intervention in family matters via this apparatus improved the position of minor children only in those families that owned enough property and were able to leave an inheritance, and it thus contributed to the reinforcement of the simple-family structure only in these strata. In this way, the link between the simple-family structure and the social classes that made a fortune during the economic growth in the port cities was developed, and, at the same time, mutual interests connected these social strata to the reformed state. It should be noted, however, that, as shown by the loan to Uncle Khalil, the way in which the personnel of the court and orphan fund implemented the instructions regarding borrowing money from orphans reproduced the legal notion of gender and family in the new institution. The instructions enhanced a notion that stressed the individual instead of the family by maintaining an account for each orphan, from which money was to be borrowed and to which it was to be paid back, regardless of accounts of other orphans in the same family. However, the clerks of the court and the orphan fund in Jaffa conducted Khalil's loan as a family matter, and the orphans' accounts were treated as forming a group of heirs according to Muslim inheritance law. Thus, although the orphan funds may have contributed to changing the construction of the family among the affluent strata, some of the deep-rooted legal notions of family nevertheless continued to shape this new construction.

In the meantime, in the construction of the family as it related to poor people of the urban lower-middle and lower levels who attended the court, the prevailing notions of family and social justice remained intact, and, as I illustrated in chapter 4, maybe became even more prominent, reinforcing the structure of the patrilineal family. Thus, not only was the map of family notions in society gradually changing, but the social stratification and the dividing lines between lower and the middle classes were also being transformed and redefined. In the following chapters, I explore other aspects of this development as it took place inside as well as outside the court.

6

Attorneys and the Justice of the Qadi

The Judge's Discretion

THE EMERGENCE of the professional attorney *(wakil da'awi)* in the Jaffa and Haifa *shari'a* courts in the late nineteenth century had a significant impact on their legal culture. Legal representatives *(wukala, sing. wakil)* had appeared in *shari'a* courts for centuries. They were laymen who were not engaged in advocacy and did not charge their clients.[1] This type of representation was compatible with the *shari'a* court's legal culture in spite of all the changes the court had gone through during its long history and the differences between the wide range of local cultures of which it was part. The new professional attorney—who apparently emerged as a result of the late-nineteenth-century innovations in the judicial system, in particular the foundation of the *nizamiye* courts—did not replace the prevailing lay representative, but rather coexisted with him.[2] A practicing advocate, he was integrated into the routine of the *shari'a* court, which means that the concept of advocacy, although foreign to the *shari'a* court legal culture, did not contradict it. Furthermore, a study of interactions between the attorneys and the judge in court indicates that the attorneys, although challenging the judge's professional exclusivity, did not essentially change the pattern of his work and the ways he employed legal dis-

---

1. Jennings 1975; El-Nahal 1979, 25–26, 29, 36, 48, 50; Gerber 1988, 204–6; Marcus 1989, 107; İnalcık 1991, 5. On women and the changes in the concept of legal representation, see also Agmon 1995, 56–79.

2. For the circumstances of the foundation of the Bar Association in Istanbul, see Özman 2000, 331–33.

cretion. The attorneys' activity in court led mainly to an emphasis on social differentiation between the litigants and a reinforcing of the procedural aspects in the prevailing legal culture. At the same time, their contribution highlighted elements of social justice resulting from the judges' use of legal discretion. From this point of view, then, the following discussion on professional attorneys in the *shariʿa* court also offers a refutation of the Weberian notion of "kadi-justice" and other similar concepts.

Weber argued that in legal systems such as the *shariʿa* court, forming part of patrimonial societies, the judge used his legal discretion arbitrarily because he had to reach decisions without any clear legal frame of reference. The implementation of Muslim law—divine, comprehensive, and above any legislative power—had necessitated substantial interpretation. Its jurisprudence was never formulated in legal codes, and its interpretations in the form of legal opinions (sing. *fatwa*) are not structured as legal precedents on which the judge could have relied. The court work was based on a single judge. His relations with the mufti, whose duty was to interpret Muslim jurisprudence by addressing legal questions, were loosely defined. The legal procedure did not require the judges to specify reasons for their decisions, while at the same time they worked in a cultural environment in which local traditions and customary laws prevailed side by side with the *shariʿa* law. Furthermore, in the Ottoman Empire judges were state employees who also applied laws and regulations promulgated by the rulers *(kanun)*. Against this background, Weber characterized the discretion of the *shariʿa* judge as irrational, and the term that he used in this context, "kadi-justice," became a synonym for traditional but not exclusively Muslim court systems.[3]

Some of the scholarly works on legal history have reinforced this image of the *shariʿa* judge as lacking legal guidance and hence reaching arbitrary decisions. The nature of Muslim jurisprudence has attracted scholarly attention for many years. The conservative approach in legal history claimed that the way to legal interpretation *(ijtihad)* had been blocked at a relatively early stage in Muslim history, preventing judicial innovation. This approach depicted the Muslim legal system as based on a separation between theory and practice:

3. Weber 1968, 3, 976–78 (the term *kadi-justice* was borrowed by Weber from Richard Schmidt, his colleague at Freiburg University); Turner 1974, 107–21. On the status of local customs in Muslim jurisprudence, see Hallaq 2002.

while theory stagnated, a variety of practical solutions were adopted to fit a changing reality. This description might well support the conclusion that the judge made arbitrary legal decisions under such circumstances. However, paradoxically, the revisionist approach to the prevention of *ijtihad* did not improve the image of the judge. The critique of the conservative notion of juridical stagnation argues that the chain of innovative jurists (muftis) had actually never been broken. This claim focuses on uncovering innovative aspects in these jurists' work and its continuity—in other words, on reinforcing the significant role influential muftis played in the legal system.[4]

The accepted and basically fair characterization of Muslim jurisprudence as one predominated by jurists has nevertheless somewhat overlooked the judge's contribution to the continuity of the legal system and the significant role played by the court under his lead in mediating between Muslim societies and the development of Muslim jurisprudence.[5] The description of the judge as poorly educated, of a lower moral standard, and liable to be influenced by local notables fails to explain how this court system remained relatively stable over such a long period and over a vast and diversified region (Messick 1993, 143–45; see also Powers 1994). The entitling of the *shari'a* court as a *"qadi* court" in many scholarly works points to a logical flaw that may have sustained the imbalanced evaluation of the judge's function in the Muslim legal literary tradition, an evaluation made without sufficient empirical research. My hypothesis is that scholars, even if they rejected the notion of "kadi-justice" in their own description of the *shari'a* court, were misled into expecting to find prominent judges who had left a personal mark on the judicial system because they noticed that after a long history of institutionalization, this court was still headed by a single judge. Disappointed at not finding such notable figures, they overlooked the fact that under the prevailing concepts of judge and court, they were looking in the wrong places and reaching incorrect conclusions.

A close reading of a substantial number of court case records and an analysis of their production process enable us to trace the mark left by a judge

4. For the fundamental critique of the conservative approach to Muslim jurisprudence, see Hallaq 1984. Brinkley Messick, in his thought-provoking legal anthropological study of Yemen since the late Ottoman period, presents the development of the poor reputation of the judge's position in Muslim legal literature (1993, 142–46).

5. See, for example, Messick 1986, 1993, 146–51.

not so much as an individual, but rather as a figure representing the concept of arbitration (and sometimes mediation). The legal culture of the *shari'a* court, in particular the position of the judge as the sole legal expert with the exclusive authority to make legal decisions in the court arena, shaped this essential feature of arbitration. As arbitrator, the judge sorted out feasible solutions for people's conflicting interests, solutions for which the *shari'a* law in its broader sense constituted a binding conceptual framework. The judge was positioned at the crossroads of an ongoing encounter among *shari'a* law as an abstraction that required constant concretization, the Ottoman rulers' instructions, local traditions, and local societies' changing needs. He faced the heavy task of combining and mediating between these varied features and cultural resources. Although he shared this responsibility with several assistants and advisors, on the court scene he was the sole decision maker, so that implicit rather than explicit arbitration was the strategy he employed in dealing with this complicated task.

When I first read the court records, I was puzzled by the position and intentions of judges who ignored contradictions and white lies in litigants' versions. One might easily conclude that no principle at all, but rather arbitrary judgment, was behind their decisions. However, the records' laconic style and the lack of recorded legal reasoning amplified my initial feeling that some organizing principle did prevail in the court, and because that principle was clear to all in the courtroom, it was not explicitly registered. This conclusion motivated me to look further for an explanation. From an early stage when I began to read these records, for instance, it became obvious to me that an element of bargaining played a major role in the give-and-take at court, and I integrated this understanding in my 1995 analysis of women in court.[6] However, it was the difference between recorded deliberations in which professional attorneys were involved and those cases in which the litigants appeared independently that provided me with the missing key to understanding the judge's performance in a sociolegal context.

6. The social bargaining highlighted in Lawrence Rosen's analysis, in spite of being strongly criticized for the neo-Weberian concept it reinforces, nevertheless seems to offer a viable explanation for the situation as recorded in the court records. See Rosen 1989, 11–19; Gerber 1994, 10–12, 17–18, 25–42; Agmon 1995, 79–94; Shahar 2000b, 23–24. On the judge as mediator, see also Peirce 2003 and Ergene 2004.

The Emergence of Professional Attorneys

The attorneys, whose involvement in the legal arena became widespread in the course of the Tanzimat, presented a challenge to the judge, who up to this point was used to enjoying professional exclusivity in the courtroom. This challenge looked like a twist in the judge's arbitration role: he now had to sanction one of two opposed versions presented by competing lawyers. This shift from arbitration to judgment may be deemed a linear passage from a traditional court to a modern court. According to this logic, arbitration is conceived of as a traditional approach sustaining the concept of "kadi-justice," wherein the judge is more after sorting out a compromise between disputed parties and less concerned to find out who might have broken the law and decide the case accordingly. Judgment, in contrast, is modern in its focus on revealing the truth about the disputed parties' versions in legal terms and therefore on reaching decisions, an approach that requires the lawyers' professional knowledge and identifies it with "the truth."

However, a closer look at the interaction between the judge and the attorneys offers a different perspective on this passage to modernity that challenges both the traditional versus modern dichotomy and the rational versus arbitrary dichotomy. From this perspective, the confrontation between the attorney's professional skills and the judge's attitude toward his new colleagues produced a situation in which the judge controlled both arbitration and judgment in the *shari'a* court, with the professional attorney virtually becoming a kind of court staff member.

Readers of court records from various places and periods are familiar with the earlier figure of the legal representative *(wakil)*, who continued to function in court during and after the Tanzimat. Meanwhile, the professional attorney *(wakil da'awi)* appeared on the legal scene[7] while the *wakil*, a layman who was assigned literally to replace a litigant in court, had no other role, and he fulfilled this one voluntarily (Jennings 1979).[8] This representative was frequently a relative of the absent litigant, particularly when the latter was a woman. This concept of legal representation is clearly illustrated by cases in which the de-

---

7. See note 34 in chapter 4.

8. The office of *wakil* was open in principle to men and women, Muslim and non-Muslim alike. In practice, however, it became a male-dominated office. I never came across women who served as legal representatives, nor did I read about such cases in other studies. See also note 1.

fendant did not show up, and the court assigned an ad hoc representative *(wakil musakhkhar)* to replace the absentee in court. In the period under discussion, it was usually one of the professional attorneys whom the judge assigned for this task, yet another indication of the attorneys' involvement in the work of the court. However, the ad hoc representative's function in court was similar to that of the old *wakil* even though the person assigned to fulfill the task was a professional attorney: he only replaced the absent litigant, but did not make any use of his legal knowledge to serve the litigant's best interests.[9] However, when the same person functioned as *wakil da'awi,* he worked for a fee and displayed his legal knowledge, serving the clients' interests to the best of his ability. Thus, the professional attorneys held a different legal position than that of the old representatives and fulfilled legal requirements beyond those expected of their lay colleagues.

The new profession was never officially introduced into the *shari'a* court system, but rather gradually penetrated from the *nizamiye* court system. In the *Mecelle,* the code prepared during the 1870s for the civil and *shari'a* courts, the definition of *legal representative* was compatible to that of the lay *wakil* (*Mecelle,* Article 1458), probably because the *Mecelle* consisted of the *shari'a* civil and procedural laws codified as a statute. The new profession of attorney was officially introduced into the *nizamiye* courts via administrative regulations issued in 1876, initially for implementation only in Istanbul. In the same year, the *Mecelle* committee accomplished its work and submitted the new code. A year later the instructions regarding the work of professional attorneys in *nizamiye* courts became applicable to the rest of the empire (Özman 2000, 328). More regulations regarding legal practice in the *nizamiye* courts and the professional education required of attorneys were issued in 1879. Attorneys in the *nizamiye* courts were required to have a legal education. However, the Ottoman law school was not fully developed at the time; there was no professional inspection of practicing attorneys, and most of the steps toward systematic professionalization of legal advocacy were initiated only after 1908.[10]

The attorneys who represented litigants in the *shari'a* courts of Jaffa and

---

9. See chapter 7 for the case of Hasan, who sued his ex-wife Hind and demanded custody of their minor daughter; Hind did not show up to court and was represented by an ad hoc representative appointed by the court, Sheikh Muhammad al-Salah, who normally functioned as a professional attorney.

10. Reid 1981, 75–80, 83–84; Özman 2000, 328–29; see also notes 11 and 13.

Haifa were clearly familiar with the law, although I have no direct evidence regarding their education. In terms of ethnic and religious backgrounds, they formed as diversified a group as the urban communities in which they lived, including Arab and Turkish Muslims as well as Jews and Christians of different sects, which meant that their legal education was probably also acquired at a variety of schools.[11] They were not officially part of the court personnel, but were hired privately by litigants, yet a central core of attorneys represented most litigants in each city and are usually mentioned in the records as being "from among the *wukala da'awi* in Haifa/Jaffa." They spent a substantial amount of time at court and became involved in legal procedures other than the legal representation of their clients. For example, as I mentioned earlier, the judge would sometimes assign one of them to represent absent litigants as *wakil musakhkhar* or ask them to confirm the validity of a recorded procedure by signing its protocol as notaries *(shuhud al-hal)* or to serve in a special delegation of experts for the court *(ahl al-Khibra)*.[12] At a certain point during their legal career, some served as scribes or legal assistants at court. Others began their career as attorneys and were appointed later to legal state positions, such as *qadi* or mufti.[13] Thus, although they were private lawyers and were hired and paid by the people who required their legal services, they also became part and parcel of the court operation. Their profession served as a focal point for a variety of positions that, although not state positions, were also open to educated jurists, of whom many were members of the established ulama families.

11. Only as late as 1915 did the Ottoman authorities try to gain control over the profession of advocacy in *shari'a* courts by limiting it to law school graduates with at least five years of practice. See Yazbak 1998, 52.

12. See, for example, the following records: HCR, *Jaridat al-Dabt* 5, 24 S 1332/22 I 1914, 108, case 81; 10 Ra 1332/6 II 1914,123, case 86; 10 Ra 1332/6 II 1914, 129, case 89. And JCR, *Hujaj* 83, 7 Z 1317/8 IV 1900, 64–65, case 1113. See also the data about some of the attorneys in this group in Agmon 1995, 56–60.

13. One *shari'a* judge from Aleppo began his career as *wakil da'awi* after acquiring a legal education in a *madrasa* (his father was a *madrasa* teacher too) and was then appointed as *shari'a* judge and to other legal positions. In 1913, at the age of thirty-seven, he took the exams of the College for Shari'a Judges in Istanbul, apparently following the regulations that forced judges to do so (Albyrak 1996, 1: 131). Sheikh Muhammad Tawfiq al-Dajani, mufti of Jaffa since 1908, practiced law as a *wakil da'awi* at the court of Jaffa at the turn of the century (JCR, *Hujaj* 83, 4 Za 1317/6 III 1900, 23–24, case 1048) before being appointed to succeed his cousin as mufti following the latter's death in 1908 (SA dos. 3102).

The attorneys' clients, usually affluent, tended to be involved in property cases more than in questions of personal status.[14] They often gave the lawyers a general power of attorney to represent them in any legal instance and with regard to any situation that might emerge, whether they were plaintiffs or defendants. It is plausible that such comprehensive powers of attorney, given by litigants to professional attorneys in cases deliberated in the *nizamiye* court system, opened the way to professional representation in the *shariʿa* court system as well, for, as I mentioned earlier, litigants often moved between the two systems. The power of attorney also frequently included representation of clients in economic transactions, particularly with regard to real estate.[15] In court, the attorneys used their legal skills intensively to serve their clients' best interests: they raised procedural claims to gain more time or to change the course of the trial for their clients' benefit; they argued with their rival colleagues; they advised the judge how he should pursue the case; and they raised new claims every so often in the course of the trial. The outcome was that cases in which they took part were longer and legally more complicated and the verdicts less predictable.[16]

14. This situation resulted both from the socioeconomic structure of the population in which the propertied families (who were also the ones who tended to hire attorneys) were fewer than the families with modest means and from upper-class families' tendency to avoid bringing their domestic disputes to the court. See Agmon 1995, 67–71, 157–65.

15. See data about the various types of power of attorney in Agmon 1995, 57. As to the flexibility of the division of labor between the civil and the *shariʿa* courts, the *shariʿa* court records under observation include many civil cases and evidence of cases that had moved between the two legal instances. For example, in a lawsuit presented at the *shariʿa* court of Haifa in early 1889, the plaintiff, Abraham Cohen, a Jew from Haifa holding French citizenship, sued Sheikh ʿAli Abu al-Hijja, from the neighboring village ʿAyn Khud, to whom he had leased out five fields near the village of Ijzim (which Sheikh ʿAli in turn leased out to a woman from Ijzim). Cohen claimed that Sheikh ʿAli had failed to meet the conditions of their contract. In his response, Sheikh ʿAli mentioned that this lawsuit had been deliberated a year earlier in the civil court *(al-mahkama al-bidaʾiyya),* and he presented a document with the decision reached at that court. HCR, *Sijill* 1305–1309/1888–92, 1 Ca 1306/3 I 1889, 69–70, case 189.

16. See, for instance, Amina and Salim's case in chapter 4. This case was settled after only four court sessions because the parties reached an agreement outside the courtroom. Many other cases in which professional attorneys were involved, however, took many more sessions and a longer time, as I demonstrate later in this chapter.

The Judge and the Attorneys

In Husun and Muhammad's case (chapter 5), the judge conducted the trial single-handedly and within two court sessions settled the dispute, a complex of claims and counterclaims, in Husun's favor. By using his discretion to place the burden of proof on Muhammad, who was unable to substantiate his version, the judge gave Husun the opportunity to prove hers merely by swearing to the truth of her claims. In many other cases, however, the judge sought legal and other assistance from various experts. He had at his disposal a team of legal and technical experts whom he deployed according to the requirements of specific cases. Sometimes he would seek the mufti's advice on juridical questions as a means to exclude a testimony or to invalidate a contract signed out of court, thereby gaining support from another professional jurist in guiding disputes toward solution.[17]

Another kind of expert was the court deputy, usually one of the scribes or legal assistants, whom the judge would send to examine and report back on issues located outside the courtroom, such as a conjugal dwelling *(maskan shar'i)* or the proximity of a certain window to the neighboring house. The judge would also request experts in various fields to share their professional experience in connection with a matter under dispute, such as the division of common property or the agrarian status of certain real estate. When litigants reached a compromise while their case was still under deliberation, the judge would legalize and adopt the agreement. The judge used all these tools, together with the procedural tools, to achieve feasible and socially balanced solutions. Feasible solutions, then, were at the heart of the process, which involved a variety of procedures and experts and was presided over, but not arbitrarily so, by the judge. The professional attorney, as I demonstrate in the following case, gave this pattern of conduct a fresh twist.

This case was, in fact, two cases, both dealing with the same domestic dispute simultaneously over a period of six months during 1913–14. Their records end with only a partial decision.[18] In both cases, the wife, Khadaja Abu

17. See the Abu Basha case described later in this chapter.

18. JCR, *Hujaj* 152, 2 Za 1331–5 C 1332/3 XI 1913–1 V 1914, 3–4, 9, 14, 29, 251, 254, 257, 275, case 2; 2 Za 1331–10 C 1332/3 XI 1913–6 V 1914, 5–7, case 3. These records demonstrate the registration practice developed by the Jaffa court scribes when implementing the instruc-

Radwan from Jaffa, sued her husband, Hasan al-Basumi from Ramla. Neither Khadaja nor Hasan appeared in the Jaffa court, each being represented by an attorney. Both attorneys were members of the established Dajani family in Jaffa: Sheikh Muhammad ʿAli Efendi ibn Sheikh Muhammad Abu al-Suʿud al-Dajani represented Khadaja, the plaintiff; and Sheikh Mustafa Efendi ibn Sayyid Hasan ibn Sheikh Salim al-Dajani represented Hasan, the defendant. As mentioned in chapter 3, many positions in the Jaffa legal system, including muftis, court scribes, and attorneys, were held by members of the Dajani family. For instance, the mufti at the time of the trial, Sheikh Muhammad Tawfiq, was a cousin of Sheikh Mustafa, Hasan's attorney. He had been appointed mufti five years earlier following the death of the former mufti, another cousin of both Mustafa and Sheikh Tawfiq. Khadaja's attorney, Sheikh Muhammad ʿAli Efendi al-Dajani, was the brother of Ahmad Raghib Efendi, the *başkatib* of the court. Among his clients were members of notable families, such as the Husayni family of Jerusalem.

The judge during that period was Mehmet Sadık Efendi, a man in his mid-fifties, of medium height and with blue-gray eyes, from Alaʿiyye in the district of Antalya. He was an experienced judge who had acquired his religious and legal education first in his hometown and then in the Süleymaniye mosque in Istanbul. After passing the College for Shariʿa Judges exams in his early thirties, he was appointed and served on seven different courts throughout Anatolia, the Balkans, and Libya, before arriving in Jaffa in 1911. In 1913, before he had completed his service in Jaffa, the regulation restricting judges' term of service to two years was cancelled, and he stayed on there. In October 1915, he

---

tions about protocols (chapter 4): cases 2 and 3 were brought before the judge one after the other on the same day. To each record the scribe allocated two pages in the volume of protocols in advance. When the scribe wrote down the protocol of case 2, he first filled the two pages (pp. 3–4). The records of two court sessions and part of the third were written on these two pages before the scribe ran out of space. He was in the middle of a sentence when he reached page 5, a page filled by the record of case 3, so he continued the record of case 2 on several other pages throughout the volume. Most of these pages were originally allocated to cases that were cancelled or to cases that turned out to be much shorter than the space reserved for them. Case 3 included a smaller number of sessions and required much less space than case 2. In addition, the following case (for which page 7 was reserved) was cancelled; three lines for this case were recorded and then erased, and the scribe was able to register the entire record of case 3 consecutively on these three pages.

was dismissed following a complaint that related to his previous term of judgeship in Bafra (near the Black Sea). Two years later he died at the age of fifty-eight (SA dos. 1095; *İlmiye Salnamesi,* 275). Khadaja and Hasan's case was brought up at court when he had already served for more than two years in Jaffa, so he was probably already familiar with the local community and local court culture. He seems to have conducted the deliberations attentively, listening to the attorneys who tried to influence him, considering their demands, and making his own decisions as to how to pursue the case: at each stage, after the record specified the attorneys' disputed views or after a comment by one of the attorneys determining the prevailing legal situation, the judge's decision regarding the next stage in the trial was registered, followed by his signature. The record of the two cases stopped before he reached his final decision, so his role can be followed only up to that point. Yet a close look at the records reveals some interesting exchanges between the judge and the two attorneys, enabling a better understanding of the interaction between them.

Dajani versus Dajani

This convoluted dispute offers a sense of the court dynamics in cases in which attorneys were involved. A short summary of the story presents the basic complications: Hasan had married Khadaja one and one-half years prior to the lawsuits. Khadaja was apparently very young; according to her attorney, she was a minor at the time. Hasan committed himself to pay her 20 LF prompt dower and provide furniture and household items for her use in their conjugal dwelling. According to Khadaja's version, he paid 18 LF and still owed her 2 LF and the furniture. He brought her to his house in Ramla, which she had to share with his mother. The latter treated her badly, hit and injured her. He was not at home most of the time and when he was, he also hit her. Finally, Khadaja left her husband's house and returned to her father's house in Jaffa, leaving behind her entire wardrobe. Khadaja's attorney mentioned all these details at one point or another in the course of the deliberations, but not in a narrative structure. Accordingly he demanded that Hasan pay his debts, arrange a conjugal dwelling for Khadaja in Jaffa, return her clothes, and in the meantime pay her maintenance. Hasan's attorney basically denied all these claims and demanded that Khadaja be forced to return to his house or else be considered a rebellious wife. The judge sent one of the scribes to check Hasan's house, who found it unsuitable as a conjugal dwelling. Hasan was obliged to make the necessary arrangements. He followed the order and improved his house while objecting to Khadaja's demand that he arrange a conjugal dwelling in Jaffa and pay her maintenance. Hasan was forced to pay Khadaja the 2 LF she demanded from the prompt dower and 1 beşlik a day in maintenance. The rest of the issues remained open as the deliberations in Khadaja's two lawsuits against Hasan stopped suddenly.

In the first and more complicated case record, Muhammad ʿAli Efendi al-Dajani, Khadaja's attorney, told the court that about one and one-half years earlier his client had married the defendant, Hasan. According to their marriage contract, Hasan had to pay Khadaja a dower of 20 LF at the time of the marriage and another 10 LF later on (as deferred dower). In addition to the prompt dower, he committed himself to giving her furniture—a bureau and a mirror, mattresses, blankets, pillows—to the total value of 12.5 LF.[19] He paid her 18 out of the 20 LF agreed on, and the marriage was consummated while she was still a virgin. She asked him to pay the remaining 2 LF of the prompt dower, but he unlawfully refused. Sheikh Muhamad ʿAli requested that the court force Hasan to pay his debt and, in the meantime, to pay maintenance.

Sheikh Mustafa, Hasan's attorney, responded to the claim by saying that as soon as the plaintiff could prove her version, his client would be willing to pay the rest of the dower and meet the additional conditions. Meanwhile, he requested that the court either force Khadaja to return to live with her husband (muʿashara) or declare her a disobedient wife (nashiz). He also denied the plaintiff's attorney's claim concerning the dower (in spite of what he had said about his client's willingness to pay provided that Khadaja proved her claim).

Sheikh Muhammad ʿAli requested that the defendant, Hasan, clarify whether he had married Khadaja on the condition that he would pay the above dower, whether he had had intercourse with her, and what portion of the dower he had paid at the time of the marriage. Sheikh Mustafa confirmed that the marriage and the sexual relations had indeed taken place. He claimed,

19. These items apparently constituted the *jihaz*, household items that the groom supplied for use in the couple's household. Legally, they belonged to the bride, and in case of temporary separation or termination of the marriage she was entitled to them. The term *jihaz*, however, was not mentioned in the record. See chapter 4 for Amina and Salim's case, in which Amina also demanded furniture and household items that probably constituted her *jihaz*. About the value of the LF and other coins, see chapter 4, "A Note on Money and Daily Conditions."

however, that the entire dower was paid to Khadaja and requested postponement of the deliberations till the following day.

At the next session, which took place more than two weeks later, he repeated his claim that Hasan had paid the entire prompt dower and had fulfilled the additional conditions (with regard to the furniture). Khadaja's attorney said that his colleague in fact had acknowledged the disputed matter, and therefore he should prove the alleged payment. In other words, he advised Judge Sadık that because his colleague's response ought to be considered a counterclaim, the judge should require him to prove his claim. This was also the judge's understanding of the situation because he ordered Hasan's attorney to bring witnesses to the next court session, five days later. At the beginning of that session, Hasan's attorney named ten witnesses. Two of them confirmed Hasan's version of the marriage, the sums involved in the dower, the payment of the entire amount, and the additional conditions.

At this stage, the judge would normally have conducted the procedure of checking the witnesses' credibility *(tazkiya)*. In this case, however, when the deliberations were resumed a couple of days later, Khadaja's attorney objected to the testimony and raised a new claim: he argued that at the time of her marriage one and one-half years earlier, Khadaja had been a minor *(saghira)* and had reached puberty only recently. My interpretation is that when Khadaja's attorney brought up the question of her minority in order to establish his objection to the testimony, his logic was that had the witnesses attended the ceremony as they testified, they would have alluded to the issue of the bride's guardian (which was mandatory in cases of a minor bride). They never mentioned it, so their testimony was not valid. However, Judge Sadık thought otherwise: he did mention that when the bride is a minor, her guardian *(wali al-nikah)* must give his consent (and hence must attend the event). However, to his mind, because Khadaja's attorney had not raised this point earlier and the testimony was in keeping with his original claim, she could not be considered to have been a minor at the time of the marriage. He then ordered that the procedure of *tazkiya* should be carried out.

I assume that whether Khadaja was or was not legally a minor at the time of her marriage, she must have been very young, an important factor in explaining her position in Hasan's household, particularly with regard to her mother-in-law and the reasons for her escape, which emerged later in the record. Her father (who appeared in court later) was apparently her legal guardian, which means that even if under the circumstances she or her natal family were regretting this marriage, she was not legally entitled to ask for its cancellation on the grounds of *khiyar al-bulugh* (the right of a minor bride to cancel her marriage as soon as she reached puberty); according to the Hanafi school, this option was open to minor brides only when the guardian was not the father or the agnate grandfather. Thus, her attorney's maneuvers might have been intended to push Hasan to initiate a divorce or at least to improve Khadaja's position in his household. Be the goal of the lawsuit as it may, Khadaja's situation is yet another illustration of my argument about women's divided loyalties and obligations (Agmon 1998) and about the vulnerability of minors, especially females, in the family.[20]

Khadaja's attorney did not give up. At the following session, after the witnesses' credibility was confirmed, he claimed that the defendant had publicly admitted his debt in this court (apparently referring to the exchange between him and Hasan's attorney during the first court session) and thereby had invalidated his own proof. He then raised a new claim: he demanded that Hasan be ordered to prepare a conjugal dwelling *(maskan shar'i)* for Khadaja, as she had left his house in Ramla because of his family's mistreatment of her. Hasan's attorney rejected his colleague's claim and demanded that the court force Khadaja to return to her husband's house. Judge Sadık instructed Khadaja's attorney to prove his claim regarding the house and rejected his repeated claim for the debt. The continuation of the trial was postponed once more.

When the trial resumed, Khadaja's attorney told the court that Hasan's mother used to strike Khadaja and injure her and to give her bad food; Hasan himself was absent most of the time, but when he was at home, he also would hit her. The attorney claimed that Khadaja wished to prove this by requesting that her husband take an oath. He was apparently unable to produce witnesses for the maltreatment his client said she received at the hands of her mother-in-law, although he did not state this inability explicitly, or at least the records do not mention it. According to the procedure in a situation like this, the party that cannot provide the court with eyewitnesses is entitled to ask that the other party swear to the truthfulness of his or her claim, in which case the judge has to decide in favor of the party who took the oath. Judge Sadık, however, was not in a hurry to follow this line of action. Instead, he asked Hasan's attorney

20. See chapter 5 and further discussions on these issues in chapter 7.

to respond to the claim about the injury caused to Khadaja. At the same time, he reconsidered the issue of the dower that seemed already settled and ordered Hasan to swear that he had paid the 2 LF.

Hasan himself was present at the next session and was requested to take an oath. He refused, so Judge Sadık ordered him to pay his debt. Hasan paid the 2 LF to Khadaja in the presence of her attorney and her father.

At face value, this development meant that Hasan indeed owed Khadaja this sum and that her attorney was right about the flaws in the testimonies of Hasan's witnesses. It illustrates the efficiency of the oath as evidence (see also the discussion of the case of Husun versus Muhammad in the previous chapter). It is also plausible that this shift in the decision about the debt was owing to the new claim about maltreatment, seemingly the main problem requiring solution in this case. Hence, Hasan might have been willing to give up what he had almost gained in terms of the dower (whatever the truth about who owed what to whom) in order to pursue a solution to the question of his wife's running away. At this point in the record, after Hasan paid his debt, his attorney rejected Sheikh Muhammad ʿAli al-Dajani's claim about the injury and demanded that Khadaja return to live with her husband *(muʿashara)* in Ramla, in the conjugal dwelling he had prepared for her; otherwise, she should be determined a rebellious wife. The judge finally ordered Khadaja's attorney to prove the claim of injury.

At the next session, Muhammad ʿAli repeated what he had said about Khadaja's situation when living with Hasan's mother in Ramla. He demanded appropriate maintenance according to her social position and a conjugal dwelling that would be at arm's length from both her husband's family and hers. Muhammad ʿAli rejected the possibility that the judge would force him to prove his client's injury, even though she was able to do so, and stated that he had submitted the matter to the mufti. Hasan's attorney insisted on his client's demand for either *muʿashara* in Ramla, as he had no house other than that of his family, or *nushuz* (a statement that she was a disobedient wife). The judge decided to send one of the court's scribes to check the house, this way ignoring both Khadaja's attorney's claim that her husband's family treated her badly and his recommendation regarding who should present the proof in the matter.

At the next session, the scribe reported at length to the court about the house in the neighborhood of al-Bashawiyya in Ramla, describing it as having a communal toilet and other facilities. The judge consequently instructed

Hasan to make the necessary changes.[21] Hasan's attorney, Sheikh Mustafa al-Dajani, stated that his client was willing to make the required arrangements in the house and that his wife should return. Sheikh Muhammad ʿAli asked that the court order Hasan to pay maintenance to his wife until the house was ready. The judge accepted this demand. Muhammad ʿAli noted that the requested sum of maintenance was 1 beşlik. Sheikh Mustafa repeated his client's willingness to prepare a conjugal dwelling, but rejected the demand for alimony. The scribe was sent once again to check the house and reported that this time it met the requirements.

The last session started with Sheikh Muhammad ʿAli al-Dajani claiming again that the house was in Ramla and that his client had been injured while living there. He was willing to prove this claim and requested that the court order the defendant to prepare a conjugal dwelling elsewhere for his client's safety . Sheikh Mustafa rejected these claims and demanded that the court order the plaintiff to return to the house in Ramla, as it had been legally approved. At this point, the record ends with neither a verdict nor a reference to another session.

In the second case involving the same couple, which started on the same day as the first, Khadaja's attorney claimed that when his client had run away from her husband's household, she had left there her clothes, including dresses, suits, shirts, and other items, the total value of which was 1,332 kuruş. He asked the court to order Hasan to give back Khadaja's belongings. Hasan's attorney responded that only some of these items were in his client's possession. At the second court session of the case, he denied the entire claim, and the burden of proof was imposed on his colleague, Sheikh Muhammad ʿAli al-Dajani. The judge asked Hasan's attorney again about the claim, and he responded that Khadaja had the said items with her in her father's house and that she had used them. The burden of proof was imposed once again on Khadaja's attorney, who requested that Hasan take an oath because Khadaja was unable to bring witnesses to support her claim.

21. The husband was legally obliged to provide his wife with a separate house, but this demand was rarely implemented or even demanded by women who came to court to ask for a conjugal dwelling. In this case, the necessary arrangements probably meant that the wife would have a separate toilet and kitchen in her husband's household. See also Amina and Salim's case in chapter 4 and the discussion on family experiences in chapter 7.

Sheikh Mustafa al-Dajani promised that his client would come to court and take an oath. The last session took place five days after the last session of the other case. Hasan came to court. The beginning of his oath is registered in the record, and then the record ends, and it is clear that there was no continuation: there is no reference to such continuation, nor is there any continuation without a reference; the page on which the record ends contains only the few lines of the beginning of the oath, and the scribe had scribbled over the rest of the page in order to make sure that no unlawful text would be added (JCR, *Hujaj* 152, 10 C 1332/6 V 1914, 7, case 3). The form of the record suggests that for some reason the parties continued their dispute outside court. It also indicates that session protocols were actually recorded during or shortly after the time the respective sessions took place (see chapter 4).

Abu Basha versus Abu Basha

During the period of the deliberations in the Khadaja versus Hasan case, an additional lawsuit was brought before Judge Sadık. In this case, another couple, unhappily married (or, rather, divorced, as the record gradually reveals), appeared at court without representation. Comparing this case to Khadaja and Hasan's case offers another perspective in the discussion about the judge as an arbitrator within the legal concept of social justice and the way in which he tackled the challenge represented by the attorneys.

The former husband and wife in this case were members of the same extended family, Abu Basha, although they were not first cousins. The wife, Jamila, claimed that her husband, Al-Sayyid, still owed her 3 out of 20 LF of the prompt dower he had taken upon himself to pay to her when they were married six years earlier. She also mentioned that the deferred dower was 5 LF. According to her claim, seven months before the trial, when she asked him to pay the 3 LF and he refused, she had left the house with Ahmad, their two-year-old son, leaving behind various household items (probably her *jihaz*) and clothing valued at 10 LF. She asked the court to oblige her husband to pay her his debt in addition to maintenance and child support and to return her belongings.

Al-Sayyid responded by telling an entirely different story. He claimed that in fact they had divorced seven months earlier following a dispute that had broken out between them when he returned from a business trip to Tiberias and found out that various articles were missing from their store, for which

Jamila was responsible in his absence. He acknowledged the sums of the dowers and his fatherhood of Ahmad, claiming that Ahmad was three years old, rather than two, and said that in a written divorce agreement they had signed in the presence of witnesses, Jamila had released him from all his financial obligations to her *(bara'a)* in return for a full divorce and hence had no grounds for further demands.

Judge Sadık placed the burden of proof on Al-Sayyid. The latter brought four witnesses who fully confirmed his version. The divorce agreement was also checked, and then two of the witnesses were summoned again to confirm the claim that Ahmad was three years old and that Jamila had agreed to take care of him without payment. At this point, Judge Sadık sent the divorce agreement to the mufti, Sheikh Muhammad Tawfiq al-Dajani, asking whether Jamila's renunciation of alimony and child support without specifying the sums in question was in keeping with the law. The mufti confirmed her right to give up her dower and alimony, but not the child support. Following this response, Jamila demanded 3 beşlik in child support. Al-Sayyid said he could not afford to pay this sum and claimed that Jamila should be deprived of the right to take care of Ahmad altogether because she was untrustworthy *(ghayr amina)*. Judge Sadık rejected this claim on the basis that it was presented too late in the proceedings. Jamila said that Al-Sayyid could afford to pay the sum she demanded because he owned a house in the neighborhood of Manshiyya (at the northern end of Jaffa), which he rented out. The judge summoned witnesses to testify as to Al-Sayyid's financial situation, and on this basis he instructed him to pay 1 beşlik a day in child support and a caretaker wage *(ujrat al-hadana)* to his ex-wife.[22] The case was deliberated over a period of five weeks. About a month after it was settled, Judge Sadık restated the divorce of renunciation in the margins of the last page of its record, and after another month the couple came and signed a new statement to the effect that Jamila was to have custody of Ahmad, and his father would pay child support.[23]

22. Legally, the father should have paid the mother a wage for taking care of his minor children in addition to child support. The records rarely mention this right. The judge mentioned the letter of the law following the consultation with the mufti apparently to enable Jamila to reclaim the highest possible sum.

23. JCR, *Hujaj* 152, 10 M–6 R 1332/9 XII 1913-4 III 1914, 105–8, 112–14, 119–20, case 50. See also Agmon 1996.

The Litigants and Their Proceedings

The information about the dowers, marriage gifts, maintenance, and child support of the two disputing couples—Khadaja and Hasan, Jamila and Al-Sayyid—indicates a similar economic position for both couples. The sum both Khadaja and Jamila were to receive for daily maintenance, the former for her own expenses and the latter for her son's, was 1 beşlik (about 3.5 kuruş), a medium-size sum according to the three-level system of daily support per capita that prevailed at the Jaffa and Haifa courts. The other sums of money and the furniture and clothes also indicate a higher- to middle-level economic position. They were clearly better off than the couples whose marital relations were discussed in the previous chapter (Muhammad and Hajar, and Muhammad and Husun).

Socially, however, the Abu Basha couple represented a different middle-class pattern from Khadaja and Hasan: Al-Sayyid and Jamila were involved in some sort of trade; after six years of marriage, they had only one son, who was two to three years old. Judging by the fact that most of their witnesses lived in Manshiyya, a relatively new neighborhood populated largely by immigrants, some from affluent and respected families, it is likely that the Abu Bashas also lived in that neighborhood—one of the identifying witnesses for Jamila mentioned that she was his neighbor—and that Al-Sayyid also owned and rented out a house there. It is possible that he lived in the house he rented out, as did other small property owners.[24] Al-Sayyid signed the record with his name, and Jamila signed with a personal seal. Thus, the Abu Basha couple belonged to a socioeconomic group of small entrepreneurs, several of whom had immigrated to the growing port cities from neighboring towns and villages or lived in villages that had developed into suburbs of the port cities. They had managed to accumulate some wealth, yet did not adopt upper-class manners, so they—not even the woman, Jamila—would not hire attorneys to represent them in court. On the contrary, Jamila demonstrated particular resourcefulness at court (Agmon 1998).

24. See the discussion of the lawsuit of the father against his son in chapter 5 and the discussion of living conditions in chapter 7. The Murtada family, the family of the judge from Damascus (chapter 3), rented a house in the Manshiyya neighborhood; Yusuf Haykal's grandmother (discussed in chapter 7) moved there to live with her son's conjugal family.

Khadaja and Hasan's families, in contrast, either considered themselves upper class or maybe were upwardly mobile, so they did not attend the court, but preferred to hire attorneys to represent them, a pattern that became a symbol of upper-class status during this period (Agmon 1995, 57–60, 157–71). When demanding maintenance on her behalf, Khadaja's attorney stressed that the sum should represent her social standing, which may have been somewhat higher than Hasan's. (Although asking for "appropriate" maintenance was a legal convention, this idiom was rarely used in the Jaffa court record.) We know that Khadaja's family, Abu Radwan, was connected through marriage to the Haykal family, a respected and wealthy family in Jaffa. Members of both the Haykal and the Abu Radwan families signed the protocol of the first session at Sheikh Husayn's trial, described in chapter 3, after Sheikh Husayn mentioned his long list of notable witnesses.[25]

The length and intricate nature of the deliberations in the lawsuit of Khadaja against Hasan, which was no more complicated than the Abu Basha case, clearly stemmed from the attorneys' involvement in the former. The attorneys argued with each other, advised the judge how to deliberate the case, raised new claims, requested postponements, and used every procedural trick in order to serve their clients' best interests. I assume that the separation of this dispute into two cases also resulted from this line of action and was made at Khadaja's request, although it is hard to ascertain in what way this division was meant to be advantageous. After half a year, this double dispute ended without a legal decision. At the same time, the judge was able to deliberate and decide the Abu Basha case, which required the summoning of a relatively large number of witnesses and consultation with the mufti, in a much more focused manner. The main legal decision, that the divorce agreement would be changed to enable Jamila to receive child support and a caretaker wage, was reached within five weeks without any delay. It then took another couple of months before the judge restated the conditions of the renunciation divorce and officially implemented it, but during these two months no further deliberations were recorded for this case. Altogether, this record reflects a three-month-long case that resulted in a court decision, whereas Khadaja and Hasan's case took six months and was not concluded in court.

25. See the discussion on the Haykal family in chapter 7.

Taming the Attorneys

Most important to this discussion is the interaction between the judge and the attorneys and the way it reshaped legal procedure. As shown, the attorneys frequently advised the judge as to the legal terms he should use for their claims. For example, Hasan's attorney asked several times that the court either force Khadaja to return to live with her husband *(mu'ashara)* or declare her a disobedient wife *(nashiz)*. After he made this demand for the first time, the protocol of the following session was recorded as if the session had been conducted by the two attorneys alone: Khadaja's attorney phrased the legal questions that the defendant should answer, and Hasan's attorney responded. Later, after the testimony of Hasan's witnesses had been heard, Khadaja's attorney pointed to flaws in it, a role normally played by the judge. In the Abu Basha case, for instance, after hearing the testimonies on the contents of the divorce agreement, Judge Sadık suspected that the agreement contained legal flaws and decided to seek the mufti's advice in the matter.

Nevertheless, although it seems from the record that the judge allowed the attorneys considerable leeway to raise claims, argue with each other, and try to push the deliberations in a direction favorable for their respective clients, he did intervene whenever he found it necessary and did not automatically heed the attorneys' advice: for example, right after Khadaja's attorney contested the testimony of Hasan's witnesses, the judge ignored him and instructed the attorneys to proceed with the *tazkiya*. He apparently was not convinced that the testimonies were untruthful and was determined to carry on with them. However, he changed his mind after the *tazkiya* and before making his final decision. According to the official procedure, he could have continued on this course of action and decided that Hasan had proved his claim regarding the dower. However, he decided to reexamine these testimonies after all by instructing Hasan to take an oath on the matter, although the reasons for changing his mind and accepting Khadaja's attorney claims about the testimonies are not specified in the record and not even written by the judge in the margins, as was sometimes done. The result—Hasan's refusal to take the oath—justified this decision. Thus, the judge, although preserving his legal authority by fending off some of the attorneys' demands, was also relying on their expertise to support his discretion.

Because of the attorneys' involvement, did the judge's work as arbitrator between two disputing parties turn into ruling between two opposing versions of truth? At first glance, it may seem that in cases where the litigants appointed attorneys to represent them, the judge found himself on the legal stage surrounded by two professional jurists whose goal was different from his: he worked as an arbitrator to achieve a fast and feasible decision, whereas they concentrated on obtaining as favorable a verdict as possible for their clients. In consequence, the legal procedure became longer and more unpredictable. It also became more legally elaborate: not only did the attorneys make use of their legal skills, but the judge also tended to explain his legal decisions during the deliberations, a tendency that was not typical of the court record in general (and that was amplified by the introduction of recording protocols, see chapter 4). In addition, certain legal procedures, such as the examination of the conjugal dwelling that Hasan was asked to prepare, were apparently applied more meticulously when the attorneys were breathing down the judge's neck. The focus of the legal deliberations was also more dispute oriented, and the rendering of the opposition between two competitive versions more poignant. All the deliberations in Khadaja and Hasan's case did not even end with a decision.

Yet a closer look at the case records of the two disputing couples leads me to a different conclusion. The judge's arbitration in the Abu Basha case is evident in the record. The trial began with the presentation of two opposing versions. In the recorded process of examining the facts mentioned in the claims, which the judge pursued without any procedural delay, one version, the husband's, was exposed as true, whereas the other version was shown as false. From the perspective of truthfulness, the judge could have easily dismissed Jamila's claim against her husband as unfounded after hearing the testimonies on the divorce agreement and seeing the agreement itself. Had he thought the agreement illegal, he could have either pointed out its flaws or sent it to the mufti at that stage. However, he continued. After he heard not just two but four witnesses to the agreement, he asked the husband to prove his claim about his son's age, and then, when only the procedure of the *tazkiya* remained to be conducted before the inevitable decision in favor of Al-Sayyid was taken, he sent the divorce agreement to the mufti. The latter then enabled him to reach a decision by which Jamila would not leave the court empty-handed. It seems odd that an experienced judge such as Mehmet Sadık Efendi did not notice the basic legal flaw in the divorce agreement—that Jamila had given up a financial right, child support, that was not hers to begin with. Yet, according to the record, it had escaped his notice up to this point. Even the question he put to the mufti did not focus on this legal problem, but rather indicated that he suspected the divorce agreement was somehow not flawless. After nothing else worked in Jamila's favor, Judge Sadık involved the mufti, hoping to pursue a compromise. The mufti's juridical opinion indeed allowed for some changes to the agreement. Another plausible interpretation of the judge's conduct is that he did recognize the legal flaw in the divorce agreement but was trying to push the litigants to correct it by reaching a compromise. When this did not happen, and in order to stress the legal ground for the reconsideration of the entire agreement, he sent it to the mufti (which indeed led to rephrasing the entire agreement).

This record clearly illustrates the concept of arbitration because, unlike many other records, it shows from an early stage that one party told what actually had happened regarding the disputed matter, whereas the other one lied. Yet the judge was not interested in the truth as such, but rather in responding to the needs that had led to the appeal by finding a compromise between the litigants' opposing interests. Thus, the narration of this case advanced from the issue of truth, which was pushed aside—no compromise was possible there—toward the issue of interests, or the realm of arbitration. At the same time, the arbitrated decision was strictly in keeping with the law. Moreover, it corrected an unlawful agreement. Judge Sadık used his discretion when recognizing that Jamila and her minor son, of whom she had custody, found themselves in a radically inferior situation, and he worked to adjust this socioeconomic imbalance according to the legal definition of social justice. His main tool in so doing was the law of procedure rather than the substantive law, although in this particular case the substantive law could also provide a solution. As I mentioned in the previous chapter, this choice suggests that judges were accustomed to view legal procedure as the realm for employing their discretion.

According to Khadaja and Hasan's case record, however, the disputed issue was somewhat evasive because the attorneys obscured it by raising new claims every so often and by arguing procedural questions. At first, the dispute was apparently about the prompt dower. Then the question of Khadaja's majority was raised incidentally, followed by the issue of the treatment she had received from Hasan and his family. This latter issue raised the question of the conjugal dwelling and the conditions for the couple's reunion. The demand for a judgment between two opposing versions of truth, typically posed to the judge by the attorneys, can be detected in this case record with regard to each new claim the attorneys raised as the case progressed. This is why, at first glance, the judge's decisions seem inconsistent and give the impression that he was too busy controlling the two attorneys and thus giving up his role as arbitrator.

However, when we look at the judge's decisions from the point of view of arbitration, they seem less inconsistent. The first issue was the dower. Judge Sadık deliberated it as usual, and when he was close to a decision in favor of Hasan, the claims about the maltreatment Khadaja had received in Hasan's house brought to the forefront the issue that probably motivated Khadaja to run away to her natal family and hence became the main problem that needed to be solved. Thus, after the *tazkiya* of Hasan's witnesses in the dower issue was carried out, Hasan was summoned by Judge Sadık, who asked him first to take an oath with regard to the dower. When he refused, he was instantly forced to pay the debt. In this way, Judge Sadık achieved three aims: the issue of the dower was proved and decided in Khadaja's favor; this decision was part of the deliberation on the couple's marital dispute as a whole; and it was initiated by the judge, not by Khadaja's attorney. The judge then moved on to the question of injury. In spite of all her attorney's efforts to prevent a decision that would force Khadaja to return to live with her husband, the judge pursued a solution that would facilitate such a return.

The Judge's Justice

We will never know just how the dispute between Khadaja and Hasan actually ended out of court. We may, however, consider some plausible scenarios in order to understand better the judge's discretion in this case. According to the indications mentioned earlier, had the case continued, the verdict would have forced Khadaja to live in the repaired residence that Hasan prepared for her. Not only did the judge's instructions before the record ended point in this direction, but the record of Khadaja and Hasan's second case also indicates that a verdict in favor of Hasan was only a matter of time: it ends at the point at which Hasan was taking an oath about Khadaja's belongings, the disputed issue in the second case, and a procedure that would ultimately lead to a verdict in favor of the party taking the oath. Furthermore, this happened only five days after the record of the last session of the couple's first case also came to an end. These indications, in addition to Khadaja's attorney's efforts to prevent a decision that would approve the conjugal dwelling in Hasan's family's house in Ramla and would force his client to live there, lead me to suggest that Khadaja's attorney stopped the trial.

We may recall that although Hasan, like any other husband, only had to announce a divorce if he desired one, Khadaja, like all wives, needed his consent in order to get a divorce. This consent at the least would have left her without financial rights, as shown in the Abu Basha case. Indeed, had Khadaja (or her family or both) objected to the idea of her return to Hasan's house in Ramla, a court decision in the matter would have been the worst scenario from her point of view since refusal to return would legally have put her in the position of a rebellious wife: not a divorcée and, at the same time, one not entitled to any financial support from her husband. Remaining in her natal family's household without either a court decision or divorce and financial support was better because it would have left her the option to renegotiate her status with her husband from a somewhat better position later on. Because she was threatened by a possible court decision that would be so damaging for her future, it was in her best interest to stop the deliberations at that point.

Another plausibility is that the parties negotiated outside the court while the deliberations in court continued and then stopped the legal proceedings as they reached an agreement. Court records in general include many agreements that the parties brought to the court for legalization, as shown in Amina and Salim's case (chapter 4). In fact, even fictitious disputes were brought up in court in order to subject to legal scrutiny and approval any agreements already reached outside the court.[26] The fact that such agreements were recorded means that at least one of the parties involved in each agreement, usually the plaintiff who had initiated the lawsuit, was interested in its legal approval.

In Khadaja and Hasan's case, no such agreement can be traced in the records. This does not necessarily mean that no agreement was reached between them, but only that they did not legalize it. Khadaja would probably have been interested in legalizing any agreement dealing with either a divorce or maintenance payments without divorce that would allow her to live with her natal family. However, for the reasons I mentioned earlier, she would probably

26. See a discussion of such a case in Agmon 1998, 489–90.

not have been interested in legalizing an agreement leading to her living with Hasan. He, however, would probably have been keen to legalize such an agreement; that was his attitude during the entire course of the trial, as recorded in the protocol. Yet as a defendant he could not have forced the plaintiff to implement the legal procedure, though he could have initiated a new lawsuit in the matter. However, it is rather clear from the protocol records that Judge Sadık was not in a hurry to force Khadaja to return, although he did pursue the deliberations in this direction. Thus, for the purposes of this discussion, we might assume, based on the fact that the records of the couple's two parallel lawsuits stopped without a court decision, that either Khadaja remained with her family and that there was no change in the disputing couple's legal status, or that she returned to her husband on the basis of some sort of understanding between them (or their families) that was not legalized.

The feature of arbitration as part of the way in which Judge Sadık handled the deliberations is clearly inscribed in this record. Furthermore, the nature of this arbitration can also be traced: although Judge Sadık recognized that Khadaja was in trouble when she lived in her husband's household, he insisted on pushing her to return. At the same time, he forced Hasan to make some changes to the house. In addition, his consideration of an inquiry into the injury issue as well as the fact that he brought up the question of the dower after it was almost decided against Khadaja might be interpreted as a warning to Hasan that he ought to put some serious effort into treating his wife better. In other words, Judge Sadık's arbitration aimed at maintaining the marriage.

It is impossible to ascertain how badly Khadaja was treated in her husband's house, yet the judge apparently thought that her complaints in the matter were serious, and her attorney repeatedly emphasized this issue. Moreover, shortly before the record ended, he insisted that his client would be at risk if forced to return to live in that house even after it was repaired and approved by the court. The judge's discretion in this case reinforces the view of the family as the main framework responsible for social justice. Economically, Khadaja was not in dire straits: she was still married, and her husband did not want to divorce her and was willing to follow the court's instructions about the conjugal dwelling. The judge, then, did not encourage a separation or divorce, but rather urged the couple and their families to reconnect the bonds that had tied them together. Thus, Khadaja's distress in Hasan's household was not considered a violation in terms of the legal notion of social justice.

The judge did not give up his arbitration as a result of the attorneys' representation of the litigants. The legal process took more time and became more disputatious, and the proceedings were more elaborate, yet at the end of the day the attorneys were incorporated into the legal culture of the court, and, generally speaking, arbitration rather than judgment remained a major feature of the judge's discretion. At the same time, the incorporation of attorneys into the court culture also reshaped this culture, just as the number of cases in which attorneys represented litigants in court grew. As soon as hiring attorneys became an accessible option in *shari'a* courts, people of upper-class background and wealth, who were used to employing agents and dealers for running their business interests, began to authorize agents to represent them—not only in economic disputes, but also in personal-status disputes—in the various court systems and new legal proceedings that developed during this period.

The incorporation of the attorneys into the court resulted in a dual-track legal proceeding: one track in which litigants came to court and brought their claims and requests before the judge, and another track in which attorneys came instead and employed their legal knowledge in their clients' service. Thus, certain segments of the society ultimately kept away from the court, mainly upper-class and nouveau riche families, whereas the lower and middle strata, including upstart families that had not (yet) adopted upper-class etiquette, constituted the lion's share of the litigants who appeared in court. This pattern reinforced the legal notion of social justice as described in chapter 5.

However, the two tracks of court proceedings, with and without attorneys, were not oblivious to one another. Rather, they were interrelated. After all, the same judge and court personnel moved along both tracks, with and without attorneys, and the same lay people—witnesses, litigants awaiting their turn, and their companions—constituted the audience at legal proceedings other than their own. All were exposed to the features of the cases with attorneys—their procedural articulation and antagonistic attitudes. For the court personnel, these features, in particular the meticulousness regarding procedures, were significant owing to the considerable growth of the population in the port cities during that period, which complicated the court's work. This growth and the short terms served by judges ultimately restricted the judge's ability to rely on local knowledge, reinforcing procedures such as sending the court deputy to check the situation of a conjugal dwelling and report back. It is more difficult to ascertain how much the lay audience's exposure to the features of cases

with attorneys, like their exposure to the procedures of recording the protocols (chapter 4), altered their understanding of the court culture. However, it
seems reasonable to assume that when the people who constituted this ever-
changing audience required the court's services, they would bring with them
whatever they had learned from their experience in the audience and would
use it as they saw fit, which in turn would reflect on the reconstruction of the
court culture.

Finally, the professional attorneys' activities and the way they were incorporated into the court culture, like the other innovations in the *shariʿa* court
discussed in the previous chapters, contributed to the re-constitution of the
urban classes and their stratification. Obviously, this process took place
mostly outside the legal arena. However, one of the salient features of this
process—namely, the separation between the social classes, in particular the
detachment of the urban upper class from the lower levels (an issue further
discussed in the next chapter)—was boosted in court by the attorneys' activities and by the prevailing upper-class cultural conception of the need to hire
their services.

Part Four

◆   ◆   ◆

Reshaping Solutions

7

Family Experiences

IN THE PREVIOUS CHAPTERS, I examined a number of case records, mainly exploring changes that took place in the court culture and legal concepts of family, gender, and social justice during the era of reform. In this chapter, I focus on family experiences of the urban middle class, leaving aside the courtroom and concentrating on those individuals whose family realities are inscribed in the court records.

The *shariʿa* court was accessible to all: upper and lower classes, men and women, Muslims and non-Muslims, city dwellers and non–city dwellers. However, in the period under discussion, the court served mainly the urban middle and lower strata, mostly Muslims of both sexes, both as a result of the legal reforms and their repercussions on court culture and because of the rapid growth of the port cities in the nineteenth century. Upper-class families' tendency to avoid bringing their domestic disputes to court and the concentration on family matters in the *shariʿa* court as a result of the development of other court systems resulted in underrepresentation of the upper class in court. At the same time, the constant immigration to and urban growth of the port cities contributed to the growth of the middle and lower strata. However, although the *shariʿa* court maintained its user-friendly attitude, which appealed mainly to these two strata (who in addition could not afford to hire attorneys), the court fees probably prevented the very poor from applying to the court in the first place. In the course of the nineteenth century, the *shariʿa* courts received from Istanbul a list of fixed prices for their various services, and they had to keep records of their financial accounts (HCR, *Daftar al-ʿAʾidat al-Sharʿiyya* 1319–24/1903–1908). The charges probably kept certain segments of the lower class out of court, with the results that this stratum was underrepresented and the middle class overrepresented.[1]

In the period under discussion, the emerging urban modern middle classes were gradually turning into major sociopolitical actors in their societies. Their history, however, more specifically their family history, has barely been written, in no small part owing to the lack of sources documenting their way of life and experiences at a microhistorical level. Hence, the urban elite in the Ottoman-Arab provinces has been the subject of most of the local histories in the field, whereas the rest of the urban population has remained nameless, faceless, vaguely defined groups.[2]

As noted in chapter 2, the middle class discussed here is not a tightly knit social group, but rather a number of segments in the urban communities of the port cities. Judging by their socioeconomic position as reflected in the court records, they clearly did not belong to the upper class, nor were they extremely poor. One can distinguish at least two levels, to which I have referred as the "higher-middle" and "lower-middle" levels respectively. The former level included small real-estate owners, and the sums of money mentioned in their legal cases as income, dowers, alimony, and child support were of medium size according to the three-level system of daily payments (chapter 4). The people discussed in the previous chapters belonging to the higher-middle stratum include Amina and Salim (chapter 4); Muhammad and his son, Qasim (chapter 5); Uncle Khalil, his nieces Farida and Nazira, his nephew Tahir, and his sister-in-law Maryam (chapter 5); and Jamila and Al-Sayyid Abu Basha, as

---

1. Scholars who studied Ottoman *shariʿa* court records of earlier periods observed similar tendencies (Hanna 1995, 55; Peirce 2003, 6). On the instructions about fees for court services, see chapter 3.

2. About the sources for family history, see chapter 2. As to local histories that deal with the elite families, see, for instance, Schilcher 1985; Marcus 1989; Zeʾevi 1996; Meriwether 1999. Hanna 1998 represents an exception in its unfolding of a merchant family's experiences in seventeenth-century Cairo, as does Peirce 2003 in the stories of three sixteenth-century Aintaban women. Fawwaz (1983) and Doumani (1995) produced rare studies using family archives from Beirut and Nablus, respectively, and Khater (2001), in his study of the emergence of the middle class in Lebanon, reconstructs the experiences of Lebanese emigrants to America and those who returned to Lebanon at the turn of the twentieth century. Toledano offers a detailed reconstruction of the social stratification of mid-nineteenth-century Cairo and the lifestyles of various urban strata and rural immigrants (1990, 155–77, 196–248).

3. A boat at the entrance to the port of Jaffa. From the studio of Bonfils, c. 1870. Courtesy of the Middle East Department, University of Chicago Library.

well as Khadaja and Hasan (chapter 6). Khadaja and Amina (but not their husbands) possibly came from upper-class families, or at least from middle-class families of higher position than that of their husbands.[3] Hasan and Hind, whose case is unfolded in this chapter, also belonged to this level. Those in the lower-middle level were worth smaller sums, and there is no indication that they owned any real estate (although the lack of indication may have resulted solely from the nature of their court cases). Muhammad and Hajar, Muhammad and Husun, and Tamam, whose case records were unfolded in chapter 5,

---

3. The legal principle of socioeconomic equality *(kafa'a)* between the groom's and bride's families is not mentioned in their case records. In fact, in spite of the rapid population growth and social mobility that must have encouraged situations in which inequality in marriage was likely to occur, this terminology was hardly ever used in records dealing with domestic disputes. It is difficult to ascertain why this was so, particularly because it is the absence of the term *kafa'a* rather than its usage that requires explanation. A possible interpretation is that the very circumstances that promoted more pluralistic marriages rendered the legal term *equality* ineffective for dispute resolution.

seemed to belong to this level.[4] Other features typical of members of the middle class were that they made a living in various state services or worked in private services, small trade, construction, or agriculture, and many of them had migrated to the port cities from nearby villages and towns or from more distant regions in Syria, Egypt, and Anatolia.

Owing to their nature, court records cannot replace historical sources such as diaries and memoirs in providing the point of view of people of modest socioeconomic position, yet such sources are not known to exist for these lower- and middle-level strata. The potential of the court records in this respect should not be ignored, particularly when it comes to the encounter between values and ideals embedded in the legal notion of the family and the realities faced by the urban middle class. Valuable information about topics such as family bonds, household formation and structures, relations between housemates and neighbors is likely to be inscribed inadvertently in protocols recording bitter disputes. These records tend to be relatively long and detailed and to include a variety of legal proceedings, such as several testimonies on the disputed issue, correspondence with the mufti, reports by experts or court delegations, and documents from other official departments. They provide varied information not so much in the form of direct responses to legal questions, but rather as details buried within the lines. Furthermore, a record sometimes includes several interpretations of the same topic or event, particularly when many witnesses testified or when a certain issue was raised several times, each time somewhat differently, in the course of deliberations. Some of the case records unfolded in the previous chapters suit this description well.

Issues inscribed in these court records relate to the space occupied by middle-class families in the port cities and to the nature of ties and relations that evolved in this space and shaped it. Studies in the social history of Ottoman-Arab premodern urban societies show, for instance, that small households and a close proximity with non–family members were common historical phenomena among the urban nonelite strata.[5] I argue that these characteristics were cultural norms that the circumstances of rapid growth in the port cities in the late nineteenth century did not change, not necessarily for lack

---

4. In addition, Sheikh Husayn (chapter 3) and Judge Abu al-Nasr, who presided at his trial, belonged to the upper class, as did Yusuf Haykal (discussed later in this chapter).

5. See references in note 10.

of choice. Close proximity among neighbors should be understood as part of the premodern semifamilial culture of the urban middle and lower classes, not as an inevitable compromise of the poor with reality; the passage to modernity in the period under consideration did not change this middle-class cultural norm, but rather reinforced it. Another issue considered here is the gendered construction of the middle-class family. I argue that women experienced the family very differently from men owing to the court's reinforcement of the patrilineal family and to the circumstances in the port cities that encouraged small household structures and hence stressed the vulnerability of middle-class women and children. I further argue that the construction of the family in the upper class contributed to reducing this sort of vulnerability at those levels.

Family Households

As indicated in chapter 5, Muhammad ibn Qasim Hasun al-Sharut claimed that he was in dire straits and so asked the court to force his son, whom he claimed was better off, to support him.[6] This case facilitates a look into two questions: What type of household structure was widespread among the middle class, and was the structure of households determined mainly by the economic means of the families involved? The disputed issue in the Hasun case, as to who was better off, the father or his son, resulted in a fairly detailed account of the financial situation of both men, especially the father, Muhammad, whose lawsuit was based on the claim that he was impoverished. These details were embedded in further information about the urban conditions for and the lifestyle of the two litigants. In addition, the recorded identification of the witnesses who testified in this case provides snippets of information about aspects of the social environment and networks of the father and son, both of modest background.

The father and son had moved to Haifa from al-Tira, a neighboring village on the lower western slopes of Mount Carmel, a few kilometers south of Haifa and a couple of kilometers from the Mediterranean shore. Other villagers from al-Tira had moved to Haifa and lived in Wadi al-Nisnas, which is sometimes also referred to in the court records as "the Western Quarter" *(al-mahalla al-gharbiyya)*. Wadi al-Nisnas was built in the course of the nineteenth

---

6. HCR, *Jaridat al-Dabt* 5, 12 Za 1331–17 M 1332/X–XI 1913, 7, 18, 20–22, 26–27, 55, 72, case 52. See the discussion in chapter 5.

century on the northern slope of Mount Carmel, southwest of the city walls, when the pressure of immigration to Haifa led to the construction of new houses outside the walls (Yazbak 1998, 194–95, 199–200).[7] Muhammad al-Hasun, all the witnesses brought by his son to testify to his father's economic position, and the *tazkiya* witnesses lived in this neighborhood, and most of them were explicitly mentioned in the record as people who had moved to Haifa from al-Tira. Thus, like immigrants everywhere, the villagers from al-Tira also tended to stick together for security and support in their new location, even though they came from a relatively nearby village; it might have been easier for them, in comparison to newcomers from distant regions, to keep close ties with their relatives and support groups living there.[8]

Muhammad and his adult son did not live under the same roof. Each headed and supported a simple-family household of his own. Muhammad had built a small house in Wadi al-Nisnas and registered it at the land-registration office *(tapu)* in town. According to the official registration, his house consisted of only one room, so probably even if he had wanted to keep his multigenerational family in one joint household, it would have been impossible. However, from the testimonies, we learn that Muhammad had extended his house, adding two more rooms and a place for animals; he rented out one of these extra rooms, while Qasim and his dependents lived elsewhere, probably in the same neighborhood. A large joint-household structure among the urban middle class was probably not widespread, as indicated by this record and the other case records discussed here.

Muhammad lived with his second wife and four minor children in his one-room house. He supported this family by selling vegetables while riding a donkey through the streets of Haifa. He earned 5–7 beşlik (about 17–25 kuruş) a day from his trade. In addition, after enlarging his house, he rented out one of the extra rooms. Altogether, his simple-family household consisted of six

7. It is possible that Muhammad had moved to Haifa only a few years before suing his son: a man of the same name and lineage was mentioned as an identifying witness from the village of al-Tira in a case record registered in 1901 (HCR, *Jaridat al-Dabt* 14, 16 R 1319/1 VIII 1901, 1, case 1).

8. See theories on networks of immigrants supporting newcomers from their place of origin and hence encouraging more migration from one place to another in Massey et al. 1993, 448–50, 461–62. Akram Khater describes similar patterns in connection with the Lebanese emigration to America in the late nineteenth century (2001, 63, 72–74).

people, all living in one room. Next to them lived another family, or maybe a couple or a single man, who rented the extra room. In the third room, Muhammad stored his merchandise, and he kept the donkey in an additional structure that he built for this purpose. His income, including the rent he received from the extra room, probably 1 kuruş a day, would have enabled him to spend about 1 beşlik per capita per day. In comparison to the sums of daily alimonies and child support mentioned in the court records, this was a medium-size sum.[9] According to the prevailing standards of living, Muhammad was certainly not rich, but neither was he poor, and he was clearly improving his situation (apparently, he had hoped to improve it even further by leaning on his son, but failed). He lived in close proximity not only with his conjugal family, but also with his lodgers, who were not relatives and did not belong to his household, although he had financial ties with them as they paid him rent.

His elder son, Qasim, lived with his own conjugal family in a separate household. We have no specific information about the location of his house or how crowded it was. However, we do know that in addition to his wife and minor children, Qasim also supported his divorced mother. Because family households among these strata tended to be small, women were likely to change households more than once in their lifetimes, whenever they married, divorced, remarried, or were widowed. Under the circumstances of rapid change typical of this period, they sometimes also moved with the household to another town if the head of the household migrated. Thus, not only were households small, but they also tended to include more women than men, as they were joined by the single adult, divorced, or widowed daughters, sisters, or the mother of the head of the household—a structure differing from the classic simple household.

Small households among the urban middle class were neither a new phenomenon nor typical only of flourishing nineteenth-century port cities. Historians studying cities throughout the Ottoman-Arab and Anatolian provinces in different periods—Aleppo, Damascus, Cairo, Algiers, Bursa, and Istanbul—produce similar findings. They all embarked on their research equipped with the same common knowledge about the "traditional family"—namely, the extended family maintaining a joint multigenerational household—only to find

---

9. See chapter 4, "A Note on Money and Daily Conditions."

that household structures were much more variegated and that large joint-family households were quite rare among families of modest means.[10]

From the economic point of view, it is understandable that in the highly populated, major provincial towns of the seventeenth to the nineteenth centuries, families of modest means would not have been able to afford a residence large enough for a multigenerational household. However, the circumstance in the port cities in the late nineteenth century were different from those prevailing in the large provincial inland cities. In earlier periods, cities were surrounded by walls, so their expansion was limited and legally prohibited, resulting in high rents, crowded quarters, and ultimately small household structures among most of the urban population. In the second half of the nineteenth century, the city walls were ignored during the rapid urban growth, and legal changes permitted construction outside the walls. Yet real-estate prices were still high and increased as the population grew even faster than the housing area. Thus, as far as the middle and lower levels of the urban population were concerned, the economic conditions of the port cities were similar to those prevailing in the large older cities long before expansion occurred.[11]

Moreover, rapid urban growth led to the renting of small rooms to and the sharing of houses with nonrelatives, which also encouraged people who owned even a tiny property to try to rent out parts of it, as did Muhammad when his situation improved and he enlarged his one-room house. The entrepreneurship resulting from economic circumstances encouraged smaller family household structures and close proximity among nonrelatives, even among people who were somewhat better off. Thus, the assumption that only poverty and similar obstacles forced people to give up large family households needs to be reconsidered.

Cultural Ideals and Urban Realities

Amina al-Sabʿ Aʿyun and Salim Qaraman, whose domestic dispute was examined in chapter 4, lived with their baby daughter in a rented room next door to

---

10. Raymond 1985; Gerber 1989; Marcus 1989; Duben and Behar 1991; Establet and Pascual 1994; Shuval 1998; Fargues 2003. Okawara (2003), in contrast, shows that the large joint household was typical in late Ottoman Damascus.

11. Yazbak 1998, 197–99; LeVine 1999, 82–83.

their landlord.[12] There are indications that, before moving there, Amina and Salim had lived in the house of Salim's father. We know that they moved into the rented room only four months before the trial, and in her initial claim Amina mentioned the furniture she had left behind, stating that Salim had locked it up in his father's house.[13] The room was owned by someone who was not a relative, judging by his name and the fact that both Amina and Salim came to Haifa from other towns, Saida and Nablus, and hence were not likely to have many relatives in Haifa. The landlord and other neighbors were able to testify in detail in court about the couple's intimate relations. In the record of Muhammad and Qasim al-Hasun's case, Muhammad's neighbors in Wadi al-Nisnas told the court that he and his wife and children lived in one room and rented out another room. This evidence shows that unrelated families lived in the small house that belonged to one of them and that Muhammad's neighbors were also able to provide the court with accurate details about the practical arrangements inside that house, though less accurate than the testimony given by Amina and Salim's neighbors.

Such close proximity of nonrelatives who constituted separate family households living under the same roof and sharing some of the private spaces of the house—the kitchen, the toilet, the courtyard—emphasizes the need to reconsider the family structure among the urban middle and lower strata. In an article published in 1987, Janet Abu-Lughod suggested a reconsideration of the cultural ideal of the family's private space among the urban lower strata (167–69). Her hypothesis, however, did not receive the attention it deserves.[14] She revisited the debate on the "Islamic city," shaking up most of the assumptions underlying that battered Weberian construction. Relating the Weberian description of the physical structure of Muslim cities as an array of narrow alleys that lack urban corporation and autonomy, she pointed to a cultural concept embodied in the alley. Because the urban poor were unable to maintain

12. HCR, *Jaridat al-Dabt* 5, 110–11, 120, 124, 131, 27 S–15 Ra 1332/13 I–14 III 1914, case 83.

13. The furniture probably consisted of the household items that Salim had bought for Amina as part of the marriage contract *(jihaz)*, to be used in their marital residence (chapter 5).

14. Avner Giladi excepted; in his book on breast-feeding, his discussion of milk relatives is inspired by this insight (1999, 27). Maternal milk is considered in Muslim jurisprudence as establishing kinship relations, so breast-feeding by a wet nurse imposes marriage prohibitions on the people involved.

seclusion and physical privacy according to the prevailing upper-class cultural ideal, they broadened the notion of private space to include the alley as a semi-private space, so that nonrelated neighbors living in the same alley were considered semirelatives for all sociocultural purposes. Ehud Toledano portrays the culture of the alleys in mid-nineteenth-century Cairo as follows: "alleys and blind alleys in a neighborhood were not considered as public domain. In them, women washed kitchen wares, children played, and men sat out and relaxed after a day's work. All met there and conversed with each other, thus using the *hara,* or neighborhood, for social interaction" (1990, 202). In light of the circumstances in which even inside the house people often could not maintain private space along family lines, Abu-Lughod's insight might also be useful in explaining why such proximity was not so unthinkable, and it might offer an interpretive framework for understanding some of the ties and relations among nonfamily housemates.

Abu-Lughod's argument should also be considered within the context of the discussion on privacy and social order. Before publishing his 1989 book on eighteenth-century Aleppo, Abraham Marcus wrote an article (1986) on privacy and the meaning of cultural ideals in the highly populated housing situation of the lower classes in Aleppo. He raises the question of how privacy was preserved by people who could not afford to live in houses big enough to separate their private space from that of other families. Was privacy important to them, and what meaning did they attach to it? He presents evidence showing that the people lived in very crowded houses and neighborhoods and were exposed to the most intimate details about each other, as in the late Ottoman port cities. In answering his questions, he suggests that privacy was grasped as consisting of two aspects: a physical privacy and a privacy of information. Physical privacy was secured in the seclusion of women and valued as highly important. The privacy of information, on the other hand, was deemed less important. In this way, Marcus reconciles the testimonies he finds in the court records that disclose intimate stories about neighbors with the purpose of many of these stories: to defend the moral value of the seclusion of women. In that manner, the urban poor maintained their own form of privacy, one that was quite different from the elite's cultural ideal, though the ideal as such was upheld.

Studying seventeenth-century Jerusalem, Dror Ze'evi has taken Marcus's interpretation one step further by showing that the importance of physical privacy motivated the violation of the privacy of information. Hence, intimate information was exposed in order to defend and reinforce the moral concept of physical privacy. In his understanding, the prevailing practice of going to the authorities and informing them about neighbors' intimate relations occurred when the relations involved were undermining the concept of physical privacy. In this way, people participated in maintaining the social order for which physical privacy served as a basic organizing principle (Ze'evi 1991, 320–24).

The choice of the term *privacy* for this discussion is somewhat misleading despite Marcus's explanation of this terminology. The cultural ideal at stake concerns neither personal privacy nor the boundaries between the individual and the public. The dividing lines do not separate individuals from one another, but rather groups defined in terms of gender and family. Thus, the concern is not privacy as such, but rather women's chastity and seclusion from nonfamily men as well as inclusion in and exclusion from the family as a means of social control (Marcus 1986, 168).[15]

Marcus's interpretation, its development by Ze'evi, and Abu-Lughod's argument presuppose that the upper class defined the cultural ideals of family and the seclusion of women for society as a whole, ideals facilitated by their spacious houses. Furthermore, this logic implies that the lower classes reconstituted the elite's ideals of family and the seclusion of women in order to keep the upper-class mode as an ideal, and that their actual lifestyle was a necessary evil resulting from poverty. There are several reasons why this line of thinking is flawed, not the least being the description of the cultural exchange between the upper and lower classes as only a top-down exchange. However, for the purposes of the current discussion, I concentrate on its main weakness: its adherence to materialistic reasoning that results in seeing poverty as a monocausal explanation. In this respect, Abu-Lughod takes the living conditions of the poor several steps beyond the materialistic explanation to suggest a lower-class cultural construction of family space.[16]

15. About the scholarly emphasis on sentiment and privacy as defining characteristics of modern families in western Europe, see Hareven 1991, 98.

16. It should be noted, however, that in his book (published three years after his article) Marcus rephrases his conclusion about the lack of privacy of information, rendering it as "cultural preference, in the sense that the community opted for a dense physical environment and for group life despite the fact that this choice inevitably limited personal privacy" (1989, 323), and interpreting this choice in the context of the security, warmth, and communality gained by a close proximity with neighbors (324).

Neighbors, Housemates, and the Semifamilial Space

Close proximity of family members and neighbors meant more, much more, than a necessary evil to people of the middle class. It played a significant role not only in maintaining social order, for which the close proximity of non-family members served as a chastity guard replacing physical seclusion, but also in providing people with a wider choice of relationships, social networks, and support, features that turned family households into a community. Furthermore, I suggest that under the circumstances of rapid urban growth and constant immigration, not only did the demand for housing increase, but also the need to boost community bonds grew, frequently through close proximity among immigrants who came from the same village or town as well as between new acquaintances.

In considering the relations between neighbors in terms of cultural norms, we should also note another cultural feature, the notions of partnership and cooperation. Anybody who reads court records more extensively cannot miss the astonishing records of partnership *(sharika)* and the common possession of property that bonded people, many of whom often held tiny shares in what might seem to be no more than a source for trouble and endless disputes.[17] The object of partnership was almost anything, and partnerships can be traced between owners of soap factories, investors, and olive oil producers; between orchard owners and orange merchants; between landlords and cultivators; and so on. The *waqf* and *musha'* systems cannot be properly understood without the concepts of partnership and cooperation.[18] Granted, these examples of partnership in possession or cooperation in management and produc-

17. See, for example, a lawsuit submitted to the Haifa court by a postman, who bought five out of twenty-four shares *(qararit)* of a horse from one of its two owners (HCR, *Jaridat al-Dabt* 5, 16 Za 1331–5 M 1332/16 X–4 XII 1913, 16, 29–30, 46, case 55). See also al-Qattan 2002, 518–23.

18. On the *waqf,* see chapter 2, note 8. As a result of the features of the *waqf,* a few generations after a family *waqf* was established, numerous distant relatives could find themselves sharing the revenues of the same property. *Musha'* was a widespread method in many rural areas, where the village rather than the household was considered as a unit for purposes of taxation. In order to deal with this situation and to reduce the risks involved in agricultural production, the villagers held the lands jointly, divided them into fields, and rotated them among themselves every couple of years. See, for example, Mundy 1994.

tion belong to the socioeconomic sphere, whereas the issue at stake—shared spaces and physical proximity in family households—requires an explanation in cultural terms. Moreover, these examples are profoundly different from one another in many respects, yet they share the deeply ingrained notions of partnership and cooperation. Hence, I mention them here as an indication that, in general, sharing was basic to rather than an option for the societies observed. In the context of the present discussion, this means that members of these communities would not necessarily avoid close proximity, and, as I have pointed out earlier, at times of rapid change close proximity might even have provided them with a greater sense of security and companionship.

The dispute between Amina and Salim from Haifa (chapter 4) illustrates my points about the middle-class semifamilial space and the cultural meaning of interaction among neighbors and nonfamily housemates. The testimonies about the quarrel between them include a few hints on the matter. Salim's witnesses mentioned that the reason for the quarrel was that Amina had borrowed 5 beşlik from her neighbors and had asked Salim to pay it back. Two out of three witnesses, the couple's landlord and another resident, described the scene in detail, and the third, another neighbor, knew all the details but said explicitly that he was not at home when it happened.[19] The landlord's testimony was the most detailed. He was present when the quarrel occurred and was directly involved. He said that the couple had lived peacefully in his house for four months; Salim had brought Amina food, and she had not complained. According to the landlord, one day Amina asked him to ask her husband to give her 5 beşlik. At that moment, Salim had arrived and brought Amina bread and meat. When she asked him for the 5 beşlik, he asked why she needed the money. She answered that she had borrowed the sum from the neighbors. He did not give her the money, she refused to take the food, and since then he had not returned or slept with her. The second witness was a neighbor who heard everything from next door (it is not clear from the record whether he lived in another room of the house or in another house, but he evidently was close enough to hear the quarrel). He repeated the testimony that the couple had lived peacefully, that Salim had supplied his wife with her necessities, and that

---

19. Hearsay was legally inadmissible (*Mecelle*, Article 1688), yet the record includes no comment about rejection by the judge, maybe because it was the third testimony, and two witnesses sufficed anyway; this witness was entitled "sheikh."

"we"—here it is not clear to whom he referred, perhaps to himself and the rest of the neighbors, or maybe to himself and his family—did not hear any quarrel about food and drink. But then twenty days prior to his testimony, he had heard Salim's wife asking Salim for 5 beşlik, and he testified about the rest of the event along lines similar to the first witness.

The testimonies indicate that the couple shared a common space at least with their landlord. The other neighbors, whether they were housemates or next-door neighbors, lived close enough to hear whatever was going on in that house. Amina was in the same room with the landlord when Salim was out. It is not entirely clear if it was the landlord or some other neighbor who lent Amina money. This was not a negligible sum of money to borrow casually, even assuming that it would be paid back by the end of the day.[20] The other sums of money mentioned in this case and in Muhammad and Qasim's case may put this sum in proportion: at the end of the trial, Amina received as daily maintenance and child support less than one-third (1.5 beşlik) of the sum she had borrowed; the daily income of Qasim, who was a professional construction worker, was lower than this sum, 15 kuruş (about 4 beşlik); Muhammad earned a somewhat higher sum of money (5–7 beşlik) per day by selling vegetables (see chapter 4, "A Note on Money and Daily Conditions"). Thus, it seems that Amina felt close enough to at least one of her neighbors to ask for such a favor and that this neighbor trusted her and wanted to help her. She also felt comfortable enough with the landlord to ask him to become involved in the issue between herself and her husband. It is not mentioned in so many words in the testimonies, but the subtext suggests that Salim was deeply offended by his wife's initiative. The landlord's testimony focused on the dialogue between Amina and himself, whereas the other neighbor concentrated on the ensuing dispute between the husband and wife. It was according to the latter's account that Salim's strong reaction was not after he heard about the loan, but rather after he heard for what purpose the money was borrowed.

20. When a woman received a court decision that forced her husband to pay her *nafaqa* (maintenance, alimony, or child support), she was legally permitted to borrow money up to the sum specified by the court, and lenders had the right to expect her husband to pay it back. This right was also mentioned in the court decision with which Amina's lawsuit ended. However, Amina borrowed the money before she had a court decision and even before she sued her husband.

Amina offended her husband twice: by not relying on him as her provider (an attitude that she reinforced by refusing to take the food he brought her) and by humiliating him when she turned to an outsider for the money. One should bear in mind that all three testimonies—though not entirely identical in their details and focus—stressed the same points: that this quarrel caused Salim to leave his wife and daughter, and that until then he had been a perfect husband and father. Because they were Salim's witnesses, this narrative was most probably expected to tip the scales in his favor, indicating that it fitted the legal concept of marital rights and duties.

The close proximity of nonfamily members dwelling under the same roof complicated the rules of the game inside the house. In a house where two or three unrelated families lived, linked only by neighborly ties, and where each family constituted a separate economic unit, more options for social interaction and maneuvering existed, and more than one center of gravity. Thus, the main repercussions of the situation in which nonfamily members shared houses and private spaces were sociocultural. The situation provided people with a human reservoir not tied to them by complex familial interests and emotions. Yet they were living as close, even closer sometimes, to nonfamily as to their own family. We do not know what sort of relations stood behind the loan that Amina took. Yet it illustrates the option with which the neighborly relations provided Amina, a member of a very small simple-family household, to break away from the inherently imbalanced relations she had as a wife and mother with her husband and the father of her baby daughter.

At the same time, Salim's reaction and the way his witnesses, his attorney, and the recording scribe interpreted the situation suggest that Amina had crossed an invisible boundary. This boundary separated men and women along family lines and kept them apart even when physically they shared the same space and were socially involved with one another. This dividing line existed not only in the minds of all the men who testified or who heard and recorded the testimonies, but also in Amina's mind. There is no indication that Amina tried to challenge the concept of family boundaries. For some reason, however, she constructed marital relations and the gendered division of labor in the family differently from Salim. We may recall that although the witnesses alleged that the couple had lived peacefully together since they had rented the room, and only the incident of the loan had brought about the dispute, Amina had hired an attorney to represent her in claims against her husband long before this incident happened, around the time when they moved into the rented room. She also had initiated the lawsuit. The record also indicates that even before the incident that brought about her lawsuit, Amina's attorney had brought up the issue of conjugal dwelling with Salim. The high sum of money she borrowed, the type of furniture she owned, her attorney's implications that she felt like a prisoner in the rented room—all suggest that Amina belonged to a higher social level than Salim.

In her initial claim, Amina mentioned furniture that she had left at her father-in-law's house (probably her *jihaz*): a closet, two big gas lamps, a bureau, and a mirror. Khadaja Abu Radwan, who ran away from her husband's house in Ramla (chapter 6), mentioned similar items in her lawsuit. The use of these and other items was growing in nineteenth-century Palestine. Many of these goods were imported from Europe or produced by local artisans who responded to the growing demand by the urban upper-class and successful middle-class families for European-style furniture.[21] It seems that Amina grew up in a family belonging to one of these levels, probably the latter. The gap between her and her husband may have resulted not so much from a difference in their class affiliation as such, but rather from the different meanings attributed to their similar social levels in their different places of origin (Saida and Nablus). Alternatively, it is possible that Amina's social position was indeed higher and that, for some reason, perhaps owing to her natal family's immigration to Haifa, she had to compromise over her groom's status. Be the source for the differences between Amina and Salim as it may, Amina apparently meant to provoke Salim by borrowing the money, as women often did in order to cope with a situation in which they were by definition inferior (Agmon 1998), so she must have been aware of the boundary she was crossing.

Women and Family Boundaries

Family boundaries, as far as middle-class women were concerned, were as intangible as the rope of an acrobat in a flying circus act: from the audience's perspective, they were invisible, yet the women necessarily remained well aware of them in order to juggle their family loyalties and obligations. In an

---

21. Agmon 1985, 83–84, 194–95, 1995, 229–37; Bahjat and al-Tamimi 1917, 1: 110–11. See also Göçek 1996, 87–116, on the growing import and consumption of Western goods in the Ottoman capital in the eighteenth and nineteenth centuries.

article dealing with this issue (Agmon 1998), I stress the different patterns of women's behavior in court according to class affiliation, patterns that reflect the differences in the way they experienced the family. I highlight the agility and resourcefulness typical of middle- and lower-class women, arguing that these characteristics resulted from a socialization that prepared them for constant physical and emotional instability in their family lives. This experience underpins the realities for middle-class women in late Ottoman Jaffa and Haifa in comparison both to their male counterparts and to women from the upper class.

The Family and the Stranger

Two lawsuits of the same divorced couple, Hasan Shahada and Hind al-Khalil from Haifa, illustrate middle-class women's realities in this period. Judging by some of the details mentioned in their case records, mainly concerning the house they owned, this couple belonged to a somewhat higher socioeconomic level than most of the others whose cases are discussed in this book. At the same time, they did not quite belong to the upper class. Al-Khalil was the name of one of the most prominent families in Haifa, but nothing in Hind's lineage or the names and titles of other family members mentioned in these two records suggests that she belonged to this notable family. On the contrary, some details in these records point to the plausibility that her family networks in Haifa were very loose. I suspect that her natal family immigrated to Haifa, possibly when her father came there in the line of duty as a state official.

The records of the two lawsuits are relatively short and contain no disputes, for Hind, the defendant, did not appear in court in either case. Furthermore, although the two records are protocols, they resemble the registration type in that they are more like summaries prepared afterward than detailed accounts of the deliberations; at certain points, the reader might even get the impression that the judge's decision was predetermined (these features are particularly salient in the second lawsuit). There are shortcuts in recording some of the regular legal formulas, and the witnesses were ready to testify in the first session, immediately after the plaintiff presented his claim. This situation does not necessarily mean that justice was distorted; it is possible that because Hind was summoned three times, according to the procedure, and did not show up, Hasan knew that she did not intend to come. When the second lawsuit was deliberated, Hind was not in town. Therefore, he might have expected that the burden of proof would be on him and so brought witnesses and was prepared. Despite their weaknesses, these two case records taken together shed light on some noteworthy points regarding middle-class women's experiences.

The two lawsuits were brought before Judge Abdülhalim in Haifa and recorded by the *başkatib* Muhyi al-Din. The first was deliberated between October and late December 1913. The second lawsuit was deliberated and decided in one session in March 1914. Hasan ibn Ahmad ibn Sheikh Shahada initiated both lawsuits against his ex-wife, Hind bint Mahmud ibn Hajj Khalil. In her absence, Hind was represented by Muhammad al-Salah, a member of a notable family in Haifa who in the past had served as a court scribe and later became a professional attorney. He frequently represented litigants in court, but in this case was appointed by the judge as an ad hoc representative *(wakil musakhkhar)* for Hind owing to her absence.[22]

In the first case, Hasan claimed that he and his ex-wife were the joint owners of a small house in Wadi al-Saliba, a neighborhood that had been built during the nineteenth century, on the northern slopes of Mount Carmel and to the southeast, outside the city walls of Haifa. Hasan described the house as having one room *('uta)*, a living room *(liwan)*, a kitchen and toilet *(muntafa'at shar'iyya)*. Because the house was indivisible, he asked Hind to share it with him. However, while she lived in the house, she was preventing him from realizing his right to possession. He asked the court to end this situation. After the ad hoc representative was appointed, Hasan brought two witnesses living in the same neighborhood; both of them repeated the description of the house and confirmed that Hind was indeed residing there. Their credibility was checked and approved. Then the ad hoc representative denied the claim concerning ownership of the house, and Hasan was asked to submit proof thereof. The same witnesses testified to Hasan and Hind's joint ownership. In the summary of these testimonies, the *başkatib* mentioned that the value of the house was 8,000 kuruş and that Hasan had requested to divide it between the two of them, but the house turned out to be legally indivisible. Thus, a coin *(qur'a)* was tossed in court, and Hasan won. Judge Abdülhalim decided that the divorced husband and wife would use the house for one year each in turn,

---

22. See chapter 6 on the ad hoc representatives. On Muhammad al-Salah, see Yazbak 1998, 141.

and because Hasan won the coin toss, he was to be the first one to do so. The ad hoc representative was ordered to inform Hind that she had to evacuate the house and hand it over to Hasan (HCR, *Jaridat al-Dabt* 5, 16 Za 1331–16 M 1332/16 X–15 XII 1913, 15, 70–71, case 54).

Some three months later Hasan came once again to the court. This time his claim dealt with the question of Fawziyya, their daughter. Because Hind again did not show up in court (the title *hurma*, "Madame," preceded her name this time), the same ad hoc representative was assigned to represent her. Hasan said that since he had divorced Hind, he was paying her 6 metalik (about 2 kuruş) a day as child support for their minor daughter, who was in her custody. After the termination of Hind's 'idda period, Hasan continued, she had married a stranger *(ajnabi)*, Mahmud ibn Muhammad al-Husayn Abu Hana from al-Tantura, a village on the seashore some thirty-five kilometers south of Haifa, and had moved there with Fawziyya. In so doing, Hind had lost her right to custody of her daughter. Hind's mother, Fatima bint Husayn al-Mubasiyya, the next custodian in line to replace the mother, was not available because she had also left Haifa and moved to Tripoli together with her son, Muhammad Wasif Efendi, who was serving there as a clerk. Thus, said Hasan, "I ask the court to order my absent ex-wife Hind to hand over my minor daughter Fawziyya to me because she [the girl] is not safe with the aforementioned husband [*likawniha ghayr ma'mun 'alyha 'inda al-zawj al-madhkur*], Mahmud Abu Hana in the village of Tantura, and to release me from paying child support." Hind's legal representative denied the claim, at which point Hasan brought forward two witnesses, one of them a former villager from Tantura, who confirmed his entire claim. Their credibility was confirmed by *tazkiya* witnesses, and the judge decided in favor of Hasan, ordering Hind, via the ad hoc representative, to hand over Fawziyya to her father, who was also absolved from paying child support (HCR, *Jaridat al-Dabt* 5, 20 R 1332/18 III 1914, 162–63, case 2).

A Woman's Domestic Cycle

Hasan and Hind's case helps us to understand better how middle-class women experienced the family and to reconstruct a plausible female life course for the women of three generations—a minor girl, her mother, and her grandmother. None of the three appeared in court: Fawziyya, the minor girl, was merely the object of the second lawsuit; her mother, Hind, was an absent defendant in both trials; and her grandmother, Fatima, was mentioned only by the way as not being available for rearing her granddaughter in Hind's place. Each belonged to a different patrilineal family that defined her first set of family loyalties and obligations, pedigree, and socioeconomic position.

Hind had been married for several years to Hasan, during which time she gave birth to Fawziyya and with Hasan purchased the small house in Haifa. The couple had probably lived with their daughter in that house. Her loyalty was then divided between her natal and conjugal families, but as long as she was married to Hasan, the father of her daughter, and did not share a household with other segments of his (and her daughter's) patrilineal family, this division of loyalties and obligations did not necessarily cause any severe conflict. From the little information about the house in the lawsuit, it appears that when Hasan divorced Hind, she intended to remain there, and he was willing to continue sharing it with her, but she did not allow him to do so. Because the description of this case is relatively "thin" and we lack Hind's legal version and some negotiations in court between the divorced husband and wife, it is more difficult to build plausible scenarios. However, based on Hasan's version alone, we can at least say that a divorced couple continuing to share one house was not unthinkable. Nevertheless, in this case Hind did consider the situation unacceptable, which led to her eviction and possibly accelerated her remarriage. It should be noted that a married couple buying a house together might be considered a feature that underpinned small households and reinforced a notion of the simple family in the middle class. However, I did not come across other case records that indicate how widespread a phenomenon it was. My impression is that it was rare. The house was small, yet it was bigger and four times more expensive than the original one-room house that Muhammad Hasun (chapter 5) built in Wadi al-Nisnas. These features gave me the impression that Hind and Hasan were better off than Muhammad and his son Qasim, who had immigrated from al-Tira.

Other details in these records indicate that Hind did not have many relatives in Haifa. Her father is not mentioned as deceased in her pedigree. Her brother (he might have been her half-brother on her mother's side; his pedigree was not mentioned) had moved to Tripoli together with her mother, and we learn that he was a state employee. He was mentioned by two given names, Muhammad Wasif, to which the title "Efendi" was added, a formula typical of Ottoman officials. This information leads me to consider the plausibility that

Hind's father was also a state employee, who had come to Haifa at some point in the course of his career and maybe was appointed later to a job elsewhere, leaving behind Hind, by then married to Hasan, his son Muhammad Wasif, and his ex-wife, Fatima, who lived in her son's household. This would explain why Hind (or any other woman in a similar situation) would have no natal family household to join as a divorcée and would be forced to find a new husband quickly, moving to a distant village, changing her entire environment and lifestyle, and risking the custody of her daughter.

In the few months after the divorce, her daughter lived with her, first in Haifa, in the small house in Wadi al-Saliba, then in Tantura. Hasan was her provider for the first three months and was to continue to pay her child support on behalf of Fawziyya. As soon as Hind remarried, her loyalties and obligations were divided among three families: her natal family, her daughter's natal family, and her new conjugal family. This situation, however, did not exist for long. Before this remarriage, assuming that Hasan sued Hind for the house immediately after he divorced her, the verdict reached three months later forced her to leave their communal house; her *'idda* period also terminated around that time. Under these circumstances, she remarried. Less than three months later Hasan sued for custody of Fawziyya and won, meaning that soon after Hind remarried and moved to Tantura, she had to hand over Fawziyya to Hasan. In terms of her family loyalties and obligations, it probably meant that Hasan's family was no longer included in Hind's list of families because she stopped receiving child support from Hasan on behalf of Fawziyya and in principle had no say in her daughter's upbringing. Her loyalties and obligations were again divided between two families. Emotionally, however, this change also meant that she was completely separated from her daughter, less than nine years of age and possibly much younger, because the available means of transportation and the cultural norms regarding women traveling alone would not have permitted Hind to travel often from Tantura to Haifa.

As to Fawziyya, according to the rule of "the stranger husband" (chapter 5), her fate as a minor child would have been the same no matter whether she was male or female. Even without the case of a "stranger husband," widespread divorce meant that young children of both sexes frequently experienced separation from one of their parents, usually first the father and then the mother, and were shunted between family households. However, boys in such cases moved back to their father's household when they were seven years old and remained there for good. Even when as adults they married and started a new simple household, this change would not cause a division in their family loyalties and obligations. Their new household merely formed a continuation of their patrilineal family. No matter how many times in their lives they would marry, divorce, or bury wives, this would not cause any rupture in their family loyalties and obligations.

Girls moved back to their father's household at the age of nine. However, for them this move was only the beginning of toing and froing between family households and accordingly divided family loyalties. Thus, when Fawziyya was separated from her father and accompanied her mother, and then when she moved back to her father, she was undergoing a process of socialization that was preparing her for constant changes of household and divided family loyalties and obligations as an adult woman.

The little information available about Hind's mother, Fatima, illustrates the later phase in women's lives in this time and place. Fatima was either a divorcée or a widow at the time of the lawsuits. She lived in her son's family household and had moved with him to Tripoli in northern Syria when he was assigned a job there in the Ottoman administration. This was the reason why she could not replace Hind in taking care of Fawziyya. Older women without a husband to provide for them would often join their adult son's household, if they had a son. This was also the case of the mother of Qasim, the professional construction worker, whose father demanded that Qasim provide for him. This meant that urban middle-class family households, although small, might still include more than two generations, and their structure would not strictly be a simple one. It also meant that wives in such households would frequently live with their mothers-in-law even when they had not moved to a joint-family household on marriage. Another point illustrated by the case of Hind's mother is that even at this stage in her life, when she was probably no longer a candidate for marriage and had settled down in what looked like a permanent home, she had to move again, this time not to another family household, but to another town.

The Stranger as Boundary

The concept of "stranger husband" is significant in this situation. As noted in the legal discourse on the family, the custody of minor children *(hadana)* was seen as a maternal, feminine right and obligation. Even in cases in which the mother lost custody, the substitute custodians first included female relatives of the mother, then female relatives of the father, and only finally the father himself and other male relatives (Motzki 1996, 134–36; Tucker 1998, 117–19; Ibn ʿAbidin n.d., 2: 633–42). Under this set of rules, particularly interesting is the rule of "stranger husband" *(ajnabi)*—that if a mother married such a man, she lost the right to custody of her minor children from her previous marriage. In chapter 5, I suggested that this rule was a sanction disciplining women who married outside the patrilineal family. Based on the interpretation of Hind and Hasan's case records, I would further argue that under the circumstances prevailing in the port cities, the sanction affected mainly the women and consequently also the children of the middle and lower classes. Practically, then, the use of this rule served as an indication of families who did not belong to the elite, a boundary bluntly unmasking the nature of the prevailing social order as being male dominated.

As I mentioned in chapter 5, the term *ajnabi* (stranger, alien) is defined by another legal term, *ghayr mahram* (permissible, not forbidden), which belonged to a separate set of rules dealing with prohibitions on marriage (Ibn ʿAbidin n.d., 2: 276–77). The latter rules defined the sort of kinship and other relations between two people that would prevent their marriage. In the context of the "stranger husband" rule, when a man married a mother of minor children to whom he was related in a way that would *not* have prohibited him from marrying one of them according to the prohibitions on marriage, he was defined as a "stranger husband," and the children had to be removed from their mother's custody. In other words, a woman who married a man who was not from a certain group of her children's agnates (not their uncle, for instance) would lose custody of her children. In the legal literature, the connection between the two terms, *ajnabi* and *ghayr mahram,* is made in passing, without further explanation, which suggests that the connection was an obvious one for the Muslim jurists.

However, in the context here, the connection is less obvious, and further discussion might shed some more light on the legal notion of the family. When the marriage prohibitions are checked carefully, it becomes clear that as soon as a man married a woman with children, the question of whether he was forbidden to marry her children owing to kinship or milk relationships became irrelevant: he was immediately prohibited from marrying them because he had married their mother. The term *not prohibited* thus serves as the default in explaining the term *stranger* and has no practical meaning as such. Furthermore, the rule applies to boys and girls alike, although from the outset, whether or not the mother's new husband was prohibited from marrying her children was irrelevant in the case of boys.

That a stranger is someone who is not an agnate is rather telling as far as the notion of the family and its boundaries are concerned. However, in the internal logic of the patrilineal family, if the term *not prohibited* is a default definition in the rules about custody, why replace it by the term *stranger?* I suggest that the explanation lies in the different perspectives from which the two terms are defined and the different messages they contain. The prohibitions on marriage are defined from inside the family. They presuppose motivation for marriage inside the family circles and set what is conceived of as necessary restrictions to this tendency. The rules of custody are defined from the opposite point of view. They set the boundaries of the family, giving the definition of a husband who stands outside these boundaries a negative meaning—a stranger, outsider, someone who is unreliable—and attach a price to such a marriage, to be paid by the woman involved and by her children.

Family and Class

In contrast to Hind and Fawziyya's case, the lifestyle of upper-class families in the port cities indicates that, practically, these rules for marriage and custody did not particularly affect such families. Descriptions taken from the first volume of the memoirs of Dr. Yousef Haikel, *Ayyam al-Siba* (Days of juvenility, 1988) illustrate the situation. The Haykal[23] family was a distinguished and wealthy family in Jaffa, connected by marriage to other upper-class families from Jaffa as well as from other Palestinian towns. Members of the Haykal family were merchants, orange grove owners, and held administrative positions in the municipality and subdistrict center. Yusuf was born in December 1907. He acquired his higher education in France and served as the last mayor of Jaffa (1945–48).[24] He published his memoirs when in his early eighties. The first volume concentrates on his childhood during the last years of the Ottoman rule, the First World War, and the early years of the British Mandate. The

23. I transliterate the names from Arabic and spell the author's name "Yusuf Haykal" (and not "Yousef Haikel" as it appears in the book).

24. After the foundation of the state of Israel, the municipality of Jaffa was unified with that of Tel-Aviv (LeVine 1999, 421).

descriptions of the first ten years of his life, which were also the last ten of Ottoman rule, deal mainly with his childhood in the compound of his natal family household near the railway station in the northeastern outskirts of Jaffa, the relations between the various branches of his extended family, his education, and the family travels out of town during the war (Haikel 1988, 13, 216–18; see also Enderwitz 2002, 66).

Haykal's memoirs are highly detailed. His descriptions about everyday life in his family household, his experiences and thoughts as a young boy, dialogues and conversations in which he took part or overheard as a child, family celebrations—all are pedantically told like scenarios for a movie.[25] Literary theorists define autobiography as a genre of fiction rather than mere positivistic documentation of personal memories. Therefore, they focus less on the factual aspect in autobiographies and more on the author's construction of the self and identity. From this perspective, which highlights the author's developmental aspect, accounts of childhood and youth are considered particularly "pure" owing to the descriptions of everyday life and family relations typically provided by their authors (Enderwitz 2002, 49–55).[26]

Even a brief look at some of the Haykal family's marital relations suffices to indicate that members of such upper-class families either intermarried or married within their own extended family, to the point that certain married couples covered both options (see fig. 4, the Haykals' family tree). Yusuf, his brother, and seven sisters were born to such a couple. Mustafa Haykal, his father, had married Zakiyya Sakajha, his mother, in 1890. Zakiyya's mother was Sayyida 'Ilmiyya Malakha, the only daughter of a wealthy man, Sayyid 'Ali Malakha. Sayyida 'Ilmiyya was married twice. Her first husband, the father of Zakiyya and of her brother and sister, was Hajj Isma'il Sakajha, a member of another rich family in Jaffa. After her first husband died, Sayyida 'Ilmiyya married 'Ali Efendi Haykal, a rich soap merchant who was also the uncle of Mustafa Haykal, who was 'Ilmiyya's son-in-law (husband of her daughter Zakiyya) and Yusuf's father. The two families were further related to each other because 'Ali's daughter from his first marriage, Fatima Haykal, was

25. Similar to the rhetorical style of Bahjat and al-Tamimi 1917. See the end of chapter 1.

26. For a broad survey on the development of literary theory on the genre of autobiography until the 1980s, see Olney 1980. See also Confino 2000 for some insightful comments on memory, oblivion, and history.

The Haykal Family

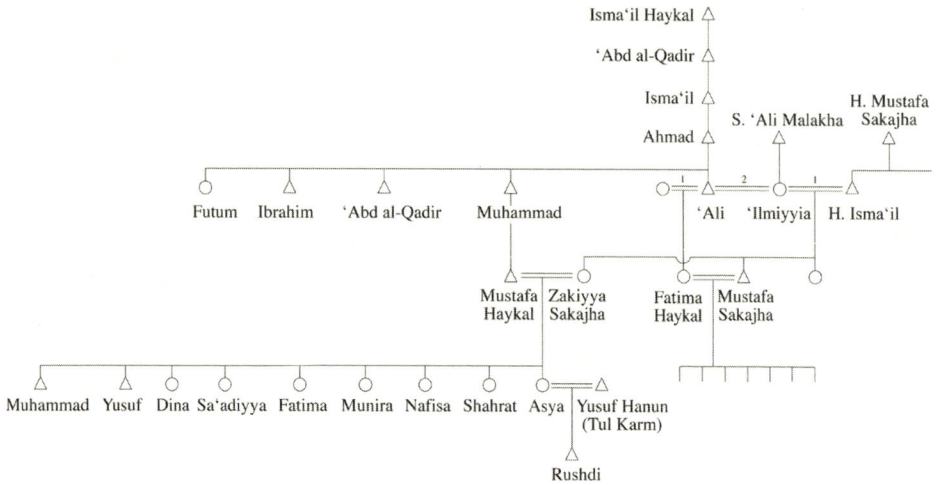

Figure 4. The Haykal family tree. Compiled by the author from Haikel 1988 and JCR.

married to his second wife's son from her first marriage, Mustafa Sakajha (Zakiyya's brother and Yusuf's uncle).[27]

Confusing? This is only a small part of the puzzle. In the context of this discussion, the description suffices to show that a case of a "stranger husband" would have been a rare situation with so much intermarriage. Furthermore, had such a situation occurred, it would have probably been easier to follow the rule without cutting the children off altogether from their mother (or from their father, in the case of a regular divorce), owing to the household formations and structures in these families.

Yusuf and his brother and sisters lived with their parents and servants in a compound consisting of two houses, a garden, a water pool, and other facilities and structures located amidst orchards, close to the train station and the cemetery, to the northeast of Jaffa (Haikel 1988, 41–44). His grandmother on his

27. JCR, *Hujaj* 83, 29 L 1317/2 III 1900, 19–22, case 1045; Haikel 1988, 7–8, 48, 216–18. See the Sakajha family tree in Agmon 1995, 161.

mother's side, Sayyida 'Ilmiyya Malakha, lived with her second husband, Yusuf's great uncle, 'Ali Haykal, on the first floor of the 'Awad house, a large dwelling in Bustrus Street, off the then new clock square of Jaffa, at walking distance from her daughter (Yusuf's mother), and her step-nephew (Yusuf's father), and their children (Haikel 1988, 7; see also Agmon 1998). Later, apparently after her second husband, 'Ali Haykal, had died, she moved to Manshiyya, the northern neighborhood of Jaffa, also at walking distance from her daughter's house. There she joined the household of her son, Mustafa Sakajha, and his wife, Fatima Haykal (the daughter of her late second husband, 'Ali Haykal, from his first marriage), and their six children, who lived on the second floor of a house known as the Za'blawi house (Haikel 1988, 48). In his memoirs, Yusuf Haykal mentions several casual visits to his grandmother in both her houses. His memoirs begin with the story of his mother going to stay at her mother's house in Bustrus Street, where she gave birth to him, her youngest son, and remained several weeks until she returned with the baby to her conjugal family house near the railway station (7–8). He also describes his uncles, aunts, and cousins, as well as his elder sister and her husband and children visiting his natal family's compound, celebrating holidays, dining and taking afternoon tea with them. His elder sister, Asya, who was married to Yusuf Hanun, originally from an established family in Tul Karm (west of Nablus), also lived close enough to pay her natal family daily visits, to leave Rushdi, her elder son, there, and to stay there herself for longer periods whenever she gave birth to a new baby. At some point after the First World War, she lived with her conjugal family next door to her parents, in one of the two houses in their compound within the orchard (45–49, 60, 109).

The structure of all the households mentioned explicitly in the memoirs was similar to the typical middle-class structure at the time, insofar as people related to each other by kin or by marriage were concerned; it consisted of parents and their offspring, a simple family, also often joined by the mother of the head of the family. The similarity in this basic structure, however, formed only one aspect of the construction of the family of these urban classes. In other aspects, they differed from each other. In the upper class, for instance, the family household also included servants. In Yusuf's account of his school days, he mentions the servant, who would accompany him to and from school and would probably be the first person to whom the boy talked about his day at school. He also mentions a maid who lived with them. It is rather striking, however, that none of the servants is mentioned by name, unlike every distant relative. Neither does Haykal mention the names of the children of their German neighbors, who used to play with the Haykal children every day (11–12, 15–18, 20, 23, 27, 29, 32–33, 36, 44, 49–51). The only name he gives of nonkin involved in the household is that of the citrus cultivator, Hajj Ahmad, who would bring fruits and vegetables to the house every other day. Yusuf Haykal begins to mention his name just before the point in the memoirs where Hajj Ahmad brought him a baby goat, to which the boy became deeply devoted (50, 53–57). However, when this story ends and the goat dies, he mentions Hajj Ahmad again as just *al-bayari*, "the citrus cultivator" (57–58). It is difficult to ascertain, however, whether keeping a distance from the servants reflects his family's attitude toward servants at the time or the way Dr. Haykal saw himself in retrospect.

Upper-class families' tendency to endogamous marriage, or marrying "their own kind"—namely, spouses from a relatively small circle of upper-class families—encouraged close daily contacts among several simple households of the same extended family. Such extended families, as in Yusuf Haykal's case, often included both the husbands' and wives' natal families. These simple families did not form one large household, yet they lived close enough to each other to allow for intensive ties and relations, horizontally between simple households of kin of the same generation, and vertically among kin of three generations. At the upper social levels, then, a person's close family was apparently extended and multigenerational, and this family consisted of several practical and emotional safety nets, in which the effects of the priority given to the male lineage as reflected in the rule of "the stranger husband" were rather subdued and less painful than among their lower-class counterparts.[28]

Marital relations between upper-class families also included families from other towns, who became part of the extended family's safety net. During the First World War, for instance, when Yusuf's parents thought that it was not safe to stay in Jaffa, the entire extended family moved to Tul Karm and for a long period of time lived close to the natal family of Yusuf's brother-in-law

28. See Fay 2003 and Cuno 2003 on the development of the notion of the simple family among the Ottoman-Egyptian elite, and Göçek 1996 on the disintegration of the Ottoman household as a social unit during the transformations of the nineteenth century and the emergence of an Ottoman bourgeoisie.

from Tul Karm, the Hanun family. Other relatives moved to Nablus during the war and were hosted by members of the ʿAshur family, to whom they were also related by marriage (59–72, 87–100).

The compound in which Yusuf, his brother and sisters, their parents, and the servants lived was large and spacious, surrounded by orchards, whereas middle-class households shared one house among two or three families, with other families living very close by or next door. Upper-class families that did not build houses by the orange groves at the outskirts of the town resided, like Yusuf's grandparents or his uncle Mustafa Sakajha and aunt Fatima Haykal, in large apartments in the modern neighborhoods built outside the city walls. ʿAli Haykal, for instance, the second husband of Yusuf's grandmother, ʿIlmiyya Malakha, owned a large house in the old city of Jaffa (217), yet he preferred to live with her in the apartment on Bustrus Street outside the old city. Although upper-class families dwelled in spacious houses consisting of many bedrooms and other facilities, the children, according to the memoirs, shared bedrooms with one another and with their parents. Only Mustafa Haykal, the head of the household, kept a room for himself (41–45). Family members living crowded together was thus not necessarily a sign of poverty. This feature provides food for thought in the discussion on the concept of privacy and also the cultural meaning of living in close proximity for the middle class.

From what we have seen so far, in the port cities simple middle-class households were widespread, and this situation was not typical of the middle class alone, nor was it a new phenomenon in Ottoman-Arab cities at large. However, the constant immigration to the port cities also involved urban communities, where many relatively small families (not only households of simple structure) were to be found. Families of upper-class immigrants could integrate through marriage alliances with local established families, and their economic resources and social status would help them in the process. What is illustrated by Hind's case is that in middle-class families the combination of modest means and a small local family potentially heightened the vulnerability of such families and of their dependent members in particular. A divorcée in a situation similar to Hind's would have had more choice and latitude if she had a larger natal family in town. Better resources would have enabled her to remain unmarried for a longer period than the three to four months during which the law obliged her ex-husband to provide for her or given her the opportunity to bargain for a less problematic remarriage.

Another plausible source of insecurity for the urban middle class might have been the growing tendency of upper-class families, like the Haykals, to move to houses outside town near the orange groves or to large new apartments in urban modern neighborhoods that were less socially heterogeneous than the old city neighborhoods. Prior to this change, the common phenomenon of the location of upper-class large houses among houses populated by people of modest background, in alleys that were often named after the elite family that lived in them, was also a reflection of the social relations between the established family and modest families of its neighborhood.[29] These relations, which historians sometimes refer to as patronage networks or factions, provided families of modest means with some security and support in rough times. The gradual disappearance of upper-class families from the old neighborhoods and their absence from some of the new ones presumably contributed to middle-class families' need to seek security and support elsewhere. This situation might have added more incentive to permit enhanced relations among neighbors and housemates of the middle classes.

Thus, the rapid growth of the port cities and the significant changes their societies underwent also intensified some of the realities of middle-class life and heightened a process of redefinition of both the middle and the upper classes. The salient features of the re-constituted middle-class include simple-family or small joint-household structures, enlarged semifamilial space, and, by default, middle- and lower-class neighborhoods detached from upper-class families' dwellings. These features indicate a certain tension within the legal notion of the patrilineal family that affected mainly the dependent members of the family, especially women and children. As I have demonstrated in earlier chapters, the redefinition of the position of the *shariʿa* court in society entailed an emphasis on features of social justice as part of the legal culture and the court's accessibility to all. However, regarding the tension inherent in the middle-class construction of the family, the reformed *shariʿa* court was less creative in offering solutions and more persistent in enhancing the notion of patrilineal principles.

29. "I walked next to the servant in our street that had our name" (Haikel 1988, 32). See also Abu-Lughod 1987, 170; Marcus 1989, 322.

8

Conclusion

Family, Court, and Modernity

IN THIS STUDY, the family has served as a unit of analysis and a conceptual framework, and the court and the texts it produced provided the arena for observing the family; at the same time, both were major objects of investigation in their own merit. In fact, the legal arena determined the tone and atmosphere of the entire study. This apparent imbalance between a dominant setting, the legal arena, on the one hand, and an understated main actor, the family, on the other, resulted in the first place from the overwhelming role played by the written sources in shaping historical reconstruction. This statement is valid for every historical reconstruction based on any kind of source material. Here, however, the methodology used for reading court records involved turning the records into an object of study and abandoning the instrumental approach to historical sources, thereby stressing the significance of the legal arena.

◆　　◆　　◆

When looked at within the legal setting, the family in late-Ottoman Jaffa and Haifa, although difficult to pin down, served as a useful category of analysis in investigating processes and mechanisms of change. This analytical framework underlined the fragmented and fluid nature of the middle class under circumstances of rapid growth in the port cities. It sustained the analysis of household structures and some of the considerations and practices that shaped them: simple-family households, often of the variety that included the mother and sometime an unmarried sister or daughter of the male head of the household, appeared as a common form among the middle class. Almost all the case records unfolded here (and many others) include evidence to this effect. Housing conditions, chain migration, and cultural norms of neighborliness and semifamilial spaces sustained both simple-family households and their close proximity to one another. As to households headed by women, the case of Hind and Hasan (chapter 7) was the only one I was able to locate in the records where this option was hinted at and evidently failed. It apparently was not a practicable option.

Although both affluent and modest middle-class families were inclined to form simple-family households, this structure represented different tendencies for each of these two groups. The orphan funds established by the Ottoman reformers encouraged the simple-family structure in the higher-middle class by defending the interests of better-off women and children within the orphans' patrilineal families. At the same time, for lower-middle-class families, in particular newcomers without many relatives in town, the structure of a simple-family household was a potential source of tensions that the legal notion of social justice was not able to remedy, as illustrated by the situation of a marriage to a "stranger husband," (chapters 5 and 7). In those families, the simple household reinforced women and children's vulnerability rather than improving their position.

The court reinforced the patrilineal family. The structural changes in the port cities, resulting from both the Ottoman reforms and rapid economic and population growth, created personal situations that often required legal solutions. These changes also shaped the *shari'a* court's open-door attitude toward its clientele and, at the same time, further exposed these clients to the legal notion of the family. However, as noted, the same structural changes reinforced family notions that undermined the patrilineal family, thereby revealing a growing tension in court between its limited ability to offer its clients practical solutions to legal issues and its user-friendly approach.

Many of these clients were newcomers to the port cities. People of varied origins and social positions immigrated to these towns for a variety of reasons, boosting the already fragmented composition of the urban middle class. State employees answered the call of duty. They were mostly lower- or medium-ranking clerks because, in Ottoman terms, Jaffa and Haifa were lower-ranking administrative centers. Villagers and townsmen from nearby and more distant places were attracted by job opportunities at the ports, the railways, and the orchards, as well as in construction, small trade, and domestic and other services. Others who had been relatively well off in their hometowns and villages were also attracted by the economic opportunities and social mobility that the port cities seemed to offer.

Men typically came alone or with small family groups—their own nuclear families with occasionally other members of their extended families. This situation was bound to create numerous tensions. For instance, as soon as the issue of marriage arose in such families, they immediately felt the lack of matches offered by one's extended family, close acquaintances, and social peers back home. Or the status of families that included potential matches for marriage in the new town may not yet have been clearly defined: under the circumstances of rapid demographic growth, neither newcomers nor long-established families in the port cities could be quite sure about the position of the other, and each may have interpreted the structure of local society very differently. Family and gender conventions added further imbalance and tensions in such a situation.

We may imagine, for instance, a state employee from a town in Syria or Anatolia looking for a husband for his daughter who had just reached puberty, but knowing that his term of service in Jaffa or Haifa would not last for long. He may have been afraid that it would take a while before he settled in his new place of service and would be able to find a good match there for his daughter, or he may simply have liked either Jaffa or Haifa, preferring that his daughter marry and stay there. Under these circumstances, he may have been willing to compromise on the social position of his daughter's future husband. Alternatively, he could marry his daughter to an immigrant whose place of origin was different from his own, but whose social position was allegedly similar. After the marriage, he, or rather the newly wedded couple, might discover that this similar social position had quite different meanings in Jaffa or Haifa than they had envisaged. Amina's marital problems (chapters 4 and 7) may have stemmed from this type of circumstance.

Having only a small family in town may have caused other sorts of tensions, as illustrated by the troubles that Hind faced after she had divorced and remarried (chapter 7). From all the details inscribed in the records of Hasan versus Hind, two elements are particularly striking because they indicate that she had no family in town and therefore was very vulnerable. The first is Hind's absence from court when two issues crucial for her future were deliberated: her rights to remain in the house she had bought together with Hasan when they were still married and to continue to have custody of her daughter. The second element is the fact that not a single family member was available either to represent her in court or to support her by taking care of her minor daughter.

◆   ◆   ◆

The family has proved to be a fairly effective framework for reconstructing certain aspects of the everyday life of ordinary people and connecting them to broader transformations of the period. And families' domestic arrangements and the relationships that evolved between members of the same family and among nonkin housemates and next-door neighbors, has proved to be particularly accessible. For instance, Muhammad Hasun (chapters 5 and 7), the villager from al-Tira, moved to Haifa and settled in Wadi al-Nisnas, near his former fellow villagers. He lived there with his second wife and four children in a one-room house he had managed to purchase, together with another person or a small family to whom he rented out one of the extra rooms he had added. He kept his donkey in a special structure built for that purpose while storing his merchandise in a third room. It is not difficult to picture his daily routine, leaving the house in the morning with the donkey carrying the vegetables, roaming the streets and selling his goods, while in his small house both his wife and his tenant's wife took care of their children, cooked, cleaned, maybe shared a backyard for some of these jobs, as their children played near them or in the alley. A similar picture can be drawn of the house where Amina and Salim (chapters 4 and 7) rented a room, which was later the scene of the quarrel that broke out between them in front of their landlord, with the rest of the neighbors listening and later telling all the details and more to those neighbors who returned in the evening.

Thus, with a reasonable degree of speculation, we can picture the crowded houses, each populated by two or three simple families—women sharing kitchens, quarreling or laughing with each other and with their husbands and their housemates, or women harassing their minor daughters-in-law (as in the case of Khadaja, who had to live with her husband Hasan's mother in Ramla [chapter 6]). Furthermore, we can link these pictures to the growth of the port cities, to immigration, to the conventions of family and gender, and to processes of social mobility. The tiny details, however—the smells and tastes, the intricate relationships, the views and feelings of the people involved in the changes to their lives, and the meanings they attributed to these changes—are still missing.

At the same time, a closer look at those accessible aspects of everyday life in middle-class families has facilitated interpretation of them, showing that individuals and families in the societies in question not only lived through the profound transformations of their time, but also reshaped them. For example, Muhammad Hasun was able to expand his one-room house, but instead of using the extra room for his family, he, like other homeowners, rented it out. In so doing, he reinforced the practice of sharing houses between unrelated families, the pattern of forming simple households, and the culture of close proximity and semifamilial spaces of the middle-class lifestyle. The court personnel in Jaffa provide another example: while applying the reform instructing them to keep the orphans' money in personal accounts in the new orphan fund (chapter 5), they calculated the sums of money borrowed from these accounts according to the gendered notion of the *shari'a* inheritance law, thereby preserving this concept in the new institution.

♦　　♦　　♦

In a short methodological essay, Natalie Z. Davis asks whether it is true that in the close examination of everyday local experiences, features of coping and sharing are overstated, whereas domination, oppression, and resistance are neglected (1990, 30–33). In other words, is the presentation of harmony inherent in the microanalytical approach? This question echoes two interrelated critical issues. One critiques the Geertzian cultural approach in anthropology (Davis 1990, 33), which strongly affected microhistorical thinking. The criticism stresses that this approach attributes one cultural voice to the observed community and hence is bound to highlight its coherence and thus to overlook aspects of disharmony. The second issue relates to "classic" social historians' (in Davis's terms) claim that as a result of analyzing small-scale units, microhistory necessarily overlooks conflict, domination, and forms of resistance in society.

Davis responds to the criticism of microhistory by calling on both micro- and macrosocial historians to balance their respective biases toward too harmonious or too conflictive a historical reconstruction. Giovanni Levi views the issue differently. As noted in chapter 2, he argues that, from the outset, microhistory concentrates on "fragmentation, contradictions and plurality of viewpoints" in society (1995, 107). Several case records presented in this book sustain Levi's claim. They demonstrate the extent to which reducing the scale of the unit of analysis and dealing with individuals in society instead of merely with statistical averages expand our understanding of the observed societies and reveal their plurality and the many ways in which they experienced transformations in their societies. As to the second concern that microhistory overlooks domination, conflict, and resistance, historians studying court records are on the contrary usually accused of overstating aspects of conflict and crisis by virtue of their use of legal texts. The court, so goes the argument, is a place where people unpack their quarrels and animosities and not their mutual affection and support. The legal context of the present study, therefore, serves as a corrective means for any bias toward cooperation and reciprocity claimed to be inherent in the microanalytical approach.

Indeed, none of the individuals and families involved in the legal disputes examined here behaved in an extraordinary manner. They did not deviate from any social norm or cultural practice, and none of them seriously challenged any system, whether prevailing or reformed. At the same time, hardly any of them could be described as typical or average. Granted, they only came to our knowledge either because they worked at the court and participated in producing its records, or because they belonged to the rank and file of the port cities and happened to require the court's services at a certain moment in their lives—not because they had reservations about the prevailing social order or ambitions to transform it. Yet, by gaining access to these moments at court, we are able to draw a broader picture of societies in transition, of domination along lines of gender and age moderated by the social justice of the court, and of the reformed state's growing involvement in individuals' lives. At the same time, these moments at court reveal these individuals' agency and sometimes their resistance to the inherent oppressive patterns and imbalances reinforced by contemporary social transformations. In their own way, according to their personal situations and individual temperaments, they lived through these shifts, made their choices in life, and in so doing reshaped the changes. Amina, who was not satisfied with her domestic conditions, was willing to provoke the gendered division of labor in the family and to apply legal pressure on her husband, Salim, in an effort to change her situation. She evidently had the means and apparently also a certain social background necessary for such initiative.

However, Tamam, the orphan girl whose uncle married her off to an impotent man (chapter 5), had neither means nor any family support. Her aid came from a friendly sheikh and his mother, who testified on her behalf in court, but prior to that she had resisted the marriage, had run away, and had appeared at court to demand its cancellation. Amina's and Tamam's cases illustrate women's agency and their resistance to oppression, in terms of both gender and age, inherent in the patrilineal construction of the family. The case of Judge Abu al-Nasr (chapter 3) is noted here as a case of an individual who, by his choices, challenged the Ottoman judicial reform and in this way contributed to reshaping certain aspects of it: for some reason, Abu al-Nasr, a member of an established ulama family in Damascus, decided at the age of fifty to become a *shariʿa* judge, although in the age of reform this meant that he had to leave his hometown and take up short-term positions in various small towns all over the Ottoman-Arab provinces. He followed the new rules regarding the service of low-ranking judges, but at the same time he managed to bypass some of them and to organize his twenty-year-long judicial career to suit his needs.

◆　　◆　　◆

The courts of Jaffa and Haifa were centers of tensions and transformations of their own. As a result of the legal reforms, their situation became quite complicated. On the one hand, they were attached to the central Ottoman chain of control and accountability, so their position was elevated and their personnel had to cope with legal innovations and an increased workload. On the other hand, under the reformed judicial system, the scope of the *shariʿa* court's legal jurisdiction was narrowed. At the same time, the local court personnel—mainly junior ulama who were either members of local families or immigrants from other Ottoman-Arab cities, serving as scribes and legal interns—worked with judges from throughout the empire who had to change posts every couple of years. The judges, experienced lower-rank jurists from either Turkish or Arab ulama families and frequent travelers who worked under conditions that increased their dependency on the local staff, at the same time faced both the challenge of new attorneys at court and the need to redefine the court's position in society. An examination of the ways in which judges handled court cases reveals that, in spite of the complex changes they had to absorb, they continued to symbolize the court's authority, dealing with legal proceedings single-handedly and performing their task as arbitrators.

This continuity also demonstrates the methods by which they used their discretion, in the process refuting the Weberian concept of "kadi-justice" and undermining the accepted wisdom that judges were insignificant in as far as the development of Islamic law was concerned. Because legal interpretation per se was not part of their territory, judges used their discretion mainly in the sphere of legal procedure. This field is often regarded as merely technical, although procedural issues are crucial for any legal decision. Judges recognized this potential, understanding their duty as shaping solutions for social problems and seeing legal procedure as the means to fulfill this duty. As shown here, Ottoman judicial reform strongly emphasized the procedural aspect of the law. While on the one hand overstated procedures encouraged bureaucratization, on the other hand the reform underpinned the main sphere of the judges' legal creativity and hence led to new openings for judicial discretion.

The court, an institution possessing a long history of adjustment to changing realities, indeed showed its capacity to deal with transformations of unprecedented intricacy. Moreover, contrary to the image of nineteenth-century reform as a top-down unifying endeavor, the personnel of the local courts were deeply involved in reforming their legal arenas, so that the culture of each of their courts represented a local version of reform. The courts were able to deal with intricate transformations, but, as noted, not without tensions, conflicts, and failures. In the court arena, both the personnel of local origin and judges from outside, coming from similar social backgrounds and sharing a vested interest in the continuity of the *shariʿa* court system, demonstrated substantial solidarity in confronting these challenges. They reshaped the balance between judges and scribes, and in spite of the profound bureaucratization of the court and the shrinkage in its authority, its doors remained open to all, and its services, in general, were in demand by the entire society. While stressing its own notion of social justice in redefining its position in society, however, the court was not always successful in confronting some of the challenges presented by the needs of middle-class families.

The court's situation was linked to the multifaceted nature of the modern Ottoman state, which has been tenaciously present in many ways, although it has not explicitly formed a unit of analysis in this study. The most salient and straightforward connection is the court's basic function as a state agent. The orphan funds demonstrate that even this function, one that constituted the main target of Ottoman reform, was less straightforward than might be expected. The establishment of orphan funds represented state intervention in the family domain. These funds were meant to work in cooperation with the local court. However, the court attached its own purpose to the orphan funds by maintaining the orphan accounts according to *shari'a* inheritance law, thereby shoring up a family notion that the new institution was attempting to undermine. At the same time, the Ottoman reformists gave the authority established for supervising orphan properties responsibility for the social security of the wives and children of deceased judges and other ulama. This responsibility was in addition to its role in supervising the orphan funds, so it redefined the relations of the state with the *ilmiye* and highlighted the judges' position as state employees.

This situation and other social and legal dynamics explored in this book illustrate, above all, the obscure and complicated nature of modernity. From the outset, one of the most fascinating features I found when looking closely at the court arena was the similarity and convergence between what is usually defined as *traditional* and what is defined as *modern*. Scholars who explore this period often construct these terms as a dichotomy, in spite of growing awareness that this binary is misleading, at least insofar as modern practices are concerned. This study focused mainly on the analysis of these practices, complemented by comments on the ways in which they were constructed in scholarly works on modernity. By investigating some of the mechanisms of change in court and family in concretely historical terms, I hope I was able to contribute to the conceptualization of "premodernity" and "modernity" as being less dichotomous and of the passage from one to the other as more complex and continuous rather than abrupt and dramatic.

By employing a hermeneutic approach in reading the records of the *shari'a* court and exploring them as a historical object, I have reconstructed some aspects of both court culture and the family patterns inscribed in them that do not easily lend themselves to interpretation by historians. As I pointed out in chapter 2, this approach and, consequently, our historical knowledge are bound to benefit from future studies aimed at filling in the lacunae in this field. However, as far as family history is concerned, the limitations of the court records as a historical source, in addition to their potential, have also been clarified. My analysis of the records in combination with only one autobiography in chapter 7 illustrates the gaps in the available information on family patterns and on the meanings of those patterns for individuals and groups. The records alone are incapable of bridging those gaps. The missing aspects are essential for exploring not only changing notions of family, but, as noted, also the prevailing discourses on modernity. I hope more autobiographies, diaries, family papers, and other similar source material, particularly from nonelite families, will become available for historical investigation and will substantiate further studies of family history in the Middle East. I also believe that further studies on the *nizamiye* courts and other nineteenth-century legal organs—in particular, studies of the daily work of such institutions—will enrich our knowledge of sociolegal processes and will enable us to draw a more nuanced picture of the family.

References

◆　　◆　　◆

Index

References

Shariʿa Court Records

University of Haifa Library, Haifa.
Al-mahkama al-sharʿiyya fi Hayfa. Vols. 1287–1334/1870–1918.
Al-mahkama al-sharʿiyya fi Yafa. Vols. 1214–1334/1799–1918.

Ottoman *İlmiye* Files

Müftülük (the former office of the Ministry of Şeyhülislâm), Istanbul.
Sicill-i ahval defterleri. 7 vols.
Sicill-i ahval dosyaları. 6,386 files.

Published Official Records

Beyrut Vilayeti Salnamesi. Years 1311–12/1893–94; 1318/1900–1901.
Düstur, birinci tertib (1st ed.). 1937–43. Vols. 1–4, Supplements 1–4, Istanbul; Vols. 5–8, Ankara.
Düstur, ikinci tertib (2d ed.). 1329–1927/1911–27. Vols. 1–12, Istanbul.
Al-Dustur. 1301/1884. An official translation of parts of the first edition of *Düstur* (*Düstur* 1) into Arabic by Nawfal, Nawfal Efendi Niʿmatulla. Beirut.
İlmiye Salnamesi. 1334/1916. Istanbul.
Mecelle-i Ahkam-ı Adliye. (*Düstur* 1, 3: 38–148; *Düstur* 1, 4: 93–115.)
Suriye Vilayeti Salnamesi. Year 1318/1900–1901.

Books, Articles, Periodicals, Dissertations, and Papers

Abou-El-Haj, Rifaat A. 1974. "The Ottoman Vezir and Paşa Households, 1683–1703: A Preliminary Report." *Journal of the American Oriental Society* 94, no. 4: 438–47.
Abu-Lughod, Janet. 1987. "The Islamic City—Historic Myth, Islamic Essence, and

Contemporary Relevance." *International Journal of Middle East Studies* 19, no. 2: 155–76.

Abu-Manneh, Butrus. 1990. "Jerusalem in the Tanzimat Period: The New Ottoman Administration and the Notables." *Die Welt des Islams* 30: 1–44.

Adams, John W. 1981. "Anthropology and History in the 1980s: Consensus, Community, and Exoticism." *Journal of Interdisciplinary History* 12, no. 2: 253–65.

Agmon, Iris. 1985. "The Development of Palestine's Foreign Trade, 1879–1914: Economic and Social Aspects" (in Hebrew). M.A. thesis, Univ. of Haifa.

———. 1995. "Women and Society: Muslim Women, the *Shari'a* Court, and the Society of Jaffa and Haifa under Late Ottoman Rule, 1900–1914" (in Hebrew). Ph.D. diss., Hebrew Univ., Jerusalem.

———. 1996. "Muslim Women in Court According to the *Sijill* of Late Ottoman Jaffa and Haifa: Some Methodological Notes." In *Women, the Family, and Divorce Laws in Islamic History,* edited by Amira El-Azhary Sonbol, 126–40. Syracuse, N.Y.: Syracuse Univ. Press.

———. 1998. "Women, Class, and Gender: Muslim Jaffa and Haifa at the Turn of the 20th Century." *International Journal of Middle East Studies* 30, no. 4: 477–500.

———. 2003a. "Fatma's Dilemma, Bertrand's Invented Marriage, and Penelope's Thread: Introductory Note to Leslie Peirce's Article." *Jama'a* 11: 109–21 (in Hebrew).

———. 2003b. "Text, Court, and Family in Late-Nineteenth-Century Palestine." In *Family History in the Middle East: Household, Property, and Gender,* edited by Beshara Doumani, 201–28. Albany: State Univ. of New York Press.

———. 2004a. "Recording Procedures and Legal Culture in the Late Ottoman Shari'a Court of Jaffa. *Islamic Law and Society* 11, no. 3: 333–77.

———. 2004b. "Social Biography of a Late Ottoman Shari'a Judge." *New Perspectives on Turkey* 30: 83–113.

———. 2004c. "Women's History and Ottoman Sharia Court Records: Shifting Perspectives in Social History." *HAWWA* 2, no. 2: 172–209.

Akiba, Jun. 2000. "The Making of a Judge in the Late Ottoman Empire: Some Observations on Social Mobility and Integration." Conference paper presented at MESA Annual Meeting, Orlando, Florida, Nov.

———. 2003. "A New School for Qadis: Education of Sharia Judges in the Late Ottoman Empire." *Turcica* 35: 125–63.

———. 2005. "From *Kadı* to *Naib:* Reorganization of the Ottoman Sharia Judiciary in the Tanzimat Period." In *Frontiers of Ottoman Studies: State, Province, and the West,* 2 vols., edited by Colin Imber and Keiko Kiyotaki, 1: 43–60. London: I. B. Tauris.

Albayrak, Sadık. 1996. *Son Devir Osmanlı Uleması (ilmiye ricalinin Teracim-i Ahvâli.* 5 vols. 1980. Reprint. Istanbul: Istanbul Büyükşehir Belediyesi.

Bahjat, Muhammad Bey, and M. Rafiq Bey al-Tamimi. 1917–18. *Wilayat Bayrut*. 2 vols. Beirut: Matbaʿat al-Iqbal.

Barbir, Karl. 1980. *Ottoman Rule in Damascus, 1708–1758*. Princeton, N.J.: Princeton Univ. Press.

Baron, Beth. 1993. "The Construction of National Honor in Egypt." *Gender and History* 5: 244–55.

———. 2005. *Egypt as a Woman: Nationalists, Gender, and Politics*. Berkeley and Los Angeles: Univ. of California Press.

Berk-Seligson, Susan. 1992. *The Bilingual Courtroom: Court Interpreters in the Judicial Process*. Chicago: Univ. of Chicago Press.

Bonine, Michael E. 1998. "The Introduction of Railroads in the Eastern Mediterranean: Economic and Social Impacts." In *The Syrian Land: Processes of Integration and Fragmentation. Bilad al-Sham from the 18th to the 20th Century*, edited by Thomas Philipp and Birgit Schaebler, 53–78. Stuttgart: Franz Steiner Verlag.

Booth, Marilyn. 2001. "Women and Islam: Men and the 'Women's Press' in Turn-of-the-20th-Century Egypt." *International Journal of Middle East Studies* 33, no. 2: 171–201.

Bowen, John R. 1988. "The Transformation of an Indonesian Property System: Adat, Islam, and Social Change in the Gayo Highlands." *American Ethnologist* 2: 274–93.

Braudel, Fernand. 1966. *La Méditerranée et le monde méditerranéen à l'époque de Philippe II*. 1949. Reprint. Paris: A. Colin.

Burke, Edmund, III, ed. 1993. *Struggle and Survival in the Modern Middle East*. London: I. B. Tauris.

Burke, Peter. 1990. *The French Historical Revolution: The Annales School, 1929–89*. Stanford, Calif.: Stanford Univ. Press.

———. 1995. "Overture: The New History, Its Past and Its Future." 1992. Reprinted in *New Perspectives on Historical Writing*, edited by Peter Burke, 1–23. Philadelphia: Pennsylvania State Univ. Press.

Campos, Michelle U. 2003. "A 'Shared Homeland' and Its Boundaries: Empire, Citizenship, and the Origins of Sectarianism in Late Ottoman Palestine, 1908–13." Ph.D. diss., Stanford Univ.

Christelow, Alan. 1985. *Muslim Law Courts and the French Colonial State in Algeria*. Princeton, N.J.: Princeton Univ. Press.

Clancy-Smith, Julia. 2002. "Marginality and Migration: Europe's Social Outcasts in Pre-colonial Tunisia, 1830–81." In *Outside In: On the Margins of the Modern Middle East*, edited by Eugene Rogan, 149–82. London: I. B. Tauris.

Cohen, Amnon. 1973. *Palestine in the 18th Century: Patterns of Government and Administration*. Jerusalem: Magnes Press.

Cohn, Bernard S. 1965. "Anthropological Notes on Disputes and Law in India." *American Anthropologist* 67, no. 6: 82–122.

————. 1981. "Anthropology and History in the 1980s: Toward a Rapprochement." *Journal of Interdisciplinary History* 12, no. 2: 227–52.

————. 1996. *Colonialism and Its Forms of Knowledge: The British in India.* Princeton, N.J.: Princeton Univ. Press.

Confino, Alon. 2000. "Traveling as a Culture of Remembrance: Traces of National Socialism in West Germany, 1945–1960." *History and Memory* 12, no. 2: 92–121.

Coontz, Stephanie. 1992. *The Way We Never Were: American Families and the Nostalgia Trap.* New York: Basic Books.

Cuno, Kenneth M. 1995. "Joint Family Households and Rural Notables in 19th-Century Egypt." *International Journal of Middle East Studies* 27, no. 4: 485–503.

————. 1999. "A Tale of Two Villages: Family, Property, and Economic Activity in Rural Egypt in the 1840s." In *Agriculture in Egypt from Pharaonic to Modern Times,* edited by Alan K. Bowman and Eugene Rogan, 301–29. Oxford: Oxford Univ. Press.

————. 2001. "The Reproduction of Elite Households in Eighteenth-Century Egypt: Two Examples from al-Mansura." In *Etudes sur les villes du Proche Orient, XVI–XIX siècle: Hommage à André Raymond,* edited by Brigitte Marino, 237–61. Damascus: IFEAD.

————. 2003. "Ambiguous Modernization: The Transition to Monogamy in the Khedival House of Egypt." In *Family History in the Middle East: Household, Property, and Gender,* edited by Beshara Doumani, 247–70. Albany: State Univ. of New York Press.

Dabbagh, Mustafa M. 1988. *Biladuna Filastin.* Vol. 4, part 2: *Fi al-Diyar al-Yafiyya;* vol. 7, part 2: *Fi Diyar al-Jalil—Jund al-Urdun.* 2d ed. Kafar Kara', Israel: Dar al-Shafaq lil-Nashr wal-Tawzi'.

Davis, Natalie Z. 1981. "Anthropology and History in the 1980s: The Possibilities of the Past." *Journal of Interdisciplinary History* 12, no. 2: 267–75.

————. 1983. *The Return of Martin Guerre.* Cambridge, Mass.: Harvard Univ. Press.

————. 1990. "The Shapes of Social History." *Storia della Storiografia* 17: 28–35.

Deringil, Selim. 1998. *The Well-Protected Domains: Ideology and the Legitimation of Power in the Ottoman Empire, 1876–1909.* London: I. B. Tauris.

————. 2003. " 'They Live in a State of Nomadism and Savagery': The Late Ottoman Empire and the Post-colonial Debate." *Comparative Studies in Society and History* 45: 311–42.

Divine, Donna R. 1994. *Politics and Society in Ottoman Palestine: The Arab Struggle for Survival and Power.* Boulder, Colo.: Lynne Rienner.

Dostal, Robert J., ed. 2002. *The Cambridge Companion to GADAMER.* Cambridge: Cambridge Univ. Press.

Doumani, Beshara. 1985. "Palestinian Islamic Court Records: A Source for Socioeconomic History." *MESA Bulletin* 19: 155–72.

————. 1995. *Rediscovering Palestine: Merchants and Peasants in Jabal Nablus, 1700–1900.* Berkeley and Los Angeles: Univ. of California Press.

————. 1998. "Endowing Family: Waqf, Property Devolution, and Gender in Greater Syria, 1800 to 1860." *Comparative Studies in Society and History* 40: 3–41.

————. 2003. "Introduction." In *Family History in the Middle East: Households, Property, and Gender,* edited by Beshara Doumani, 1–19. Albany: State Univ. of New York Press.

Duben, Alan. 1985. "Turkish Families and Households in Historical Perspective." *Journal of Family History* 10: 75–97.

————. 1990. "Understanding Muslim Households and Families in Late Ottoman Istanbul." *Journal of Family History* 15: 71–86.

Duben, Alan, and Cem Behar. 1991. *Istanbul Households: Marriage, Family, and Fertility, 1880–1940.* Cambridge: Cambridge Univ. Press.

Eickleman, Dale F. 1985. *Knowledge and Power in Morocco: The Education of a Twentieth-Century Notable.* Princeton, N.J.: Princeton Univ. Press.

Eldem, Edhem, Daniel Goffman, and Bruce Masters. 1999. *The Ottoman City Between East and West: Aleppo, Izmir, and Istanbul.* Cambridge: Cambridge Univ. Press.

Enderwitz, Susanne. 2002. "Palestinian Autobiographies: A Source for Women's History?" In *Writing the Feminine: Women in Arab Sources,* edited by Manuela Marín and Randi Deguilhem, 49–72. London: I. B. Tauris.

Ener, Mine. 2003. *Managing Egypt's Poor and the Politics of Benevolence, 1800–1952.* Princeton, N.J.: Princeton Univ. Press.

Ergene, Boğaç. 2003. *Local Court, Provincial Society, and Justice in the Ottoman Empire: Legal Practice and Dispute Resolution in Çankırı and Kastamonu (1652–1744).* Leiden: E. J. Brill.

————. 2004. "Pursuing Justice in an Islamic Context: Dispute Resolution in Ottoman Court of Law." *Political and Legal Anthropology Review* 27, no. 1: 67–87.

————. Forthcoming. "Evidence in Ottoman Courts of Law: Oral and Written Documentation in Early-Modern Courts of Islamic Law." *Journal of the American Oriental Society.*

Esposito, John L. 1982. *Women in Muslim Family Law.* Syracuse, N.Y.: Syracuse Univ. Press.

Establet, Colette, and Jean-Paul Pascual. 1994. *Familles et fortunes à Damas: 450 foyers Damascains en 1700.* Damascus: Institut Français de Damas.

Fahmy, Khaled. 1997. *All the Pasha's Men: Mehmed Ali, His Army, and the Making of Modern Egypt.* Cambridge: Cambridge Univ. Press.

Fargues, Philippe. 2003. "Family and Household in Mid-Nineteenth-Century Cairo." In *Family History in the Middle East: Household, Property, and Gender,* edited by Beshara Doumani, 23–50. Albany: State Univ. of New York Press.

Faroqhi, Suraiya. 1999. *Approaching Ottoman History: An Introduction to the Sources.* Cambridge: Cambridge Univ. Press.

Fawwaz, Leila Tarazi. 1983. *Merchants and Migrants in Nineteenth-Century Beirut.* Cambridge, Mass: Harvard Univ. Press.

Fay, Mary Ann. 1993. "Women and Households: Gender, Power, and Culture in Eighteenth-Century Egypt." Ph.D. diss., Georgetown Univ., Washington, D.C.

———. 2003. "From Warrior-Grandees to Domesticated Bourgeoisie: The Transformation of the Elite Egyptian Household into a Western-Style Nuclear Family." In *Family History in the Middle East: Household, Property, and Gender,* edited by Beshara Doumani, 77–97. Albany: State Univ. of New York Press.

Filastin (Jaffa). 1911–14. Biweekly edited by Yusuf al-ʿIsa.

Findley, Carter V. 1980. *Bureaucratic Reform in the Ottoman Empire: The Sublime Porte, 1789–1922.* Princeton, N.J.: Princeton Univ. Press.

———. 1986. "The Evolution of the System of Provincial Administration as Viewed from the Center." In *Palestine in the Late Ottoman Period: Political, Social, and Economic Transformation,* edited by David Kushner, 3–29. Leiden: E. J. Brill.

———. 1991. "Mahkama (2): The Ottoman Empire (ii): The Reform Era (ca. 1789–1922)." In *Encyclopedia of Islam,* 2d ed., 6: 5–9. Leiden: E. J. Brill.

Fortna, Benjamin C. 2002. *Imperial Classroom: Islam, the State, and Education in the Late Ottoman Empire.* Oxford: Oxford Univ. Press.

Foucault, Michel. 1979. *Discipline and Punish: The Birth of the Prison.* Translated by Alan Sheridan. New York: Vintage.

Geertz, Clifford. 1973. "Thick Description: Toward an Interpretive Theory of Culture." In *The Interpretation of Cultures,* edited by Clifford Geertz, 3–30. New York: Basic Books.

———. 1983. *Local Knowledge.* New York: Basic Books.

Gerber, Haim. 1980. "Social and Economic Position of Women in an Ottoman City, Bursa, 1600–1700." *International Journal of Middle East Studies* 12, no. 3: 231–44.

———. 1985. *Ottoman Rule in Jerusalem, 1890–1914.* Berlin: Klaus Schwarz Verlag.

———. 1988. *Economy and Society in an Ottoman City: Bursa, 1600–1700.* Jerusalem: Hebrew Univ.

———. 1989. "Anthropology and Family History: The Ottoman and Turkish Families." *Journal of Family History* 14, no. 4: 409–21.

———. 1994. *State, Society, and Law in Islam: Ottoman Law in Comparative Perspective.* Albany: State Univ. of New York Press.

Ghazzal, Zouhair. 1996. Review of Colette Establet and Jean-Paul Pascaul's *Familles et fortunes à Damas: 450 foyers damascains en 1700* (Damascus: Institut Français de Damas, 1994). *International Journal of Middle East Studies* 28, no. 3: 431–32.

———. 1998. "A Reply to André Raymond." *International Journal of Middle East Studies* 30, no. 3: 474–75.

Giladi, Avner. 1992. *Children of Islam: Concepts of Childhood in Medieval Muslim Society.* London: MacMillan.

———. 1999. *Infants, Parents, and Wet Nurses: Medieval Islamic Views on Breastfeeding and Their Social Implications.* Leiden: E. J. Brill.

Gilbar, Gad G. 2003. "The Muslim Big Merchant—Entrepreneurs of the Middle East, 1860–1914." *Die Welt des Islams* 43, no. 1: 1–36.

Ginio, Eyal. 2002. "Migrants and Workers in an Ottoman Port: Ottoman Salonica in the Eighteenth Century." In *Outside In: On the Margins of the Modern Middle East,* edited by Eugene Rogan, 126–48. London: I. B. Tauris

———. 2003. "Living on the Margins of Charity: Coping with Poverty in an Ottoman Provincial City." In *Poverty and Charity in Middle Eastern Contexts,* edited by Michael Bonner, Mine Ener, and Amy Singer, 165–84. Albany: State Univ. of New York Press.

Ginzburg, Carlo. 1980. *The Cheese and the Worms: The Cosmos of a Sixteenth-Century Miller.* Translated by John Tedeschi and Anne Tedeschi. Baltimore: John Hopkins Univ. Press.

———. 1992. *Clues, Myths, and the Historical Method.* Translated by John Tedeschi and Anne C. Tedeschi. 1989. Reprint. Baltimore: John Hopkins Univ. Press.

———. 1993. "Microhistory: Two or Three Things That I Know about It." *Critical Inquiry* 20: 10–35.

Göçek, Fatma Müge. 1996. *Rise of the Bourgeoisie, Demise of Empire: Ottoman Westernization and Social Change.* Oxford: Oxford Univ. Press.

Gregory, Brad S. 1999. "Is Small Beautiful? Microhistory and the History of Everyday Life." *History and Theory* 38, no. 1: 100–111.

Grondin, Jean. 2003. *The Philosophy of Gadamer.* Translated by Kathryn Plant. Chesham, England: Acumen.

Al-Hafiz, Muhammad M., and Nazar Abaza. 1986. *Ta'rikh Ulama Dimashq fi al-Qarn al-Rabi ʿ ʿAshar al Hijri.* Vol. 1. Damascus: Dar al-Fikr.

Hagopian, V. H. 1907. *Ottoman-Turkish Conversation-Grammar: A Practical Method of Learning the Ottoman-Turkish Language.* London: n.p.

Haikel, Yousef. 1988. *Ayyam al-Siba. Suwar min al-Hayya wa-Safahat min al-Ta'rikh.* Amman, Jordan: Dar al-Jalil lil-Nashr.

Hallaq, Wael B. 1984. "Was the Gate of Ijtihad Closed?" *International Journal of Middle East Studies* 16, no. 1: 3–41.

———. 1998. "The Qadi's Diwan (Sijill) before the Ottomans." *Bulletin of the School of Oriental and African Studies* 61: 415–36.

———. 2002. "A Prelude to Ottoman Reform: Ibn ʿAbidin on Custom and Legal Change." In *Histories of the Modern Middle East: New Directions,* edited by Israel Gershoni, Hakan Erdem, and Ursula Woköck, 37–61. Boulder, Colo.: Lynne Rienner.

————. 2002–2003. "The Quest for Origins or Doctrine? Islamic Legal Studies as Colonialist Discourse." *Journal of Islamic and Near Eastern Law* 2, no. 1: 1–31.

Hanıoğlu, M. Şükrü. 1995. *The Young Turks in Opposition*. Oxford: Oxford Univ. Press.

Hanna, Nelly. 1995. "The Administration of Courts in Ottoman Cairo." In *The State and Its Servants: Administration in Egypt from Ottoman Times to the Present*, edited by Nelly Hanna, 44–59. Cairo: American Univ. in Cairo Press.

————. 1998. *Making Big Money in 1600: The Life and Times of Ismaʿil Abu Taqiyya, Egyptian Merchant*. Syracuse, N.Y.: Syracuse Univ. Press.

Hareven, Tamara K. 1991. "The History of the Family and the Complexity of Social Change." *American Historical Review* 96: 95–124.

Hathaway, Jane. 1997. *The Politics of Households in Ottoman Egypt: The Rise of the Qazdağlis*. Cambridge: Cambridge Univ. Press.

————. 2004. "Rewriting Eighteenth-Century Ottoman History." In *New Historiographies of the Ottoman Mediterranean World*, edited by Amy Singer, special issue of *Mediterranean Historical Review* 19, no. 1: 28–52.

Hill, Enid. 1979. *Mahkama! Studies in the Egyptian Legal System: Courts and Crimes, Law and Society*. London: Ithaca Press.

Hirsch, Susan F. 1994. "Kadhi's Courts as Complex Sites of Resistance: The State, Islam, and Gender in Postcolonial Kenya." In *Contested States: Law Hegemony and Resistance*, edited by Mindie Lazarus-Black and Susan F. Hirsch, 207–29. New York: Routledge.

————. 1998. *Reasoning and Preserving: Gender and the Discourses of Disputing in an African Islamic Court*. Chicago: Univ. of Chicago Press.

Hoexter, Miriam. 1998. *Endowment, Rulers, and Community: Waqf al-Haramain in Ottoman Algiers*. Leiden: E. J. Brill.

Ibn ʿAbidin, Muhammad Amin. n.d. *Radd al-Muhtar ʿala al-Durr al-Mukhtar. Hashiyat Ibn ʿAbidin*. 5 vols. Beirut: Dar Ihya al-Turath al-Arabi.

Iggers, Georg G. 1997. *Historiography in the Twentieth Century: From Scientific Objectivity to the Postmodern Challenge*. Hanover, N.H.: Wesleyan Univ. Press.

İnalcık, Halil, 1965. "Adaletnameler." *Belgeler* 2: 49–145.

————. 1991. "Mahkama (2): The Ottoman Empire (i): The Earlier Centuries." In *Encyclopedia of Islam*, 2d ed., 6: 3–5. Leiden: E. J. Brill.

Jennings, Ronald C. 1975. "The Office of Vekil (Wakil) in 17th-Century Ottoman Sharia Courts." *Studia Islamica* 42: 147–69.

————. 1979. "Limitations of the Judicial Powers of the Kadi in 17th C. Ottoman Kayseri." *Studia Islamica* 50: 151–84.

Johansen, Baber. 1981. "Sacred and Religious Elements in Hanefite Law—Function and Limits of the Absolute Character of Government Authority." In *Islam et poli-*

tique au Maghreb, edited by Ernest Gellner and Jean-Claude Vatin, 281–303. Paris: CNRS.

Kandiyoti, Deniz. 1998. "Afterword: Some Awkward Questions on Women and Modernity in Turkey." In *Remaking Women: Feminism and Modernity in the Middle East,* edited by Lila Abu-Lughod, 270–87. Princeton, N.J.: Princeton Univ. Press.

Kark, Ruth. 1990. *Jaffa: A City in Evolution, 1799–1917.* Jerusalem: Yad Izhak Ben-Zvi Press.

Karpat, Kemal H. 1985. *Ottoman Population, 1830–1914: Demographic and Social Characteristics.* Madison: Univ. of Wisconsin Press.

Kayalı, Hasan. 1997. *Arabs and Young Turks: Ottomanism, Arabism, and Islamism in the Ottoman Empire, 1908–1918.* Berkeley and Los Angeles: Univ. of California Press.

Keyder, Çağlar. 1999. "Peripheral Port-Cities and Politics on the Eve of the Great War." *New Perspectives on Turkey* 20: 27–46.

Keyder, Çağlar, Y. Eyup Özveren, and Donald Quataert. 1993. "Port- Cities in the Ottoman Empire: Some Theoretical and Historical Perspectives." In *Port Cities in the Eastern Mediterranean,* edited by Çağlar Keyder, Y. Eyup Özveren, and Donald Quataert, special issue of *Review* 16, no. 4: 519–58.

Khater, Akram F. 2001. *Inventing Home: Emigration, Gender, and the Middle Class in Lebanon, 1870–1920.* Berkeley and Los Angeles: Univ. of California Press.

Khoury, Dina R. 1997. *State and Provincial Society in the Ottoman Empire: Mosul, 1540–1834.* Cambridge: Cambridge Univ. Press.

Kogacıoğlu, Dicle. 2003. "Law and Everyday Life in Turkey: Developmentalism and the Reproduction of Inequalities." Ph.D. diss., State Univ. of New York, Stony Brook.

Kramer, Lloyd S. 1989. "Literature, Criticism, and Historical Imagination: The Literary Challenge of Hayden White and Dominick LaCapra." In *The New Cultural History,* edited by Lynn Hunt, 97–128. Berkeley and Los Angeles: Univ. of California Press.

Kühn, Thomas. 2003. "An Imperial Borderland as Colony: Knowledge Production and the Elaboration of Difference in Ottoman Yemen, 1872–1918." In *Borderlands of the Ottoman Empire in the 19th and Early 20th Centuries,* edited by Eugene Rogan, special issue of *MIT Electronic Journal of Middle East Studies* 3: 5–17.

Kunt, Metin. 1983. *The Sultan's Servants: The Transformation of Ottoman Provincial Government, 1550–1650.* New York: Columbia Univ. Press.

Kupferschmidt, Uri M. 1986. "A Note on the Muslim Religious Hierarchy Towards the End of the Ottoman Period." In *Palestine in the Late Ottoman Period: Political, Social, and Economic Transformation,* edited by David Kushner, 123–29. Jerusalem: Yad Yizhak Ben-Zvi Press.

Layish, Aharon. 1975. *Women and Islamic Law in a Non-Muslim State: A Study Based on Decisions of the Shari'a Courts in Israel.* Jerusalem: Israel Universities Press.

———. 1991. *Divorce in the Libyan Family: A Study Based on the Sijills of the Shariʿa Courts of Ajdabiyya and Kufra.* New York: New York Univ. Press.

———. 2000. "Reformist Matrimonial Legislation and the Collapse of the Muslim Patrilineal Family." *Awraq* 21: 57–80.

Le Roy Ladurie, Emmanuel. 1978. *Montaillou: Cathars and Catholics in a French Village, 1294–1324.* Translated by Barbara Bray. London: Scolar Press.

Levi, Giovanni. 1995. "On Microhistory." 1992. Reprinted in *New Perspectives on Historical Writing,* edited by Peter Burke, 93–113. Philadelphia: Pennsylvania State Univ. Press.

LeVine, Mark. 1999. "Overthrowing Geography, Re-imagining Identities: A History of Jaffa and Tel Aviv, 1880 to the Present." Ph.D. diss., New York Univ.

Levy, Zeʾev. 1986. *Hermeneutics* (in Hebrew). Tel Aviv: Sifriat ha-Poalim.

Lewin, Linda. 1992. "Natural and Spurious Children in Brazilian Inheritance Law from Colony to Empire: A Methodological Essay." *The Americas* 68, no. 3: 351–96.

Lewis, Bernard. 1968. *The Emergence of Modern Turkey.* Oxford: Oxford Univ. Press.

Magnússon, Sigurdur Gylfi. 1995. "From Children's Point of View: Childhood in Nineteenth-Century Iceland." *Journal of Social History* 29, no. 2: 295–323.

———. 2003. "The Singularization of History: Social History and Microhistory within the Postmodern Knowledge." *Journal of Social History* 36, no. 3: 701–35.

Makdisi, Ussama. 2002. "Ottoman Orientalism." *American Historical Review* 107, no. 3: 768–96.

Malti-Douglas, Fedwa. 1991. *Woman's Body, Woman's Word.* Princeton, N.J.: Princeton Univ. Press.

Mannaʿ, Adel. 1986. "The District of Jerusalem Between Two Invasions (1798–1831): Administration and Society" (in Hebrew). Ph.D. diss., Hebrew Univ., Jerusalem.

———. 1995. *Aʿlam Falastin fi Awakhir al-ʿAhd al-ʿUthmani, 1800–1918.* 1986. Reprint. Beirut: Institute for Palestine Studies.

Maʾoz, Moshe. 1968. *Ottoman Reform in Syria and Palestine, 1840–1861: The Impact of the Tanzimat on Politics and Society.* Oxford: Clarendon Press.

Marcus, Abraham. 1983. "Men, Women, and Property: Dealers in Real Estate in Eighteenth-Century Aleppo." *Journal of Economic and Social History of the Orient* 26, no. 2: 137–63.

———. 1986. "Privacy in Eighteenth-Century Aleppo: The Limits of Cultural Ideals." *International Journal of Middle East Studies* 18, no. 2: 165–83.

———. 1989. *The Middle East on the Eve of Modernity: Aleppo in the Eighteenth-Century.* New York: Columbia Univ. Press.

Marino, Brigitte, and Tomoki Okawara. 1999. *Catalogue des Registres des Tribunaux Ottomans conservés au Centre des Archives de Damas.* Damascus: Institut Français de Damas.

Massey, Douglas S., Joaquin Arango, Graeme Hugu, Ali Kouaouci, Adela Pellegrino, and J. Edward Taylor. 1993. "Theories of International Migration: A Review and Appraisal." *Population and Development Review* 19: 431–66.

McCarthy, Justin. 1990. *The Population of Palestine: Population Statistics of the Late Ottoman Period and the Mandate.* New York: Columbia Univ. Press.

Meriwether, Margaret L. 1996. "The Rights of Children and the Responsibilities of Women: Women as Wasis in Ottoman Aleppo, 1770–1840." In *Women, the Family, and Divorce Laws in Islamic History,* edited by Amira El-Azhary Sonbol, 219–35. Syracuse, N.Y.: Syracuse Univ. Press.

———. 1999. *The Kin Who Count: Family and Society in Ottoman Aleppo, 1770–1840.* Austin: Univ. of Texas Press.

Meriwether, Margaret L., and Judith E. Tucker. 1999. "Introduction." In *Social History of Women and Gender in the Modern Middle East,* edited by Margaret L. Meriwether and Judith E. Tucker, 1–24. Boulder, Colo.: Westview Press.

Mernissi, Fatima. 2000. "The Muslim Concept of Active Women's Sexuality." In *Women and Sexuality in Muslim Societies,* edited by Pinar Ilkkaracan, 19–35. Istanbul: Women for Women's Human Rights.

Merry, Sally E. 1988. "Legal Pluralism." *Law and Society Review* 22, no. 5: 869–96.

Messick, Brinkley. 1986. "The Mufti, the Text, and the World: Legal Interpretation in Yemen." *Man* 21: 102–19.

———. 1993. *The Calligraphic State: Textual Domination and History in a Muslim Society.* Berkeley and Los Angeles: Univ. of California Press.

Miller, Ruth Austin. 2003. "From Fikh to Fascism: The Turkish Republican Adoption of Mussolini's Criminal Code in the Context of Late Ottoman Legal Reform." Ph.D. diss., Princeton Univ.

Mir-Hosseini, Ziba. 1997. *Marriage on Trial: A Study of Islamic Family Law: Iran and Morocco Compared.* London: I. B. Tauris.

———. 1998. "Marriage et divorce: Une margine de negociation pour la femme." In *Femme en Iran: Pressions sociales et strategies identitaires,* edited by Nouchine Yavari-d'Hellencourt, 95–118. Paris: Harmattan.

Mitchell, Timothy. 1991. "The Limits of the State: Beyond Statist Approaches and Their Critics." *American Political Science Review* 85, no. 1: 77–96.

Moore, Erin P. 1994. "Law's Patriarchy in India." In *Contested States: Law Hegemony and Resistance,* edited by Mindie Lazarus-Black and Susan F. Hirsch, 89–117. New York: Routledge.

Moors, Annelies. 1995. *Women, Property, and Islam: Palestinian Experiences, 1920–1990.* Cambridge: Cambridge Univ. Press.

———. 1999. "Debating Islamic Family Law: Legal Texts and Social Practices." In *Social History of Women and Gender in the Modern Middle East,* edited by Margaret L. Meriwether and Judith E. Tucker, 141–75. Boulder, Colo.: Westview Press.

Motzki, Harald. 1996. "Child Marriage in Seventeenth-Century Palestine." In *Islamic*

Legal Interpretation: Muftis and Their Fatwas, edited by Muhammad K. Masud, Brinkley Messick, and David S. Powers, 129–40. Cambridge, Mass.: Harvard Univ. Press.

Muir, Edward, and Guido Ruggiero, eds. 1991. *Microhistory and the Lost People of Europe.* Translated by Eren Branch. Baltimore: Johns Hopkins Univ. Press.

Mundy, Martha. 1994. "Village Land and Individual Title: *Musha'* and Ottoman Land Registration in the 'Ajlun District." In *Village, Steppe, and State: The Social Origins of Modern Jordan,* edited by Eugene Rogan and Tariq Tell, 58–79. London: British Academic Press.

———. 1995. *Domestic Government: Kinship, Community, and Policy in North Yemen.* London: I. B. Tauris.

El-Nahal, Galal H. 1979. *The Judicial Administration of Ottoman Egypt in the Seventeenth Century.* Chicago: Bibliotheca Islamica.

Najmabadi, Afsaneh. 1998. *The Story of the Daughters of Quchan: Gender and National Memory in Iranian History.* Syracuse, N.Y.: Syracuse Univ. Press.

———. 2005. *Women with Mustaches and Men Without Beards: Gender and Sexual Anxieties of Iranian Modernity.* Berkeley and Los Angeles: Univ. of California Press.

Okawara, Tomoki. 2003. "Size and Structure of Damascus Households in the Late Ottoman Period as Compared with Istanbul Households." In *Family History in the Middle East: Households, Property, and Gender,* edited by Doumani Beshara, 51–75. Albany: State Univ. of New York Press.

Olney, James. 1980. "Autobiography and the Cultural Moment: A Thematic, Historical, and Bibliographical Introduction." In *Autobiography: Essays Theoretical and Critical,* edited by James Olney, 3–27. Princeton, N.J.: Princeton Univ. Press.

Owen, Roger. 1981. *The Middle East in the World Economy, 1800–1914.* London: Methuen.

Özkaya, Yücel. 1985. *XVIII. Yüzyılda Osmanlı Kurumları ve Osmanlı Toplum Yaşantıs.* Ankara: Kültür ve Turizm Bakanlığı.

Özman, Aylin. 2000. "The Portrait of the Ottoman Attorney and Bar Associations: State, Secularization, and Institutionalization of Professional Interests." *Der Islam* 77, no. 2: 319–37.

Pamuk, Şevket. 2000. *A Monetary History of the Ottoman Empire.* Cambridge: Cambridge Univ. Press.

Peirce, Leslie P. 1993. *The Imperial Harem: Women and Sovereignty in the Ottoman Empire.* Oxford: Oxford Univ. Press.

———. 1997. "Seniority, Sexuality, and Social Order: The Vocabulary of Gender in Early Modern Ottoman Society." In *Women in the Ottoman Empire,* edited by Madeline C. Zilfi, 169–97. Leiden: E. J. Brill.

———. 1998a. "Le dilemme de Fatma. Crime sexuel et culture juridique dans une cour ottomane au debut de temps modernes." *Annales: Histoire, Sciences Sociales* 53: 291–320.

———. 1998b. " 'She Is Trouble . . . and I Will Divorce Her': Orality, Honor, and Representation in the Ottoman Court of 'Aintab." In *Women in the Medieval Islamic World: Power, Patronage, and Piety,* edited by Gavin R. G. Hambly, 269–300. New York: St. Martin's Press.

———. 2003. *Morality Tales: Law and Gender in the Ottoman Court of Aintab.* Berkeley and Los Angeles: Univ. of California Press.

———. 2004. "Changing Perspectives of the Ottoman Empire: The Early Centuries." In *New Historiographies of the Ottoman Mediterranean World,* edited by Amy Singer, special issue of *Mediterranean Historical Review* 19, no. 1: 6–27.

Philipp, Thomas. 2001. *Acre: The Rise and Fall of a Palestinian City, 1730–1831.* New York: Columbia Univ. Press.

Pick, Walter P. 1990. "Meissner Pasha and the Construction of Railways in Palestine and Neighboring Countries." In *Ottoman Palestine, 1800–1914: Studies in Economic and Social History,* edited by Gad G. Gilbar, 179–218. Leiden: E. J. Brill.

Powers, David S. 1989. "Orientalism, Colonialism, and Legal History: The Attack on Muslim Family Endowments in Algeria and India." *Comparative Studies in Society and History* 31, no. 3: 535–71.

———. 1994. "Kadijustiz or Qadi-Justice? A Paternity Dispute from Fourteenth-Century Morocco." *Islamic Law and Society* 1, no. 3: 332–67.

Al-Qattan, Najwa. 1996. "Textual Differentiation in the Damascus Sijill: Religious Discrimination or Politics of Gender?" In *Women, the Family, and Divorce Laws in Islamic History,* edited by Amira El-Azhary Sonbol, 191–201. Syracuse, N.Y.: Syracuse Univ. Press.

———. 2002. "Litigants and Neighbors: The Communal Topography of Ottoman Damascus." *Comparative Studies in Society and History* 44, no. 3: 511–33.

Quataert, Donald. 1994. "The Age of Reforms, 1812–1914." In *An Economic and Social History of the Ottoman Empire, 1300–1914,* 2 vols., edited by Halil İnalcık and Donald Quataert, 2: 759–943. Cambridge: Cambridge Univ. Press.

———. 2000. *The Ottoman Empire, 1700–1922.* Cambridge: Cambridge Univ. Press.

Rafeq, Abdul-Karim. 1970. *The Province of Damascus, 1723–1783.* 1966. Reprint. Beirut: Khayats.

Raymond, André. 1973–74. *Artisans et commerçants au Caire au XVIIIe siècle.* 2 vols. Damascus: Institut Français de Damas.

———. 1984. "The Population of Aleppo in the Sixteenth and Seventeenth Centuries According to Ottoman Census Documents." *International Journal of Middle East Studies* 16, no. 4: 447–60.

———. 1985. *Grandes villes arabes à l'époque ottomane.* Paris: Sindbad.

———. 1998. "A Response to Zouhair Ghazzal's Review of *Familles et fortunes à Damas: 450 foyers damascains en 1700* (Damascus: Institut français de Damas, 1994), by Colette Establet and Jean-Paul Pascual, in IJMES 28, 3 (1996): 431–32." *International Journal of Middle East Studies* 30, no. 3: 472–74.

Reay, Barry. 1996. *Microhistories: Demography, Society, and Culture in Rural England, 1800–1930.* Cambridge: Cambridge Univ. Press.

Redhouse, Sir James W. 1890. *A Turkish and English Lexicon.* Constantinople: n.p.

Reid, Donald M. 1981. *Lawyers and Politics in the Arab World, 1880–1960.* Chicago: Bibliotheca Islamica.

Reilly, James A. 2002. *A Small Town in Syria: Ottoman Hama in the Eighteenth and Nineteenth Centuries.* Bern: Peter Lang.

Rogan, Eugene L. 1999. *Frontiers of the State in the Late Ottoman Empire: Transjordan, 1850–1921.* Cambridge: Cambridge Univ. Press.

Rosen, Lawrence. 1978. "The Negotiation of Reality: Male-Female Relations in Sefrou, Morocco." In *Women in the Muslim World,* edited by Nikki R. Keddie and Lois Beck, 561–84. Cambridge, Mass.: Harvard Univ. Press.

———. 1989. *The Anthropology of Justice: Law as Culture in Islamic Society.* Cambridge: Cambridge Univ. Press.

Rubin, Avi. 2000. "Bahjat and Tamimi in Wilayat Beirut: A Journey into the Worldviews of Two Ottoman Travelers at the Turn of the 20th Century" (in Hebrew). M.A. thesis, Ben-Gurion Univ. of the Negev, Beersheba.

———. Forthcoming. "Ottoman Modernity: The Nizamiye Courts in Late Nineteenth Century." Ph.D. diss., Harvard Univ.

Rugh, Andrea B. 1988. Review of Judith E. Tucker's *Women in Nineteenth-Century Egypt* (Cambridge: Cambridge Univ. Press, 1985). *International Journal of Middle East Studies* 20, no. 1: 118–21.

Sabean, David W. 1990. *Property, Production, and Family in Neckarhausen, 1700–1870.* Cambridge: Cambridge Univ. Press.

———. 1998. *Kinship in Neckarhausen, 1700–1870.* Vol. 2. Cambridge: Cambridge Univ. Press.

Said, Edward W. 1978. *Orientalism.* New York: Pantheon.

Sanders, Paula. 1991. "Gendering the Ungendered Body: Hermaphrodites in Medieval Islamic Law." In *Women in Middle Eastern History: Shifting Boundaries in Sex and Gender,* edited by Nikki R. Keddie and Beth Baron, 74–95. New Haven, Conn.: Yale Univ. Press.

Schilcher, Linda S. 1985. *Families in Politics: Damascene Factions and Estates in the 18th and 19th Centuries.* Stuttgart: Franz Steiner Verlag.

———. 1998. "Railways in the Political Economy of Southern Syria 1890–1925." In *The Syrian Land: Processes of Integration and Fragmentation, Bilad al-Sham from the 18th to the 20th Century,* edited by Thomas Philipp and Birgit Schaebler, 97–112. Stuttgart: Franz Steiner Verlag.

Schölch, Alexander. 1982. "European Penetration and the Economic Development of Palestine, 1856–82." In *Studies in the Economic and Social History of Palestine in the 19th and 20th Centuries,* edited by Roger Owen, 10–87. Oxford: Oxford Univ. Press.

Scott, Joan W. 1988. *Gender and the Politics of History.* New York: Columbia Univ. Press.

———. 1995. "Women's History." Reprinted in *New Perspectives on Historical Writing,* edited by Peter Burke, 42–66. Philadelphia: Pennsylvania State Univ. Press.

Shaham, Ron. 1997. *Family and the Courts in Modern Egypt.* Leiden: E. J. Brill.

———. 2001. "Yatim." In *Encyclopedia of Islam,* 2d ed., 11: 299–300. Leiden: E. J. Brill.

Shahar, Ido. 2000a. "The Dabt (Protocol), the Sijill (Verdict), and Their Context: The Politics of Court Record Production." Paper presented at the International Workshop on Text, Context, and the Constitution of Difference, Ben-Gurion Univ. of the Negev, Beersheba.

———. 2000b. "Palestinians in an Israeli Court: Culture, Control, and Resistance in the Shari'a Court of West Jerusalem" (in Hebrew). M.A. thesis, Hebrew Univ., Jerusalem.

———. 2005. "Practicing Islamic Law in a Legal Pluralistic Environment: The Changing Face of a Muslim Court in Present-Day Jerusalem." Ph.D. diss., Ben-Gurion Univ. of the Negev, Beersheba.

Shammas, Anton. 2001. *Arabesques: A Novel.* Translated by Vivian Eden. 1988. Reprint. Berkeley and Los Angeles: Univ. of California Press.

Sharpe, Jim. 1995. "History from Below." 1992. Reprinted in *New Perspectives on Historical Writing,* edited by Peter Burke, 24–41. Philadelphia: Pennsylvania State Univ. Press.

Shaw, Stanford J., and Ezel K. Shaw. 1977. *History of the Ottoman Empire and Modern Turkey.* Vol. 2. Cambridge: Cambridge Univ. Press.

Shuval, Tal. 1998. *La ville d'alger vers la fin du XVIIIe siècle: Population et cadre urbain.* Paris: CNRS Editions.

———. 2000. "Households in Ottoman Algeria." *Turkish Studies Association Bulletin* 24: 41–64.

Singer, Amy. 2002. *Constructing Ottoman Beneficence: An Imperial Soup Kitchen in Jerusalem.* Albany: State Univ. of New York Press.

Sonbol, Amira El-Azhary. 1996a. "Adults and Minors in Ottoman Shari'a Courts and Modern Law." In *Women, the Family, and Divorce Laws in Islamic History,* edited by Amira El-Azhary Sonbol, 236–56. Syracuse, N.Y.: Syracuse Univ. Press.

———. 1996b. "Introduction." In *Women, the Family, and Divorce Laws in Islamic History,* edited by Amira El-Azhary Sonbol, 1–20. Syracuse, N.Y.: Syracuse Univ. Press.

———. 1996c. "Law and Gender Violence in Ottoman and Modern Egypt." In

Women, the Family, and Divorce Laws in Islamic History, edited by Amira El-Azhary Sonbol, 277–89. Syracuse, N.Y.: Syracuse Univ. Press.

Starr, June. 1992. *Law as Metaphor: From Islamic Courts to the Palace of Justice.* Albany: State Univ. of New York Press.

Stone, Lawrence. 1981. "Family History in the 1980s: Past Achievements and Future Trends." *Journal of Interdisciplinary History* 22, no. 1: 51–87.

Tilly, Charles. 1987. "Family History, Social History, and Social Change." *Journal of Family History* 12: 319–30.

Toledano, Ehud R. 1989. Review of Judith E. Tucker's *Women in Nineteenth-Century Egypt* (Cambridge Univ. Press, 1985). *Middle East Studies* 25, no. 1: 113–19.

———. 1990. *State and Society in Mid-Nineteenth-Century Egypt.* Cambridge: Cambridge Univ. Press.

———. 1997. "The Emergence of Ottoman-Local Elites (1700–1900): A Frame-work for Research." In *Middle Eastern Politics and Ideas: A History from Within,* edited by Moshe Ma'oz and Ilan Pappe, 145–62. London: I. B. Tauris.

———. 1998. "Social and Economic Change in the 'Long Nineteenth Century.' " In *The Cambridge History of Egypt,* 2 vols., edited by Martin W. Daly, 2: 252–84. Cambridge: Cambridge Univ. Press.

———. 2002. "What Ottoman History and Ottomanist Historiography Are, or, Rather, Are Not." *Middle Eastern Studies* 38, no. 3: 195–207.

———. Forthcoming. *Silent and Absent in the Islamic Middle East: Voices of the Enslaved in the Long–Nineteenth Century.* New Haven, Conn.: Yale Univ. Press.

Tucker, Judith E. 1985. *Women in Nineteenth-Century Egypt.* Cambridge: Cambridge Univ. Press.

———. 1998. *In the House of the Law: Gender and Islamic Law in Ottoman Syria and Palestine.* Berkeley and Los Angeles: Univ. of California Press.

Turner, Bryan S. 1974. *Weber and Islam: A Critical Study.* London: Routledge and Kegan Paul.

Tyan, Emile. 1955. "Judicial Administration." In *Law in the Middle East,* 2 vols., edited by Majid Khadduri and Herbert J. Liebesney, 1: 236–78. Washington, D.C.: Middle East Institute.

Wall, Richard, Jean Robin, and Peter Laslett, eds. 1983. *Family Forms in Historic Europe.* Cambridge: Cambridge Univ. Press.

Weber, Max. 1968. *Economy and Society: An Outline of Interpretive Sociology.* Edited by Guenther Roth and Claus Wittich. New York: Bedminster Press.

Wolf, Arthur P., and Susan B. Hanley, 1985. "Introduction." In *Family and Population in East Asian History,* edited by Susan B. Hanley and Arthur P. Wolf, 1–13. Stanford: Stanford Univ. Press.

Würth, Anna. 1995. "A Sanaa Court: The Family and the Ability to Negotiate." *Islamic Law and Society* 2: 320–40.

Yazbak, Mahmoud. 1997. "Nabulsi Ulama in the Late Ottoman Period, 1864–1914." *International Journal of Middle East Studies* 29, no. 1: 71–91.

———. 1998. *Haifa in the Late Ottoman Period, 1864–1914: A Muslim Town in Transition.* Leiden: E. J. Brill.

Yngvesson, Barbara. 1993. *Virtuous Citizens, Disruptive Subjects: Order and Complaint in a New England Court.* New York: Routledge.

Zarinebaf-Shahr, Fariba. 1996. "Women, Law, and Imperial Justice in Ottoman Istanbul in the Late Seventeenth Century." In *Women, the Family, and Divorce Laws in Islamic History,* edited by Amira El-Azhary Sonbol, 81–95. Syracuse, N.Y.: Syracuse Univ. Press.

Ze'evi, Dror. 1991. "An Ottoman Century: The Sancak of Jerusalem in the 17th Century" (in Hebrew). Ph.D. diss., Tel Aviv Univ.

———. 1995. "Women in 17th-Century Jerusalem: Western and Indigenous Perspectives." *International Journal of Middle East Studies* 27, no. 2: 157–73.

———. 1996. *An Ottoman Century: The District of Jerusalem in the 1600s.* Albany: State Univ. of New York Press.

———. 1998. "The Use of Ottoman Shari'a Court Records as a Source for Middle Eastern Social History: A Reappraisal." *Islamic Law and Society* 5: 35–56.

Zerdeci, Hümeyra. 1998. "Osmanlı Ulema Biyografilerinin Arşiv Kaynakları (Şer'iyye Sicilleri). *M.A. thesis, Istanbul Univ.*

Zhao, Zhongwei. 2001. "Registered Households and Micro-social Structure in China: Residential Patterns in Three Settlements in the Beijing Area." *Journal of Family History* 26, no. 1: 39–65.

Zilfi, Madeline C. 1997. " 'We Don't Get Along': Women and *Hul* Divorce in the Eighteenth Century." In *Women in the Ottoman Empire: Middle Eastern Women in the Early Modern Era,* edited by Madeline C. Zilfi, 264–96. Leiden: E. J. Brill.

Index

Italic page number denotes illustration.